HAITI

HAITI

The Tumultuous History—
From Pearl of the Caribbean
to Broken Nation

Philippe Girard

 St. Martin's Griffin New York

www.stmartins.com

Designed by Newgen Imaging Systems (P) Ltd., Chennai, India

Library of Congress Cataloging-in-Publication Data

Girard, Philippe R.
    Haiti : the tumultuous history : from pearl of the Caribbean to broken nation / Philippe Girard.
        p. cm.
    Includes bibliographical references and index.
    ISBN 978–0–230–10661–1 (trade paperback)
    1. Haiti—History. I. Title.
    F1921.G47 2010
    972.94—dc22   2010021390

Our books may be purchased in bulk for promotional, educational, or business use. Please contact your local bookseller or the Macmillan Corporate and Premium Sales Department at (800) 221-7945, extension 5442, or by e-mail at MacmillanSpecialMarkets@macmillan.com.

First published as *Paradise Lost* by Palgrave Macmillan, a division of St. Martin's Press LLC

First St. Martin's Griffin Edition: September 2010

D   20 19

Contents

Illustrations

All figures provided by the author except the following: figure 1.1 provided courtesy of the Central Intelligence Agency; figure 1.2 provided courtesy of the University of Texas Libraries (University of Texas at Austin); figures 8.1, 9.1, and 9.2 provided courtesy of the U.S. Department of Defense's Defense Visual Information Center.

INTRODUCTION

Haiti in Ruins

Port-au-Prince was its proud, vibrant, and impoverished self as the afternoon of January 12, 2010, neared its end. The white presidential palace, aglow in the declining sun, rose from the Champ de Mars plaza amidst monuments dedicated to Haiti's founding fathers, the statue of the unknown maroon, and the national pantheon celebrating the country's past. The descendants of Haiti's greatest generation could be found everywhere: muscular men pulling wooden carts stacked high with tires and water jugs, *marchandes* (female market sellers) selling their colorful wares, overloaded *taptaps* and *publiques* (public taxis and buses) snaking their way through the congested streets—two million people in all, from the sprawling slum of Cité Soleil in the north to the concrete shacks hanging perilously from the hillsides to the city's east and south.

People walked, argued, worked—or tried to—and yet no discernable wealth seemed to be produced. Sidewalks overflowed with minuscule stalls from which vendors sold crackers by the unit, tiny mangoes, and individual cigarettes. Aside from the occasional diplomat, journalist, or humanitarian worker, hotels and restaurants catering to foreigners were empty. Near the iron market, entire streets were lined with beautiful Haitian paintings for sale, the vendors waiting patiently for tourists who had stopped coming thirty years before. The hustle and bustle of the Caribbean metropolis was a sight to behold, but these men, women, and children often looked desperate, and many were hungry.

Particularly difficult to ignore was the fact that much of Port-au-Prince, the "prince's port" and the capital of the second-most populated nation in the Caribbean, was an open dump. Entire sections of the city were shantytowns built with discarded cardboard and sheet metal. Even in more affluent neighborhoods, where concrete two-story houses were the norm, piles of uncollected garbage lined the streets, while gaping potholes opened onto ill-maintained sewers chock-full with debris. Nondescript dogs, all bones and skin, wandered around; they were not the only hungry beings to be found, however. Most heartbreaking was the sight of the city's homeless children, many of them survivors of a form of child slavery known locally as *restavek,* and for whom the sewers were a primary source of food, water, shelter—and occasionally a final resting place.

Even in the best of times, life in Port-au-Prince was a hardscrabble struggle for survival, difficult enough for hundreds of thousands of Haitians to entrust their lives to makeshift boats in the hope of reaching the distant shores of Florida. But the early afternoon of January 12, seen retrospectively, was a blissful time. The real nightmare was yet to come.

At 4:53 P.M. a massive earthquake struck nearby Léogane. Within fractions of a second, all of Port-au-Prince was shaking violently. Walls jerked erratically, roofs collapsed, and cracks ripped the pavement apart. The sound was indescribable: falling concrete crushing anything in its path, people crying out in terror, the earth rumbling deep within—then, after thirty-five interminable seconds, the eerie silence of a collapsed metropolis that in an instant had lost over two hundred thousand souls. Some people fell to their knees to pray. Others frantically dug through the rubble with their bare hands to search for relatives, but before the damage could be assessed with any precision the Caribbean sun set abruptly, leaving survivors to endure an agonizing pitch-dark night pierced by the wails of the mourning and the moans of the injured.

It was only with daybreak on Wednesday morning that the full extent of the physical damage became apparent. Rumors of an incoming tsunami had proven false, but the earthquake's magnitude (7.0) and the epicenter's proximity to the capital (sixteen miles) had wreaked massive havoc. Even the hills surrounding the city, their flanks scarred by landslides, bore the mark of the earthquake. Entire neighborhoods had been leveled, as if by a bombing raid. In schools, shops, hospitals, and homes, falling concrete slabs had killed or trapped hundreds of thousands of hapless victims and left a million people homeless.

Cemeteries, their tombs cracked open, could barely accommodate those already interred there, let alone the recently deceased throngs. As morgues filled beyond capacity, dozens—then hundreds, then thousands—of bodies were lined up along the sweltering streets, waiting to be dragged to the anonymity of a mass grave. In the jagged strata of the collapsed city the dead, the living, and the dying were now indistinguishable. "We no longer cried for the dead" during funerals, a reporter for the Haitian daily *Le Nouvelliste* later noted. "There were too many of them, and not enough tears."[1]

The shock waves that rippled through the concrete had cracked or destroyed most permanent buildings in town but, ironically, the shacks of the shantytowns—the supple structures of which were largely quake-proof—had proven more resistant. In the aftermath of the earthquake, the city turned into a Tartar camp of old hovels, fresh rubble, and new lean-tos erected by homeless survivors. Even the lucky few whose houses still stood slept in the streets for fear of an aftershock. The slums of Port-au-Prince, which for four decades had slowly eaten at the city's outskirts, had now swallowed it entirely.

Neither God nor country had been spared: the roof of the national cathedral had collapsed, as had those of the Episcopal cathedral, the Ministry of Justice building, and the presidential palace. The National Assembly building was severely damaged, as was city hall. Particularly worrisome for future rescue operations was the fact that the country's physical and political infrastructure had received a heavy blow. Toussaint Louverture Airport and the seaport were too damaged to be of immediate use. Hotels Oloffson and Montana, traditional haunts of moneyed visitors on humanitarian missions, were heavily damaged, as were the headquarters of the United Nations (UN) mission at the Christopher Hotel. The UN special envoy, Hédi Hannabi, had been killed along with several members of his staff, as had Archbishop Joseph Serge Miot and two senators. President René Préval had survived, but both his house and his office in the presidential palace were in ruins, and he was left to wander the streets on a motorcycle to assess the damage. He was shocked and homeless, just like many of his people. Haiti was in ruins.

Haiti in the News

Haiti rarely makes the headlines unless it is hit by some catastrophe, either natural or man-made, and it had largely dropped from public view since a coup d'état and a string of hurricanes in 2004, and then food riots and more hurricanes in 2008. Its omnipresence on the airwaves in the days and weeks that followed the January 12 earthquake was a clear indication of the magnitude of the disaster that had befallen the country. Across the globe, people who had barely ever heard of Haiti sat trans-fixed before their television sets, moved by the images of collapsed schools, amputated survivors, helpless orphans, and the half-collapsed presidential palace that came to symbolize Haiti's hapless state.

For such a catastrophe to strike the poorest country in the Western Hemisphere—one already afflicted by a long list of economic, political, and environmental ills—seemed singularly cruel. It was not long before rumors spread that a cataclysm of such biblical proportions could only be preordained and that the earthquake was actually the latest plague sent by a wrathful God. Throughout the Caribbean, the word was that Haiti was simply cursed; Haitians had invited the devil's attention by invoking his name one time too many in Voodoo (Vodou, Vodun) ceremonies and were now paying the price. In a reference to the ties between Haitian slave rebels and the Voodoo religion, U.S. televangelist Pat Robertson similarly claimed that Haiti was being punished for having contracted a "pact with the devil" during its war of independence two centuries earlier.[2] (The reality was more prosaic: Port-au-Prince sits near the juncture of three tectonic plates that had been accumulating pressure since the last major quake in 1770.)

Aside from the occasional prophet of doom, the people of the world were deeply moved by Haiti's plight and responded with great generosity. A call for ten-dollar cell phone text donations brought the American Red Cross five million dollars in twenty-four hours. The United States, though mired in two overseas wars and recovering from a recent great recession, dispatched Marine units, helicopters, and the USNS *Comfort* and other support ships—ten thousand troops in the first week alone, not counting the UN mission already on site and countless nongovernmental organizations (NGOs). So many foreign governments and NGOs rushed in supplies that the airport's single runway was soon overwhelmed and flights had to be diverted to the Dominican Republic.

Despite the tragic loss of life—estimated at over two hundred thousand dead—one could find some solace in the fact that the earthquake had brought out the best in the human spirit: courage and resilience on the part of the victims, dedication and selflessness on the part of the rescuers, and generally a shared sense of humanity that transcended racial and national boundaries. Not coincidentally, the United States, France, and the Dominican Republic—three countries with which Haiti had often endured tense relations in the past—were at the forefront of the rescue effort.

Old Demons

It was not long, unfortunately, before Haiti's old demons came back to haunt it. Pat Robertson's claims notwithstanding, these demons were not *guédés* (Voodoo spirits of the dead), but age-old rivalries that had long bedeviled the country and that resurfaced in the aftermath of the January 12 earthquake. First on the scene was the prickly nationalism that is one of Haiti's enduring qualities, but which also frequently complicates its relations with its neighbors. Incoming U.S. troops were careful to introduce themselves as saviors bringing much-needed help, not as conquerors walking in the footsteps of earlier generations of U.S. invaders. Race-conscious Haitians could also not help but notice that their commander-in-chief, like virtually all Haitians, was of African descent. And yet, the sight of Black Hawk helicopters circling over the presidential palace and Marines patrolling the streets of the capital brought back painful memories of past U.S. occupations. It was not long before grumbling began about some questionable U.S. policies, such as the allocation of landing slots at the airport (which U.S. troops took over, repaired, and ran) or the high rate of amputations at the hands of a contingent of Texan doctors.

Well aware that many of his compatriots were "stigmatizing the presence of the U.S. Army," Haitian prime minister Jean-Max Bellerive reassured them that foreign forces were well intentioned and provided essential services that the country could hardly do without.[3] But his words were largely lost on the Haitian public, and rumors soon spread that the U.S. relief effort somehow fit into an elaborate imperialistic plot to take over the country. The United States had secretly developed a weapon to spark earthquakes at will so as to justify a military takeover under the guise of a humanitarian effort, according to the left-leaning *Haïti Progrès* in one of the most outlandish, but also most widespread, claims.[4] Even the more conservative *Haïti Observateur*, the organ of the affluent Haitian American community in New York, underlined the "risk inherent in any intervention of this kind" and urged Haitians to remain "vigilant" because U.S. president Barack Obama was under pressure from Republicans to continue his country's "imperial policy."[5] Farther north, a Haitian resident in Montréal similarly complained in a letter to *Le Nouvelliste* that Haiti had been "invaded by NGOs" intent on enriching themselves while undermining the authority of the Haitian state.[6]

No incident better encapsulated the tension between Haiti's desperate need for international aid and its distrust of foreign well-wishers than the arrest of ten U.S. Baptist missionaries two weeks after the earthquake on charges that they were trying to sneak thirty-three kidnapped Haitian children out of the country. If true, the charges were serious ones that amply warranted their imprisonment, but the international context in which the missionaries' case unfolded brought a nagging sense that they had become a metaphor for U.S.–Haitian relations. Even in the best of times, the Haitian judicial system rarely prosecutes anyone, so the resources it lavished on this particular case were quite extraordinary. As of 2001, 75 percent of Haitian prisoners languished in pretrial detention because they had yet to be formally charged with a crime; even as famous a captive as former prime minister Yvon Neptune had to be freed in July 2006 after government prosecutors failed to file charges during his two-year captivity.[7] In the aftermath of a devastating earthquake that had left the ministry of justice building in rubble, there seemed to be more pressing issues to address than the murky world of international adoption—such as tracking down the whereabouts of the criminals who had escaped from Port-au-Prince's national penitentiary when it collapsed during the quake.

Archival documentation for this case will not be released for a long time, but the incident left the distinct impression that Haitian prosecutors were trying, at least subconsciously, to reassert some semblance of national authority at a time when their country had effectively become a U.S. protectorate. If so, nationalistic bravado had its costs. It provided little comfort to the hundreds of thousands of orphans whom the cash-strapped Haitian government had left to fend for themselves or to rely on foreign-funded orphanages. It delayed legal international adoptions, already greatly complicated by the Haitian government's slowness in delivering requisite permits. Most tragically, it claimed the lives of many Haitian children who, maimed during the earthquake, later died on the tarmac of Port-au-Prince's airport when foreign pilots refused to fly them to surgical centers in Florida for fear that they, too, would be charged with kidnapping. Had the U.S. government been an imperialistic hegemon as its critics claimed, the diplomatic affront could even have incited it to take over the reins of government or pull out of the country altogether, leaving the Haitian government to care for its people on its own at a time of immense distress. The particulars of the case notwithstanding, this seemed to be a particularly ill-advised time to pick a fight with Haiti's powerful neighbor (the missionaries were later released before they were ever brought to trial).

The January 12 earthquake also underscored a second immutable fact of life in Haiti: that poor governance is a leading cause of the country's troubles, even during a random "act of God" like an earthquake. With building codes either nonexistent or unenforced, most structures in Haiti are built of poor-quality concrete—characterized by low amounts of cement and few steel reinforcement bars—to save on construction material. Such shabbily built structures barely stand under normal circumstances: ninety children had died fourteen months earlier when a school in nearby Pétionville suddenly collapsed on its own. In retrospect, better government regulation would likely have saved thousands of lives (sturdier structures, like the foreboding U.S. embassy, were largely unscathed; in fact, an earthquake of identical magnitude near San Francisco killed a mere sixty-three people in 1989).

People normally overlook past disputes and unite in a time of national catastrophe, but it was not long before another feature of Haitian political life—instability—reasserted itself. At issue was the attitude of President Préval (a man already prone to a self-effacing presidential style) who almost wholly disappeared from sight after the earthquake, limiting himself to a dispassionate radio address and a press conference organized by his international backers during which he stood largely speechless in the back row. Within a month, opposition politicians were openly calling for Préval's resignation for lacking leadership skills during a time of national emergency (but these politicians were not very convincing, since their main policy proposal in the aftermath of the earthquake was to propose that their lucrative term as parliamentarians, which was about to expire, be prolonged by another eighteen months on the grounds that the country was too dislocated to organize elections). A prolonged political crisis—another of Haiti's old demons—likely to paralyze the political class at a time when the nation needed it most seemed in the offing.[8] In this context, the collapsed presidential palace served as an apt symbol, not only of the massive physical destruction inflicted on Port-au-Prince, but also of the political deficiencies that had ruined the country in the first place.

Aiding Haiti

Outside the country, the January 12 earthquake breathed new life into old debates on the international community's relationship with Haiti, particularly the type of assistance it should provide as the impoverished nation struggled to rebuild. In the short term, no one questioned the legitimacy of the relief effort. As Hurricane Katrina had painfully shown in New Orleans in 2005, no country, however rich, can easily overcome the destruction of a major city on its own. Given the magnitude of the catastrophe and Haiti's scant resources, simple humanity dictated that the international community provide such essentials as field hospitals and food and water in the weeks and months to come.

More controversial was the question of how best to secure the long-term economic betterment of Haiti in ensuing years. The international community's immediate reaction, when faced with the disturbing images flooding in from Port-au-Prince, was to call for a massive aid package to help rebuild Haiti, one on the scale of the Marshall Plan in post–World War II Western Europe. It was thought that with the international community's help, the terrible earthquake might be turned into a new starting point that would lay the foundations for Haiti's long-delayed economic takeoff. Not knowing that his microphone was on, George Antoine, the Haitian consul in São Paulo, confided to a Brazilian journalist that the tragedy would prove "good to us here" because of the international attention it would generate.[9] Antoine's comment was crass but accurate: the United Nations made an immediate call for $575 million in emergency relief funds, and by the end of January Prime Minister Bellerive was in Montréal asking a gathering of international donors for $3 billion to help rebuild Port-au-Prince.

As days passed, however, skeptics in the United States and elsewhere began to question whether such a vast commitment of resources, amounting to half of Haiti's annual gross domestic product (GDP), was wise or warranted.[10] International aid to Haiti has a long and checkered history going back to Jean-Claude Duvalier, whose inauguration as president in 1971 had also been seen, in its time, as a new beginning that would usher in a different Haiti. Other fresh starts had come and gone, from Duvalier's overthrow in 1986 to Jean-Bertrand Aristide's election as president in 1990, his return from exile in 1994, and his second overthrow in 2004. Each of these milestones had brought hopes that Haiti could finally be turned around, but with each new round of aid packages all that resulted was bitter disappointment. By early January 2010—before the earthquake struck—60 percent of Haiti's budget came from foreign aid, and a staggering ten thousand NGOs were active in the country. Haiti had the highest number of NGOs per capita on the planet, but it was more impoverished and desperate than it had been in 1971.

The mixed record of previous aid packages left the international community three major policy options, which the U.S. Senate Committee on Foreign Relations discussed during a January 28 hearing. The first, backed by panelist and UN Deputy Special Envoy for Haiti Paul Farmer, was to forgive Haiti's public debt and entrust the Haitian government with a new batch of international monies, hoping that it would make better use of them than it had before. The second, presented by James Dobbins of the RAND Corporation, was to provide limited financial aid in the long term and instead improve governance in Haiti so as to provide the environment within which the private sector could bring about self-sustaining economic growth. The last was to rebuild Haiti with international funds, but to do so under strict supervision. Brainstorming aloud, Connecticut senator Christopher Dodd even evoked the possibility of turning Haiti into a protectorate or "some sort of international receivership," as he put it.[11] This most extraordinary suggestion would have brought Haiti back full circle to its early years as a colonial outpost of a Western power.

Explaining Haiti's History

Courage, suffering, incompetence, and energy: it is not difficult to understand why outsiders have always found Haiti to be at once mesmerizing and horrifying. Haiti is one of the most stunningly beautiful islands of the Caribbean. It was once home to the pre-Columbian Taino civilization, witnessed the passage of the Spanish galleons carrying the wealth of the Aztec and Inca empires, housed the legendary pirate haven of Tortuga, then saw the rise of a French plantation society that was so profitable that it earned colonial Haiti the nickname Pearl of the Antilles. But Haiti's past is also as dark as a tropical night, its violence rarely matched in the annals of human history. Over the course of its history, this country has witnessed four massacres or genocides, one of the most brutal slave systems in the Caribbean, countless civil wars and foreign invasions, and the refined cruelty of Papa Doc's torture chambers. Even today, settling a political score can mean burning someone to death or hacking a body with machetes.

Haiti might be a mere six hundred miles from the U.S. coast, but aside from AIDS, Voodoo, and boat people, the U.S. public remains generally unaware of some of Haiti's most unique features. For example, how many know that the first Spanish settlement in the New World was built in Haiti? That Haiti was richer than the United States in colonial times? That Haiti was the first free black republic in the world and the second colony in the Western Hemisphere to gain its independence? That the celebrated American ornithologist John James Audubon was born in Cayes? That the French novelist Alexandre Dumas (author of *The Count of Monte Cristo*) was the son of a Haitian general? That before 2010, U.S. troops had already landed in Port-au-Prince in 1915, 1994, and 2004? That one million Haitian Americans live in the United States today? Or that child slavery still exists in Haiti?

Adding to the general lack of knowledge of Haiti's past is the fact that Haiti is a world of its own, the main features of which are often incomprehensible to outsiders. Even though Haitians' ancestors were mostly African, they draw much of their culture from France and many of their economic aspirations from the U.S. model—only to routinely express strong anti-French and anti-American sentiments. Yet they dream of emigrating to one of these countries, while displaying a fierce and authentic pride in their *Haïti chérie*. Haiti, founded on the principle that blacks are equal to whites, remains a society divided by race to this day. Founded by slaves yearning to be free, Haiti is still home to child slaves, and sends sugarcane workers to the Dominican Republic where they work in conditions reminiscent of their ancestors two hundred years ago.

The main question outsiders often ask is this: why is Haiti so poor, so unstable, so violent? One might assume that it has always been this way, but that is not the case. Haiti's descent into the abyss of underdevelopment started two hundred years ago, when the country's economy was devastated by the war of independence, and only reached alarming proportions during the Duvalier dictatorships a generation ago. It is a recent historical phenomenon with a clearly discernable set of man-made causes.

When looking for historical insights into Haiti's current misfortune, it is easy to become lost in the mind-numbing complexity of Haiti's political life. Presidents, especially in the early twentieth century, often stay a mere few months in office before they are sent into exile or murdered. But, as is often the case in Latin America, the multiplicity of revolutions can be misleading. Haitian leaders change with dizzying rapidity; yet, beneath the surface, Haitian society displays remarkable stability. Three long-term factors, rather than the blood and gore of day-to-day politics, underpin Haitian society, as they have for all of the country's independent, and even colonial, history. The country is plagued by racial conflict; its leaders are often corrupt and uncaring; and Haitians expect foreign countries, not Haitians, to pull the country out of poverty (the January 12 earthquake was by its very nature colorblind, but the latter two factors were prominently on display).

Racial strife is as old as Haiti itself. When Christopher Columbus arrived in 1492, the indigenous Taino population in all of Hispaniola probably numbered half a million. Within two generations, it had virtually disappeared—the victim of European diseases and Spanish cruelty. When French settlers and African slaves replaced Spaniards and Taino serfs as the island's dominant and dominated races, a body of literature emerged to justify why Africans should be enslaved (such brutish creatures, their owners argued, could only work under strong leadership). Haiti's slaves revolted in 1791, launching a vicious war that culminated during 1802–1803 when each side—Napoléon Bonaparte's troops on

the one hand, Haitian rebels on the other—openly contemplated genocide in order to secure a lasting victory (the rebels won and killed or
exiled most white Frenchmen after independence).

The white population is now negligible in Haiti, but racial rivalries
remain an integral part of Haiti's troubles. Mulattoes, the distant product of unions between planters and their slaves, still tend to look down
on the majority blacks of pure African ancestry—who in turn both envy
and hate their lighter-skinned compatriots. Politicians such as Jean-
Claude Duvalier and Jean-Bertrand Aristide built much of their careers
on the darkness of their skin, which proved, according to them, that they
were "real" Haitians (or *authentiques*) as opposed to treacherous mulattoes (in a typically Haitian twist, both leaders later married rich, light-
skinned women).

Racial allegiances also complicate Haiti's foreign relations. Acting as
if white French and U.S. leaders were still slave owners intent on depriving Haitians of their hard-won freedom, Haitian politicians are quick to
denounce any offer of humanitarian help as yet another case of imperialism. Racism has even poisoned Haiti's relations with the neighboring
Dominican Republic, a former Spanish colony that occupies the eastern
two-thirds of the island of Hispaniola and whose population is noticeably lighter skinned than Haiti's because it had fewer slaves in colonial
times. In the nineteenth century, Haiti regularly invaded the Dominican
Republic and accused its neighbor of condoning slavery, while in the
twentieth century, the Dominican Republic regularly expelled (and, in
1937, massacred) its black minority.

Governing such a racially polarized society would have required a ruling class of immense political skills. Unfortunately, the Haitian intelligentsia, more often than not, has been composed of petty politicians
who only appeal to nationalism and racial pride to hide the fact that they
are spiriting away government funds. This is the second cause of Haiti's
current misfortune. Massive corruption, petty squabbles, endless revolutions, and repression have destroyed existing infrastructures, scared away
local and foreign investments, and given Haitians little incentive to better their economic well-being in an environment that does not reward
success. Even today, roads are built with international aid, schools are
funded by U.S. churches, and clinics are run by European NGOs. All the
tasks normally performed by a functioning government are neglected;
meanwhile, security forces act as a predatory institution that oppresses,
rather than protects, private individuals. Expecting nothing from their
government, Haitians consider themselves lucky to merely escape the
greedy grasp of the "Republic of Port-au-Prince," as the capital is known.

Over the course of its history, Haiti has known a few enlightened despots who hoped to foster prosperity, if not democracy, but their rule was often cut short. Toussaint Louverture, Henri Christophe, and Lysius Salomon, three of the most forceful leaders of nineteenth-century Haiti, used their dictatorial powers to develop their country's infrastructures. But all three of them were overthrown (the last two by Haitians themselves), and the improvements made during their tenure were soon abandoned. The United States' two main occupations of Haiti (1915–1934 and 1994–2000) had no more positive impact in the long run. Many U.S. officers had a genuine desire to improve Haiti, but imposing reforms from the outside only led to nationalist resentment, and foreign-built infrastructures collapsed from neglect after the departure of occupying forces.

Whether foreign countries should shoulder some of the blame for Haiti's current poverty is the third and most controversial issue in contemporary Haiti. Everyone agrees that in the 1780s, Haiti was France's most prosperous colony (even though this wealth was not equally distributed) and that Haiti is now the poorest country in the Western Hemisphere. There is widespread disagreement, however, over the roots of this dramatic shift from sugar and coffee powerhouse to impoverished people subsisting off international aid. Haitians, along with many liberals overseas, tend to blame the legacy of slavery and colonialism. Haiti, they say, was first plundered by Spanish conquistadors seeking gold, then exploited by the French planters who traded African flesh, and finally devastated during the long war of independence against France. Even after independence, it lived in the political and military shadow of the United States and saw its economy (the rice and pig industries, notably) ruined by unfair U.S. competition.

This narrative is not fully convincing, however. Haiti suffered its fair share of colonial exactions, but so did its neighbors in the Caribbean, all of which are far richer than Haiti today. All the countries in the Western Hemisphere, not just Haiti, saw their native population plummet after the arrival of European settlers. Many countries, including Canada and the United States, experienced French colonial rule, only to endure and prosper. The Caribbean islands of Guadeloupe and Martinique, still living under the "yoke" of French imperialism, are immensely richer than Haiti, which has been independent for two centuries. Cuba, Brazil, and the United States, countries that were once notable for their large slave population, have all fared better than Haiti. Being invaded and then occupied by an outside power was a common occurrence in twentieth-century history. Not just Haiti, but also France, Germany, and Japan suffered this fate. Countries whose recent history surpasses even Haiti's in its brutality—Poland, South Korea, and China—now rank among the world's fastest-growing economies. History is not an inescapable curse.

The Haitian view that foreigners are to blame for Haiti's troubles does contribute to the country's poverty—but indirectly, by making it difficult to foster a spirit of enterprise. If France and the United States are indeed responsible for all the wrongs that ever befell Haiti, as many Haitians think, then one's own actions will make little difference. Similarly, Haitian politicians frequently use theories about the colonial legacy as a convenient excuse to justify their own inability to implement development policies. In 2003, after ruling Haiti on and off for twelve years, President Aristide unveiled a plan for lifting his country out of poverty that consisted of asking France, the former colonial power, to give over $21 billion—four times Haiti's annual GDP—in aid.

Even if the colonial legacy is responsible for Haiti's problems, which is far from certain, there remains the fact that a country can change—this is the very essence of history. Haiti's poverty, relatively recent and largely man-made, is not preordained; Haitians, just like the people of any other independent nation, are the sole masters of their destiny and could easily turn their country around in the near future. Understanding this will be an essential first step toward overcoming Haiti's past.

The United States' Role

The United States has played a central role in Haiti over the past two hundred years. Aside from regularly sending troops to Haiti—particularly in the past decade—the United States has been the country's main trading partner, the preferred destination for Haitian exiles, and a six-hundred-pound political gorilla whose support (or lack thereof) can throw Haitian leaders in and out of office. For Americans intrigued by developments in their Caribbean neighbor, three questions are paramount: Should the United States care? If so, what can the United States do? And why have previous American attempts at democratizing Haiti failed so miserably?

Americans tend to agree that Haiti does matter, though not always for the same reasons. Some privately fear an invasion of dark-skinned boat people should the situation in Haiti reach a critical state; others feel a sense of duty toward their long-suffering black brothers. (These views are rarely stated this bluntly—at least in public.) U.S. policymakers, when deciding to play an active role in Haiti, also cite a variety of national security interests. In the early days of the American Republic, when

Haiti was still wealthy and mighty, the island's commerce and military potential were the main issues of concern, and John Adams and Thomas Jefferson maneuvered to secure trading rights and protect U.S. shores from the Haitian army. They succeeded admirably on both counts.

Today, there is little to be gained from trading with Haiti and little to be feared from Haiti's armed forces (they were disbanded in 1995; only the presidential band remains). What U.S. presidents fear is Haiti's weakness, not its strength. A weak Haiti is easy prey for outside powers (not so long ago, Germany and the Soviet Union were viable candidates) and an endless source of immigrants and drugs. Prodded by liberal activists eager to offset past U.S. imperialism in the Caribbean and conservative nativists who fear an influx of boat people, U.S. presidents hope to stabilize Haiti so that Haitians may stay at home. So far, this has proved a dismal failure.

As the 2010 earthquake showed, what the proper U.S. policy toward Haiti should be is also a divisive issue. Pessimists who think that Haiti is doomed to fail would be happy to isolate the island politically, as if Haiti were a sick sailor in quarantine. In practical terms, this means that a cordon of Coast Guard cutters should patrol off Haiti's coast and turn away all boat people and drug traffickers. Those more hopeful about Haiti's future genuinely believe that the United States can be a force for good in Haiti and advocate constant engagement. Over the past few decades, the United States sometimes isolated Haiti by returning refugees and establishing an economic embargo. But, more often than not, it followed the optimistic route, sending peacekeepers, giving aid, providing political advice, and hoping that an ambitious nation-building effort would turn Haiti's fortunes around.

Haitian fears of U.S. hegemonic conspiracies aside, U.S. policies in Haiti are generally underpinned by a genuine, altruistic desire to help Haitians. Many U.S. presidents have felt that their country has a historical, even messianic, mission to spread free-market democracy worldwide. Former president Bill Clinton, who has spent more time in and out of office involving himself in Haitian affairs than any other president, has done so in part because he feels a personal connection to a country where he spent his honeymoon. A strong sense of personal guilt is also at the heart of many international aid projects in Haiti, since many proponents of international aid view Haiti as a victim of foreign exploitation and think that Western powers have a duty to correct past wrongs by providing financial aid.

The goal is noble and the effort is considerable, yet Haiti remains remarkably the same: poor, unstable, violent—and, paradoxically, deeply critical of past U.S. policies. This leads to the third, most important question: why, after two major U.S. interventions (1915–1934, 1994–2000), has the long-term goal of fostering a democratic, stable, prosperous, pro-U.S. society in Haiti failed so miserably?

As this book will show, the fact that regular interventions and foreign aid packages have failed to turn Haiti around indicates that the legacy of foreign imperialism is not the main problem in Haiti; political incompetence and racial acrimony are. This fact also indicates that foreign generosity cannot be the only answer; Haitians themselves are a big part of the answer. Colonial rule died two centuries ago; the United States should now hold Haitians responsible for their country's history, including its bleakest aspects. The steady flow of foreign aid in recent times has convinced too many Haitians that outsiders will be the ones in charge of Haiti's recovery. Instead, anyone hoping to finally bring colonialism to an end must agree to put Haitians in charge of their own country's destiny. Ironically, foreigners' endless attempts to correct Haiti's political and economic life often prompt Haitians to complain that foreigners are guilty of modern-day imperialism, thus adding to the long list of colonial sins and resulting in a call for more international aid.

No one can accuse the dedicated men and women providing foreign aid of racism. And yet, the international community's insistence that French and U.S. diplomats should act as Haiti's nanny stems from a mind-set belonging to the colonial era—Senator Dodd's careless talk of a "receivership" would not have been out of place in a speech by Theodore Roosevelt or Woodrow Wilson. Even the best-intentioned NGO workers dedicating their lives to vaccinating Haitian children do so because they believe that Haitians are incapable of providing their citizens with the most basic medical care on their own. How would these workers react if Haitian doctors established rural clinics in Appalachia to treat uninsured children? Would Americans ever expect Haitian advisers to come to Florida to teach this state how to prevent electoral fraud? A truly colorblind, respectful policy would consist of giving Haitians credit for all they do, both good and bad, and expecting them to address their country's problems on their own.

History hangs like a long shadow over Haiti. The violence and exploitation of the past are difficult to forget; and yet, past ills too often serve as a convenient excuse for Haiti's present shortcomings. However painful this might be for a historian to write, Haitians would be better served forgetting their past and looking at their current problems afresh. Unfortunately, most do not, and still live in an intellectual world inherited from the colonial days. One must thus take a long step back to the depths of colonial exploitation to uncover the origins of Haitians' worldview. This, in turn, will illustrate why the United States' more recent attempts to alter Haiti's political and economic destiny have failed, and help outline a practical scenario that could once more turn Haiti into the Pearl of the Caribbean.

CHAPTER 1

The Pearl of the Caribbean: Haiti in Colonial Times (1492–1791)

European "Discovery"

In 1492, during his first voyage to the Western Hemisphere, Christopher Columbus landed in the Bahamas, then headed south for the coast of Cuba. Upon hearing that an island due east abounded in gold, pearls, and spices, he made his way across the Windward Passage, thus becoming the first European to land in Haiti. Columbus's first taste of Haiti was as bitter as it was sweet. Leaving a young boy in charge of his admiral ship so that he could take some rest on Christmas Eve, he awoke to the sound of crashing wood. The *Santa Maria* had hit a reef and soon foundered. Columbus left some crewmembers on the shore, where they built Fort Navidad, the first European settlement in the Caribbean; but these men met a tragic end, killed by the native Tainos after Columbus's departure. Luckily, Columbus noted with interest, the natives he had seen wore gold trinkets, looked submissive enough, and could presumably be enslaved without too much difficulty. As for Cuba and Haiti,

> All these islands are fertile and this one is particularly so. It has many large harbors finer than any I know in Christian lands, and many large rivers. All this is marvelous. The land is high and has many ranges of hills, and mountains incomparably finer than Tenerife [in Spain's Canary Islands]. All are most beautiful and various in shape, and all are accessible. They are covered with tall trees of different kinds which seem to reach the sky.[1]

The island was large at 29,321 square miles (present-day Haiti occupies its western third, or 10,641 square miles; the rest forms the Dominican

Republic) (figure 1.1). Most of it was mountainous. Centuries later, when questioned by Napoléon Bonaparte about the terrain French troops were likely to encounter during an expedition to Haiti, a French officer would take a piece of paper, crumble it in his hands, and answer: "this, sir, is the terrain."[2] Five main mountain ranges crisscrossed Haiti, which the French would later name Massif du Nord in the north, Montagnes Noires and Chaîne des Matheux in the west, and Massif de la Hotte and Massif de la Selle in the South. Plains—the Plaine du Nord in the north, the Plaine de l'Artibonite and the Plaine du Cul-de-Sac in the west, and the Plaine de Jacmel in the south—were few and far between. Haiti's mountains and westward orientation protected its interior from the oceanic trade winds, resulting in a climate that was dry, arid even for a Caribbean island, except in the rainy months of the summer and fall. In later years, enterprising French settlers would learn to dam the Artibonite River and irrigate the fields in Haiti's interior.

Columbus first landed on Haiti's northern coast, in a magnificent natural harbor he named Môle Saint-Nicolas, then made his way east, passing by the bay where Cap Haïtien—Haiti's largest city in colonial times—would later be built. Further south, the island resembled a giant claw. In its middle part, the coastal plain where Port-au-Prince would

Figure 1.1 Contemporary Haiti. This map does not show Navassa (La Navase), a small island located thirty-five miles southwest of Haiti and that is claimed by Haiti and the United States.

one day rise faced the beautiful island of La Gonâve. What lay in the interior and in the south—mountains for the most part, one of them capping at 2,680 meters (8,793 feet)—Columbus did not see. He named the island Española (Hispaniola) in honor of his Spanish patrons. The French would later rename the western part Saint-Domingue. In 1804, when the country declared its independence, it reverted to the pre-Columbian, native name for the island: Hayiti; Haiti.

Tainos and Spaniards

Columbus's voyages are usually labeled voyages of discovery, but he was not the first human being to lay his eyes on Haiti. The island was inhabited by approximately half-a-million native Indians called Tainos. The Amerindians of Haiti are not as famous as the Aztecs of Mexico, the Mayas of Central America, and the Incas of the Andes. Their architectural achievements were limited—thatched roof huts called *caney*, along with large ball courts for the island's most popular sport—but they had an elaborate social structure organized around local chiefs, or *caciques*. And, unfortunately, they had some gold (figure 1.2).

Figure 1.2 This vignette from an eighteenth-century Dutch map portrays the Tainos who had died two centuries earlier. Many details are fanciful; but the miners toiling in the background under the watchful eyes of idle Europeans have much to do with reality.

Columbus and later Spanish colonists were not settlers in the traditional sense of the term. They did not intend to acquire empty land, build a log cabin, and become farmers. They were *conquistadors*: they were ambitious nobles and merchants who looked down on manual labor and dreamed of conquering a strange civilization, killing its leaders, enslaving its natives, and exploiting a quick windfall of gold and spices. Killing the Taino leaders, or *caciques*, they did: the tragic story of Anacoana illustrates this well. Anacoana was a Taino Haitian princess whom the Spaniards asked to organize a big feast for Governor Nicolas Ovando. When she and other *caciques* gathered for the festivities, Spanish soldiers set the meeting hall on fire and wiped out Hispaniola's leadership; Anacoana survived the fire, only to be put on trial and hanged. Taino commoners were subsequently forced to work on gold mines and plantations.

Hatuey, another Taino *cacique*, was so revolted by the Spaniards' mistreatment of his people that he fled Haiti for Cuba. Led by Diego Velasquez de Cuellar, the persistent Spaniards landed in Cuba to pursue him. In 1512, after years of guerilla warfare, Hatuey was captured and sentenced to be burnt alive. A Franciscan friar suggested that should Hatuey repent and convert to Catholicism, his captors might show mercy and substitute garroting for the agony of death by fire. Plus, the Franciscan added, Hatuey would spend eternity in heaven. When questioned by Hatuey if Spaniards also went to paradise, the Franciscan responded that the best Spaniards did. "The best are good for nothing," Hatuey snapped back, "and I will not go where there is a chance of meeting one of them."[3] Hatuey opted for fire and hell. Bartolome de Las Casas, a young Spaniard who had initially benefited from Taino forced labor as an *encomendero* (plantation owner), was so profoundly shaken by the episode that he embraced the religious orders and spent the rest of his life defending the cause of the indigenous peoples of the Americas.

Within two generations, Spain's cruel exploitation of local laborers, combined with the plight of European diseases the Tainos had no immunity against, had resulted in the complete disappearance of the Taino population. Genocide, a word destined to become sadly notorious in the twentieth century, met its first incarnation in fifteenth-century Haiti (Spain did not intend to kill all Tainos, only to exploit their labor). By the seventeenth century, Haiti was worth nothing. Spain had killed off the natives, exploited what little gold there was, and moved on to the more promising riches of Mexico and Peru. All that remained was a small Spanish presence in the east, where the city of San Domingo presided over a hinterland backwater of cattle ranchers and colonial administrators who dreamed of leaving for the continent. Devoid of any meaningful human presence, the western part of the island was now one large tropical forest in which the cows and pigs initially introduced by Spanish colonists pullulated. Nothing remained of the native civilization that once thrived there, save for words borrowed from the Taino language and culture such as hammock (*hamaca*), hurricane (*huracan*), savanna (*sabana*), canoe (*canoa*), barbecue (*barbacoa*), and tobacco (*tabaco*). Haiti's first two hundred years of colonial rule symbolized one important rule of economic growth that Haiti was to encounter numerous times in its history: the reckless search for quick riches, with its complete disregard for individual human suffering, may result in a short-term creation of wealth, but not in long-term development.

Boucaniers, Corsaires, and Frères de la Côte

The Tainos were not the only ones to lament Spain's newfound power. Other European countries—France, England, and the Netherlands most prominently—looked in envy as galleons loaded with American gold and silver entered the ports of Cádiz and Seville. European rivalry for control of the Caribbean marked the seventeenth century, and Haiti, because of its centrality, found itself in the eye of the storm. The first French settlers were a mixed lot composed of gentlemen desirous to distance themselves from French courts, naval deserters, runaway indentured servants, and ambitious young men. Women were few in those early days; settlers formed same-sex unions, a practice inherited from the French navy and thus called *matelotage* (after *matelot*, "sailor"). Like standard brides and grooms, *matelotage* partners looked after each other, inherited from each other, and slept with each other (occasionally, they shared any available female mate); Haitian pirates later borrowed this practice. Many French settlers chose Saint-Domingue partly because Spanish presence in western Hispaniola was negligible, and partly because the wild pigs and cattle provided an inextinguishable supply of fresh meat. Hunting eventually brought more meat than they could handle. The French thus adopted the Taino tradition of slow-cooking venison on an open fire, or *boucan*, and selling beef jerky to the ships that passed by. These professionals of the art of barbecue called themselves *boucaniers*—buccaneers.

The islands of the West Indies form a long arc, stretching from Venezuela to Florida, that seals off the Caribbean Sea. To access Mexico and Panama (on the road to Peru), Spanish galleons thus had to make their way through one of the main channels dividing the islands. The Windward Passage that lies between Haiti and Cuba was one of them. The *boucaniers*, after years of seeing ships pass by their hunting grounds, reached the conclusion that seizing a Spanish galleon might provide more income than a lifetime of hunting ever could. Their main line of work subsequently switched from French cuisine to high-seas robbery. The French monarchy, still seething at Spain's newfound wealth, gave these daring men a *lettre de marque* (an official document specifying that they were on the king's service) that condoned all future violence as long as it was directed at France's enemies. These naval mercenaries, called privateers in English, were called *corsaires* in French.

French and British harassment eventually took its toll. The Spanish hold on northwestern Hispaniola became so tenuous that in 1665 France named Bertrand d'Ogeron as first governor of the French settlements in what remained, in name only, a Spanish colony. Spain finally yielded some of its Caribbean islands (whose value was limited anyhow) to European competitors and, in 1697, the Treaty of Ryswick officially gave France the western third of Hispaniola. Haiti, or Saint-Domingue as the French called their colony, was born.

For the French and the British, relying on *corsaires* was a brilliant strategy in the age of Spanish domination. Once these two countries became colonial rulers in their own right, however, their enthusiasm for privatized warfare diminished. After years of being on the predators' side, they now were likely to become the prey. They thus established their own trade routes, protected them with a national navy, and tried to forbid privateering, at least in peacetime. Abandoned by their patrons, the *corsaires* became *flibustiers* (pirates). Their lives still consisted in capturing merchant vessels, but they did so without being commissioned by a state and could expect merciless treatment if captured.

Even if their existence revolved around the sea, pirates needed a safe haven in which to spend their loot and resupply. La Tortue (Tortuga), a rocky island a few miles off Saint-Domingue's northern coast, was an ideal base. Initially, Tortuga was dominated by the Providence Company, a group of Puritans who imaginatively mixed religion and piracy. Jean le Vasseur, a dictatorial Frenchman, followed. Under his rule, Tortuga became an independent pirate state protected by a large fortress and quickly acquired a legendary status in the literature of this turbulent era. Money that had come easily was as quickly gone. Rum, women, fortunes lost in a night's gambling: the fantastic sums seized from Spanish ships did not make any lasting contribution to Haiti's economy. All that remains from this era is an interesting synonym for "pirates" that illustrates the key role Saint-Domingue's northern coast played during the age of piracy: *frères de la côte*, the brotherhood of the coast.

White Slaves and Sugarcane

After acquiring Saint-Domingue, France set up an economic model more stable than the state-sanctioned robbery prevalent in Spanish and privateering times. Settlers cultivated African and Middle Eastern crops likely to flourish in the tropical climate and fertile soil. Cotton, indigo, and coffee were among them; but none equaled sugarcane. At a time when sugar beet was not yet in wide use, sugarcane was the most efficient way of sweetening European palates. Unable to grow sugarcane at home, Europeans flocked to the Caribbean.

Sugar was the oil of the eighteenth century; all principles yielded to its needs. Major European powers fought seemingly senseless wars over controversies surrounding tiny sugar islands such as Saint Lucia and Barbados. When France lost the Seven Year War (known as the French and Indian War in the United States) in 1763, she lost virtually all her North American possessions, including Canada and the immense plain between the Appalachians and the Rocky Mountains. But, French philosophers such as Voltaire reasoned, they had saved what mattered most: Guadeloupe and Martinique. Saint-Domingue, because of its size, was the greatest and most profitable of all the sugar islands.

France also strove to attract residents more suited to the needs of empire building than the male hunters and pirates then composing the bulk of the colony's population. Attracting settlers proved to be a difficult task. Saint-Domingue was famed for quick riches, but also for tropical diseases and hard work in the sugarcane fields. Another problem was money. Traveling across the Atlantic was expensive, and Frenchmen willing to bet their lives on hopes of far-flung wealth were generally penniless. When the supply of adventurous men and women willing to pay their way proved inadequate, France resorted to an imaginative system. Colonial authorities sent *engagés* or *trente-six mois*, indentured servants who received free passage to the colonies in exchange for a three-year period of voluntary servitude.

The system led to many abuses. Drunken revelers in French ports sometimes awoke in ships bound for Saint-Domingue, having unsuspectingly signed away their freedom during a night of carousing. The king himself was known to round up criminals, orphans, and prostitutes and ship them away to clean up the streets of Paris (amateurs of French literature should refer themselves to Abbé Prévost's *Manon Lescaut*). The colony was so short on women that husbands could not afford to be too finicky about their wives' checkered past. As soon as a boatload of women landed in Saint-Domingue, men who could afford to do so purchased a bride. "I take thee without knowing, or caring to know, who thou art," the standard marriage vow went. "Give me only thy word for the future. I acquit thee of what is past." Leniency had its limits. Musket in hand, the groom added "if thou should prove false, this will certainly prove true to my aim."[4]

Even in the 1780s, at a time when the colony's financial success started attracting better citizens, Saint-Domingue continued to harbor a colorful mix of Parisian prostitutes, descendants of pirates, undesirable elements of French society, priests expelled by their national clergy, and war captives from Africa. Not surprisingly, the colony had a well-deserved reputation for being long on money and short on principles.

African Slaves

The rapid growth of Saint-Domingue's economy created an acute labor shortage. A coffee plantation employed dozens of workers; a sugar plantation required hundreds. Work was hard. To grow sugarcane, one needed to clear the land of its ancient forests, then prepare the soil (originally with an antiquated hoe, later with the more modern plow), plant the seedlings, and weed them. Ambitious irrigation projects were also required in Haiti's dry interior. Harvest time was the most strenuous season. Armed with machetes, workers made their way through canes taller than they were, razor-sharp leaves, insects, and snakes, cutting the cane as they moved along. Sugarcane sours fast, so workers then rushed to crush the cane and boil the juice, the fire adding to the tropical heat. European indentured workers could not withstand such hard work. They died by the thousands.

The dubious honor of solving the labor shortage belongs to Bartolome de Las Casas. Native populations of Latin America revere him as the Protector of the Indians, because his graphic depictions of Spanish abuse of the Tainos led the king of Spain to outlaw enslavement of most Indians in his 1542 Law of the Indies. Black inhabitants of the Americas, however, should curse his name, for Las Casas also suggested that Spain should import African slaves to make up for the dwindling pool of Indian workers (Africans, he thought, could better endure physical hardships). Such importations of African slaves remained limited at first. In 1700, there were only 9,000 slaves in all of Saint-Domingue. But in 1790, at the height of the island's prosperity, the colony imported 48,000 slaves for that year alone, and the total slave population topped 500,000. Slaves now formed the backbone of the colonial labor force. African slave workers could not withstand the hard work of sugar plantations. They died by the thousands. But the French simply imported more.

Under French law, slaves were subject to the regulations of the 1685 *Code Noir* (Black Code). These were surprisingly benign for the age. Masters could not rape their female slaves, and had to marry them and free them if they did (Art. 9). Slaves could not marry without their owner's consent—but not against the slaves' will either (Art. 10, 11). Slave families could not be separated at auction (Art. 47). Acting as stern but benevolent fathers, owners were required to feed and clothe their slaves properly, even when they grew old, and could not single-handedly resort to torture or capital punishment against their slaves; the Code even set a procedure for slaves to sue their owner for mistreatment (Art. 22–27, 42). Freed slaves immediately became full-fledged French citizens, regardless of the color of their skin (Art. 57, 59). Considering that in France the king could torture his own white citizens or jail them perpetually without trial, the *Code Noir* was a particularly enlightened piece of legislation for its time.

The king lived very far away, however, and royal governors too intent on implementing unpopular laws could be roughed up and exiled. The settlers did not abolish the *Code Noir*; they simply ignored it (this casual disregard for the law has remained a hallmark of Haitian society to the present day). Cut off from the main population centers, surrounded by hundreds of slaves, planters felt omnipotent, and they were scared. As countless anecdotes indicate, cruelty—sadism even—was seen as the only way to subdue the slaves. The Baron Wimpffen, an army officer who visited Saint-Domingue in 1788–1790, recalled in his *Voyage to Saint Domingo* (1797) that he once had dinner with a white settler who behaved with all the proper manners of a lady of the age until a servant brought an overcooked dish. The lady was incensed. She ordered the careless cook thrown into the oven and roasted.

Such mistreatment was illegal under the *Code Noir*, but planters were rarely brought to justice, and even more rarely sentenced. One case that received great attention in 1788 was that of Nicolas Lejeune, a planter who wrongly accused two female slaves of conspiring to poison him, burned off their legs to convince them to confess, then chained them and threw them in a cell. Fellow slaves alerted legal authorities, too late, unfortunately, to save the two women's lives. The planter did not question the facts; his actions clearly violated the *Code Noir*; but, he asserted, the public peace of the colony required that authorities not challenge a planter's ability to punish his slaves. He prevailed.

Slavery in Haiti and in the United States:
A Comparison

When most Americans think of the slave trade, the image that immediately comes to mind is that of Virginia or Louisiana of the 1850s. In reality, only 6 percent of the slaves taken across the Atlantic—out of a total of 10–11 million—were shipped to the United States. Many more were sold in Brazil and the Caribbean. Tiny Haiti alone, even though it abolished slavery seventy years before the United States did, imported more slaves than the United States did. Such numbers are a reflection not only of Haiti's eighteenth-century prosperity, but also of the slaves' suffering. In the United States, where the slaves lived long enough to have offspring, natural reproduction reduced the need for slave imports. In Haiti and elsewhere, slaves died in such great numbers that the pool of black labor had to be constantly replenished through the slave trade.

Scholars agree that mortality in Haiti largely exceeded that of contemporary American plantations (especially those in the mid-Atlantic region), but their views on what caused this disparity diverge, and comparative studies on the treatment of slaves have led to heated historiographical debates. American scholars tend to describe colonial Haiti as one of the cruelest slave societies in the Americas, pointing out that North American masters intimidated their slaves by threatening to ship them off to Saint-Domingue. They also draw on the anecdotal evidence relating instances of sadistic treatment of Haitian slaves to demonstrate the French masters' innate viciousness.

Differentiating shades of evil between one form of slavery and another is a complicated task; one is quickly drawn into arcane debates on the relative levels of pain inflicted by mutilation and flogging. Theories on French brutality also overlook Saint-Domingue's specific climate and economy. Tropical islands such as Saint-Domingue were plagued by yellow fever and malaria, two diseases that were poorly understood until the early twentieth century. This unhealthy climate was the prime reason for the short life expectancy; mortality was actually higher among newly arrived white settlers (including slave masters) than it was among new African slaves, who were comparatively more resistant to tropical diseases.

Because of the island's weather, Saint-Domingue's largest plantations specialized in sugarcane, not the tobacco and wheat predominant in the mid-Atlantic region; sugarcane cultivation was infamous for fostering bad working conditions regardless of the planter's nationality. Sugar was a crop that required such extensive acreage, technological expertise, manpower, and machinery that it flourished best in large plantations employing up to three hundred slaves. The start-up costs were so high that sugar-cane plantations were often in the hands of wealthy investors residing in Cap Français, or even in Paris, who hired managers to run the plantation. Paid a commission based on a year's crop, managers tended to push slaves hard to increase short-term profits, and occasionally forced them to work extra hours on rest days on separate fields owned by the manager himself. Even when the owner was present, contacts between masters and slaves were minimal on large sugar plantations, making it easier to treat as animals human beings one hardly knew. Outnumbered fifty, or even hundred, to one, planters had to resort to extreme measures to assert their control over their slaves (the situation was better in coffee plantations, more numerous but smaller than sugar plantations). Because sugar was so lucrative, planters cut down on subsistence crops, importing food instead, with disastrous conditions whenever a hurricane or war interrupted trade. Intense heat, tropical diseases, hard labor associated with the sugar harvest, and insufficient food, more than inordinate mistreatment on the part of French planters, killed 5–6 percent of the slave population every year.

The situation in the United States was comparatively better because the climate supported different crops. Plantations were smaller, rarely topping fifty slaves, with most masters owning less than ten slaves. Absentee owners were rare; American planters, who had little hope of making a quick killing in the sugar business and returning to a life of leisure in Europe, planned on spending their entire lives in the United States. Even in the Deep South, the slave population remained a minority, and planter paranoia about slave rebellion was less acute than it was in Caribbean islands where 10 percent of the population owned the remaining 90 percent. Yellow fever epidemics broke out occasionally, but with less frequency and intensity than in the Caribbean. As a result, by the time the American Civil War erupted in 1861, four million black slaves lived in the United States, a four-fold increase since the abolition of the slave trade in 1808.

Paradoxically, accounts of past French atrocities now fuel Haitian nationalism. Haitians like to argue that Haitian slavery was uniquely evil, and that Haitian slaves suffered more than anybody else did; after all, were they not the only ones who mustered enough courage to free themselves of white oppression? Haitians also claim that the rich planters of Saint-Domingue could afford higher purchasing prices than planters in other islands, and as a result commandeered the best slaves upon their arrival from the African coast. Such theories on the superiority of the Haitian racial stock must be taken with a large grain of salt.

Nationalists all over the Caribbean, it seems, always conclude that the best specimen of the slave trade were sold in the island of their birth.

Slave Resistance

What were the slaves to do? The more fearful among them decided to submit to white rule, or even to collaborate with it. Planters deluded themselves into thinking that the slaves looked up to them as friends and parents, but the conversion was rarely heartfelt. When the slave revolt began, many a planter made the painful discovery that the most prominent slaves—house servants, slave drivers—were at the forefront of the revolt, calling in no uncertain terms for the death of their beloved master. In *The New Maroons: An Essay on an Aspect of the Political Crisis* (1999), Marc-Ferl Morquette suggested that the practice of deceit in the face of superior force became so ingrained in the slaves' mind that it has remained as a feature of the Haitian national character. The history of Haiti's relations with great powers indeed includes numerous instances in which Haitian leaders played the role of the submissive friend, then raised their true colors when the balance of power became more favorable. Slavery may be long since gone; but intellectual marooning is here to stay.

Those whose hatred for slavery ran even deeper fled the plantation altogether. Despite an extensive police arsenal designed to prevent slave flight, Saint-Domingue was awash with maroons (*marrons*). Some absented themselves for a mere few days, often to protest a hired manager's excessive cruelty. Sympathetic slaves offered food, lodging, and counterfeited passes to the runaways, and tipped off search parties in the wrong directions. Other maroons left the coastal world of plantations for good, benefiting from the island's forbidding terrain to find some remote interior location and live there. They often joined bands of escaped slaves who built mountain strongholds complete with deep moats and fences of sharp stakes. Extirpating maroon communities from these hills could take years, and even such efforts were not always successful. In 1702, the French sent a first expedition to the Bahoruco region to dislodge a maroon community that had settled near the Haitian–Dominican border. The expedition failed. For decades thereafter, Bahoruco bandits continued to pillage neighboring plantations, and French columns kept on hiking to the Bahoruco region. Eighty-three years later, in 1785, the French and their Spanish neighbors finally gave up: they signed a treaty granting the maroons independence in exchange for an end to the raids on plantations. Centuries before Che Guevara and Ho Chi Minh, Haiti's black rebels had perfected all the principles of modern guerrilla warfare: operating out of an ill-defined frontier region; relying on the support of sympathetic locals; making the best of a rugged terrain; and refusing pitched battles with a superior enemy. This was a strategy later Haitian revolutionaries would implement on a large scale.

Flight brought freedom to the escapee and represented a significant financial setback for the planter, but it did little to undermine the foundations of the slave economy. While the maroons selfishly enjoyed their freedom in the mountains, the vast majority of their African brethren continued to toil in the plains. One maroon, Makandal, conceived a grander plan. Makandal was a *Congo* or *Bossale*—the term used for African-born slaves (as opposed to the second-generation *Créoles*). He had lost an arm while working on one of the large sugar plantations of the northern plain and harbored a lifelong grudge against his former French masters. He also claimed various magical powers, mixing Allah, Jesus, and African gods in one syncretic hodgepodge typical of Haiti's religious tradition. Most importantly, after running away from his plantation in 1751, he organized a vast conspiracy aimed at poisoning white Frenchmen and their cattle. For years, Makandal remained invincible; he had the ability, he said, to transform himself into a mosquito and fly away when cornered. The plot killed thousands. Finally, in 1758, the French captured him and tied him to a stake in Cap Français. As the flames consumed him, Makandal broke free of the pole, and all the slaves among the crowd gasped, "*Makandal sauvé!*" (Makandal fled!). Authorities cleared up the market square and threw him back in the fire, but, as late as the beginning of the Haitian Revolution in 1791, many slaves remained convinced that he was alive and would one day call for a day of final reckoning. They, not the rational Frenchmen of the Enlightenment Age, were right. Mosquitoes would soon decimate French ranks and help set the slaves free.

Slave Culture: Voodoo

No part of Haitian culture is more famous or more misunderstood than Voodoo. Voodoo, whose etymology goes back to a Dahomean word for "spirit," is simply a syncretic, polytheistic religion, which borrowed some of its many gods from West African and Congolese pantheons, and others from seventeenth- and eighteenth-century French Catholicism and mysticism. But Voodoo's secretive nature, vivid ceremonies, and association with revolutionary movements have given this religion a bad name. To many, Voodoo is really a satanic cult accused of practicing human sacrifice and ritualistic cannibalism; many Americans' only window into Voodoo are horror movies such as Wes Craven's *The Serpent and the Rainbow* (1988), which draw heavily on stories of possessed worshippers and living dead. Adding to the confusion, the premier disciples of Voodoo have failed to couch in writing the religion's main principles, leaving to foreign anthropologists the difficult task of describing Voodoo from the outside.

The history of Voodoo mirrors the dual origin of the Haitian people. Its central tenets derive from animistic cults of West Africa, where worship of ancestors and natural forces was common. The French unwittingly imported and merged these various cults through the Atlantic slave trade. The *Code Noir* also specified that slaves had to be baptized; so slaves were instructed by French colonial priests who often lacked theological training (the situation worsened after independence, when Haiti became infamous for its renegade priests and heresies; a concordat was finally signed in 1860). One last influence might have been sorcery, occultism, and witchcraft, which were widely popular in seventeenth-century French aristocratic society. When France acquired Saint-Domingue, the kingdom was barely emerging from a massive scandal in which prominent members of the court were convicted of celebrating black masses in which infants were executed. Male and female planters of Saint-Domingue, following the Parisian passion for occultism, practiced various enchantments on their plantations, presumably in the presence of their house slaves, who then incorporated these spells into their own Voodoo ceremonies. These mystical roots probably explain the Voodoo taste for numerology and charms. Even today, Voodoo bears the hallmarks of this slave ancestry. Uninitiated worshippers are called *bossales*, a term applied in the eighteenth century to describe the slaves who had recently landed from Africa.

Voodoo recognizes the existence of a supreme God, or *bon dieu*, but one who has little time to busy himself with the affairs of mere mortals. Practical Voodoo thus revolves around a complex pantheon of lesser gods, or *loas*, each of which has an area of expertise. Each major Voodoo divinity corresponds to a Catholic saint; so Haitian Voodoo worshippers see nothing wrong with moonlighting as devout Catholics. The most prominent *loa* is Papa Legba, father of the crossroads, who orients believers in the same fashion St. Peter does (he points to Guinea rather than Heaven). Similarly, Ogun, the *loa* of war, corresponds to the dragon-slaying St. George (Voodoo gods must know a lot about Haitian politics, for the *loa* of war also represents authority, and he is depicted either as a general or as a politician). Maîtresse Erzulie, the *loa* of maternal and physical love, is associated with the Virgin Mary. One of her incarnations Erzulie Dantó is a stolid, hard-working single mother who personifies Haitian womanhood. Erzulie Dantó is constantly quarreling with the seductress

Erzulie Freda, characterized by her beauty and preciosity. Dantó is black while Freda is mulatto; so the family quarrel probably originated with the simmering tensions between black field workers and the planters' mulatto mistresses on colonial plantations. There are hundreds of *loas*, most of them merciful, some of them more frightening, such as the Baron Samedi, the grave-digger who inspired Papa Doc, and his fellow *loas* of the *guédé* family (spirits of the dead). Interestingly, *loas* belonging to the African-born Rada family tend to be gentler than their hot-tempered Haitian cousins of the Petro cult. *Loas* can multiply or disappear; the 1915 U.S. invasion of Haiti even produced a Marine *loa* with a penchant for Bourbon and corned beef.

Voodoo relies on a network of priests and priestesses (*houngans* and *mambos*) selected for their prescience, ancestry (many are children of existing priests), or because of some unusual event (a breech birth is a particularly good omen, e.g.). The priests reside in temples called peristyles or *houmfort*. The centerpieces of the temple are a pole called *poto mitan*, often decorated with depictions of the serpent god Damballah, and an altar overflowing with Catholic and Voodoo artifacts representing the various *loas*; a nearby chapel dedicated to the favorite *loa* remains off-limits to the congregation. The priests serve as healers and advisers, but their main duty is to preside over long ceremonies designed to attract particular *loas*. Chants and dances are a prerequisite; *loas* also favor specific foods (eggs and flour for the serpent Damballah, perfume for the seductress Erzulie Freda). An animal sacrifice may be added for maximum effect. When the ceremony is successful, one or more parishioners will enter a trance and become possessed with their *loa* of choice. For example, should a person jump for a cigar, a sword, and a bottle of rum, this would be an unmistakable sign that the rowdy Ogun is present (an attendant, or *général de la place*, is on hand to keep order). *Loas* can be mischievous; it is not uncommon for a foul-talking, salacious *loa* to possess (or "mount") an otherwise mild-mannered old lady.

Most of Voodoo revolves around the hope that faith will help obtain the kind of worldly services one may expect from a Catholic saint, such as passing an exam, finding love, and succeeding in business. But the part that most fascinates foreigners, and where reliable information is hardest to come by, is the world of spells. Black magic is the realm of renegade priests, or mysterious sects; a standard *houngan* will only provide talismans to protect against another person's spell. Those operating on the fringes of Voodoo may also traffic with demons, werewolves, and *zombies*. Some of these supernatural creatures were standard features of peasant life in early modern France, where midwives whose patients lost too many infants were frequently accused of practicing witchcraft. The *zombie* phenomenon is more distinctively Haitian. *Zombies,* Haitians believe, are corpses awakened by evil spells to be transformed into brutish servants (when given a taste of salt, they awaken and run to the grave to renew their peaceful slumber). In colonial times, *zombies* served as a metaphor for slavery; many masters were accused of employing *zombies,* presumably because, to a master, the best slaves were those who worked hard and thought little.

Because of the secretive nature of the malevolent Voodoo sects, substantiating accusations of cannibalistic practices is almost impossible; the topic is so taboo that one does not even speak of human sacrifice, but of killing "goats without horns." In the 1840s, a Voodoo sect that called itself *guyons* or *loups-garous* was widely rumored to practice ritual cannibalism; alas, only one member was ever brought to a trial, in 1846, and the courts never rendered a judgment for fear the affair would further worsen Haiti's notorious reputation abroad. In 1863, a couple from Bizoton was accused of the cannibalistic murder of their young niece; this time, a thorough investigation led to the execution of the culprits and their accomplices, but it generated much unwelcome international publicity. In 1920, a Haitian rebel named Benoît Batraville took a U.S. Marine prisoner and shared his heart and liver with fellow fighters in the hope that the organs would impart wisdom and courage to those eating them. In the 1920s, Cadeus Bellegarde was arrested for killing and eating scores of Haitians in elaborate ceremonials (it is unclear whether he was a *bona fide* member of a secret cult or simply a deranged serial killer).

Voodoo's infamous reputation stems from its association with evil spells, but also from its revolutionary roots. From its origins, Voodoo was the religion of the slaves, one their master did not understand and thus could not control. Forced into the shadows, it acquired a secret, even violent, overtone that attracted rebellious slaves. Revealingly, the 1791 Haitian slave uprising was plotted during a secret Voodoo ceremony. After independence, Haitian elites did all they could to outlaw the cult, though some presidents were rumored to practice in secret what they fought in public. Toussaint Louverture, Jean-Jacques Dessalines, Henri Christophe, and Jean-Pierre Boyer all disparaged Voodoo in public; it was not until 1846 that a Voodoo ceremony was held openly in the capital. When the United States invaded Haiti in 1915, Marine officers used a provision of the Haitian Penal Code forbidding the practice of Voodoo to justify a vast campaign to destroy temples and take away sacred drums. Voodoo once again went underground and served as the main religious ally of the rebels battling the Marines. In the end, Voodoo's most potent foe has been poverty, not state repression. Voodoo is declining today because many Haitians can no longer afford to pay for offerings of rum and small animals; Haitian candidates for emigration also reason that when praying for a visa to the United States, one is better served asking the Protestant god of the Americans than local *loas* who have little sway in the U.S. Embassy. Evangelicalism is now a fast-growing religion in Haiti, because its lively practices echo those of Voodoo ceremonies, but also because it is spread by U.S. churches that finance schools and hospitals.

It is always problematic to criticize someone's spiritual beliefs. By their very nature, religions are substantiated by faith, not facts, and generate passionate, unthinking attachment to one's god(s) of choice. Yet, sociologists, such as Max Weber in his *The Protestant Ethic and the Spirit of Capitalism* (1920), have shown that a nation's main religious affiliation can determine its economic success—for example, that the Protestants' focus on critical appraisal of sources and individualism made them better suited to capitalism during the industrial revolution than their Catholic brethren. One cannot help but think that Voodoo's popularity has hindered, rather than facilitated, Haiti's development. The distant gods of monotheistic religions offer the promise of everlasting bliss in exchange for following a few rules and rituals, but they generally do not intercede on a daily basis, thus leaving more room for self-reliance and individual action. Because of its focus on the omnipresence of supernatural forces and on a *loa*'s ability to solve one's daily problems, Voodoo serves as a substitute for a rational assessment of the difficulties a parishioner should face alone. Voodoo hinders Haitians' entrepreneurial spirit by portraying godly intercession, not human activism, as the most efficient method of human betterment.

A Keg of Powder

It is easy to understand why slaves would launch an uprising. What is more surprising is that the first Haitians to raise the standard of revolt were whites and free people of color, not the oppressed black masses. The whites' main bone of contention was lack of autonomy. France had created colonies with the sole purpose of benefiting the metropolis; so all key political decisions were taken by Paris-appointed *gouverneurs* and *intendants* (the former a military officer, the latter the chief financial administrator), then imposed on planters. The planters' ire focused first and foremost on mercantilism, or *exclusif*. Under this rule, a feature of all European colonial empires until the twentieth century, Saint-Domingue was to trade primarily with the mother country. Selling colonial products to non-French merchants, even if they offered higher prices, was usually forbidden; buying manufactured goods and foodstuffs outside French ports was also prohibited. Monopolies granted to French merchants, along with a ban on manufactured products made in the colonies, further contributed to keeping the price of colonial exports low and that of colonial imports high.

By the 1790s, France had relaxed some of these rules and an active contraband trade linked Saint-Domingue to the newly independent United States, but the colonists still clamored for complete freedom of trade. When the French Revolution erupted in 1789, planters concluded that the time had come to assert their autonomy. Invoking revolutionary ideals they were flouting daily on their estates, they marginalized French envoys, created their own assembly, and petitioned Paris for a regime of colonial self-rule. The white population of Saint-Domingue was minuscule, but by 1790 it was split into a myriad of political factions divided by wealth (urban poor vs. the rich planters), politics (revolutionaries vs. monarchists), nationalism (proponents of immediate independence vs. French loyalists), and birth (Creole vs. French-born colonists). Whites executed and deported each other with abandon, oblivious to the fact that the immense black majority was on the verge of launching a general offensive.

The free population of color formed another privileged, discontented group. The dearth of available French women, male owners' complete control over their slaves had resulted in widespread miscegenation. Following in that regard a provision of the *Code Noir*, masters often manumitted their mixed-blood offspring. Other slaves bought their freedom or gained it from benevolent masters, so that by the 1790s, the number of free coloreds in Saint-Domingue (either mulatto or black) reached 30,000, roughly equal to that of whites. Whites, especially the penniless *petits blancs* (poor whites), whose sole claim to greatness was the paleness of their skin, balked at granting free coloreds the legal equality guaranteed under the *Code Noir*. As years went by, ever more stringent racial discrimination laws were introduced. The free coloreds were subjected to a mandatory period of military service, barred from certain professions, and prevented from wearing some adornments deemed too elaborate for such coarse creatures.

The free coloreds were educated, often rich, and they could not accept that the law should separate a mulatto from his white half-brother. They fought back. The 1789 French Declaration of the Rights of Man and of the Citizen, they said, granted equality to all men regardless of the color of their skin (ironically, they also claimed that the Declaration did not warrant general emancipation; the free coloreds owned slaves). In 1789, Vincent Ogé and Julien Raimond, two free people of color, traveled to Paris to petition the National Assembly for complete legal equality, including the right to elect deputies. They were outmaneuvered by the racist representatives from the colonies and obtained nothing. Ogé sneaked back undetected to Saint-Domingue, where he organized an armed rebellion, which proved as unsuccessful as his more peaceful entreaties. After a short period of fighting, Ogé and his fellow conspirators were defeated and captured. Ogé was tortured, his limbs broken on the wheel, and his severed head paraded on a pike as a warning to vindictive mulattoes.

Meanwhile, as white and mulatto slave owners fought amongst themselves, the one group that had the greatest grounds to ask for redress—the black slaves—remained still. The slaves worked on, seemingly oblivious to the political turmoil raging in Paris and Port-au-Prince. Their calm was misleading. The keg of powder would soon ignite on a stormy night of August 1791.

Colonial Legacy

The colonial era is particularly important to Haitian intellectuals, not only because it represents three hundred of the five hundred years that have elapsed since Columbus's arrival, but also because they claim that it explains many of the woes that would later plague postcolonial Haiti. Haiti, they say, suffered from arguably the harshest colonial system of its time, not once, but twice in its history—first under the Spaniards, then under the French. Just like a child who grows up in an abusive, broken home, then finds it hard to adjust to the world of adulthood, Haiti was conceived in blood, tears, and theft, hardly the best building blocks for nationhood. As Haitian president Jean-Bertrand Aristide put it succinctly in his 1993 autobiography,

> Europe owes us a debt. In fewer than fifteen years, Spain extracted fifteen thousand tons of gold here [the figure is wildly exaggerated], after having exterminated the Indians. As for France, we would never finish if we tried to recite all that it took from us. . . . The colonial powers, including the United States, must make amends for the wrongs inflicted on the colony or protectorate in those days. The debt experts, when they speak of our liabilities, need to add up the second column of their own accountability.[5]

As this excerpt suggests, colonial wrongs are not studied for their historical interest, but for their political value: arguing that Haiti is still paying the price for its colonial past is tantamount to saying that past colonial powers should indemnify Haitians. This apparently irrefutable reasoning rests on two pillars that roughly correspond to the modern legal categories of lost income and penalty for pain and suffering. First, Europeans made an undeserved profit (most of it created by unpaid Indian and African labor), which should be given back to its rightful owners. Second, the human cost was such that Europeans have a moral duty to alleviate the suffering of their victims' descendants. This argument is particularly widespread among Haitians, but it also underpins the current policy of sending foreign aid to poor countries (virtually all of them former colonies) in Latin America, Africa, and Asia.

Two important flaws make this argument morally inadequate. In modern societies, the concept of legal responsibility is individual, not collective, and limited in time, not eternal. Should a person commit a crime, this person alone will be held responsible by judicial authorities. No judge will ever prosecute a citizen because his or her first cousin happens to be a serial killer. Even this personal responsibility is limited. Statutes of limitations guarantee that an eighty-year-old man will not be prosecuted for stealing a car as a teenager. Theories on colonial legacy ignore these two important legal concepts. Individual taxpayers are held responsible for crimes committed centuries before by individuals to whom they may not even be related. For contemporary stockholders of German companies to pay compensation to heirs of enslaved World War II Jews is already a hotly debated idea; for contemporary Spaniards to pay the price for a Genoese sailor's greed half a millennium ago is simply absurd.

Attributing present-day economic performance to ancient events is an equally questionable endeavor. Economists, who cannot predict what the unemployment rate will be two quarters from now, would be hard-pressed to draw some unassailable chart proving that current policies will result in a GDP *per capita* of $23,187 in the year 2205. By the same token, describing colonial policies as the main reason for Haiti's current underdevelopment is a far-fetched idea, for a theory on economic causation spanning five centuries is unlikely to be accurate. So many random factors are involved that the end result is effectively unpredictable. Humans' ability to modify the environment they inherit from previous generations, in particular, makes it possible to reach outcomes radically different from what the historical record would warrant.

Historical inaccuracy also plagues the Haitian argument on colonial legacy. Haitians, when they refer to the enslavement of the Tainos as an example of the many wrongs inflicted on Haitians, presumably view fifteenth-century Amerindians as the ancestors of today's Haitian population. Jean-Jacques Dessalines, the first leader of independent Haiti and a prominent critic of French colonialism, even adopted the names "Army of the Incas" for his all-black army and "Hayiti" ("mountainous island" in the Taino language) for independent Saint-Domingue. History disproves those claims of pre-Columbian lineage. By the time Aristide's ancestors landed in Haiti—most of them African, a few of them French—the Tainos were long since gone, and Haiti was a *tabula rasa* in which previous history counted little. The Tainos, sadly, are nobody's ancestors. As for the Incas, they lived in the Andean mountains of Peru and Bolivia, several thousand miles to the south, and had no connection to the African-born Dessalines whatsoever.

The history of French colonialism in Haiti (1697–1804) is also cited as an uninterrupted series of crimes, slavery being the most prominent, that left Haiti with significant hurdles to overcome. However, the human cost of a policy does not always signify that its long-term consequences are nefarious. Twenty-five thousand workers died building the Panama Canal; but today the canal is a key passageway that benefits Panama's economy immensely. Slavery was horrible and unjustifiable; but, in a few decades, slaves and planters transformed Haiti's landscape for the better. When the first buccaneers landed in Haiti, the country was virtually uninhabited, and its economic output was nil. By the time the slaves revolted in 1791, large cities had sprung up, hundreds of plantations made Haiti the world's largest exporter of tropical foodstuffs, a modern road had opened between Cap Français and Port-au-Prince, irrigation had transformed the basin of the Artibonite River, skilled whites and free coloreds formed a large group of trained cadres, and close to six hundred thousand people (more than the Taino population for all of Hispaniola) called Haiti home. Haitian society, particularly its labor and racial laws, needed radical changes, but the Haitians were left with an economy transformed by decades of French investments (figure 1.3). Such a starting point was not negligible.

The only true links between colonial and contemporary Haiti are cultural. French colonization, then the African slave trade, created a hybrid culture that defines Haiti and other, smaller islands of the French West Indies. Creole, the primary language of the vast majority of Haitians, is the slaves' version of French, interspersed with words of African origin, its grammar tweaked beyond recognition. Voodoo, Haiti's most recognizable feature, appeared when African slaves, still loyal to the gods they had brought from Dahomey and elsewhere, were converted to Catholicism by colonial priests renowned as France's least rigorous theologians. Much

Figure 1.3 This frontispiece from an eighteenth-century French atlas downplays the exploitation of African slaves, but it accurately depicts the colony's great prosperity on the eve of the revolution.

of Haiti's uniqueness derives from its twin cultural ancestry—French traditions the Haitian elite prides itself on, and African traditions often concealed but nevertheless present. This cultural duality, in addition to the roads and mills and canals inherited from colonial times, enriched Haiti immensely. Haitians are right to remember slavery's evil nature, and wrong to conclude that all their problems derive from it. But, most importantly, they should not ignore the fact that their country's intricate soul was born in those troubled times.

CHAPTER 2

The Slaves Who Defeated Napoléon: The Haitian Revolution (1791–1804)

Voodoo in Gator Wood

On the night of August 21, 1791, slave representatives from all over Haiti's northern plain, the rich area surrounding Cap Français, gathered in Bois Caïman (Gator Wood) near Morne Rouge. Dutty Boukman, a Jamaican-born Voodoo priest, was there, along with Jeannot, whose hatred for the whites was notorious. Georges Biassou and Jean-François Papillon, two future leaders of the slave revolt who would later serve as generals in the Spanish army, were also in attendance. The air was dark, hot, and fiery; a tropical storm rumbled on the horizon. One slave after another emerged from the shadows, scared and thrilled. They were not allowed to sneak out of their quarters at night, and they knew that slave gatherings were strictly prohibited. With the onset of the French Revolution, rumors swirled among the planters that the Paris-based Société des Amis des Noirs had sent secret agents to Saint-Domingue to incite the slaves to revolt. Anyone accused of fomenting an uprising would likely meet an untimely and gruesome end.

There were no such agents. But the nervous planters chattered for hours about the revolution, and the many black servants who surrounded them, seemingly uninterested in such complicated political discussions, listened and drew their own conclusions. "All men are created free and equal": the unforgettable words of the French Declaration of the Rights of Man and of the Citizen could only inflame the imagination of the oppressed slaves of Saint-Domingue. The king of France had also decided to grant the slaves three days of rest a week, the slaves whispered, but the planters had conspired to keep this important decision secret. Surely, the slaves thought as they approached Bois Caïman, France would one day force the planters to implement such wondrous laws.

The rumor about an extended period of rest was false. Faced with a revolution at home, Louis XVI had little time to think about his dark-skinned subjects two thousand leagues away. But convinced that the rumor was real and that the Old Regime was crumbling, the slaves decided that the time had come to act. When everyone had finally gathered in Bois Caïman, Cécile Fatiman, a *mambo* (female Voodoo priest) and a mulatto slave of mixed Corsican and African origin, took a long, curved knife and brandished it in the air while chanting a mysterious mantra. As the congregation stood in awe, she seized a black pig and slit its throat. The look and taste of the blood left little room for doubt, Boukman proudly announced: Ogun, the god of war, wanted the slaves to revolt. Everyone took the solemn vow that they would kill white slave owners and exact vengeance from slavery. "The god of the white man calls him to commit crimes; our god asks only good works of us," Boukman added.

> But this god who is so good orders revenge! He will direct our hands; he will aid us. Throw away the image of the god of the Whites who thirsts for our tears and listen to the voice of liberty that speaks in the heart of all of us.[1]

To seal this sacred pact, each participant in turn drank the warm blood from the sacrificial pig. They also kept some of the pig's hairs to manufacture talismans that would make them invincible. As the heat and excitement reached its climax, the storm finally broke and the meeting disbanded. Drenched in blood, sweat, and rain, and surrounded by lightning and thunder, the slaves returned to their plantations. The following night, scattered revolts erupted in neighboring plantations. Soon, the entire plain was up in flames, Cap Français was besieged, and all French planters began to fear for their lives. The Haitian Revolution had begun.

The Bois Caïman ceremony features prominently in all accounts of the Haitian Revolution. The stormy setting, Voodoo gore, and vengeful pledge combine to form a startling scene that surprisingly has not yet been turned into a Hollywood epic. Historians must add a sobering caveat, however: The episode owes more to myth than to history. Most of the intriguing details were added in the nineteenth century by a Frenchman, Antoine Dalmas, who hoped to portray the slaves as savage beasts inspired by a satanic cult.[2] Slave gatherings did take place, and the slaves did revolt—but this is all we know. All the accounts remaining from this period were written by the French, who were not invited to a ceremony where their own death was being plotted. And yet, for all its inaccuracies, the Bois Caïman ceremony has become canonical; two hundred years from now, histories of the slave revolt will likely start with a detailed account of this tempestuous night. It certainly is a great story.

The Slave Revolt (1791–1792)

From the northern plain of Cap Français, the slave revolt soon spread to the western part of Saint-Domingue. Outnumbered twenty to one, the whites stood little chance of resisting the slaves' call for revenge. They hurriedly called for help from Cuba, Jamaica, Spanish Santo Domingo, the United States—even England. Despite their vested interest in seeing a white colonial hierarchy survive in the tropics, these countries sent little help.

Luckily for the white planters of Saint-Domingue, the black population was equally divided. The rebels failed to immediately direct their combined efforts on the major commercial center of Cap Français, which could easily have been taken in the early days of the revolt in a victory that would have dealt a mortal blow to the French. Worse, the four leaders who had emerged from the Bois Caïman ceremony—Jeannot, Papillon, Biassou, and Boukman—turned on themselves. Jeannot quickly became legendary for his brutality, as white prisoners who survived their captivity told stories of men lashed hundreds of times and of gunpowder rubbed into the bleeding wounds of the victims. Appalled by Jeannot's extreme cruelty, Jean-François had him arrested and executed. Jeannot's body was then hung on a butcher's hook, a reminder of the ordeal he had inflicted on many white captive. Boukman was captured while fighting French troops and decapitated; his body ended up on a French stake, like that of his idol Makandal. Internecine fighting and French repression had cut the slave leadership in half.

The primary motive of the uprising seemed transparent enough—freedom for the slaves—but the leaders' deeds did not always match their followers' creed. Rather than aligning themselves with the forces of the French Revolution, the leaders dressed themselves in royalist garb, wore the white insignia of the king, and clamored for a return to the very monarchy that had fathered slavery and imperialism. In December, in a surprising turnaround, Jean-François and Biassou offered the embattled French an enticing deal: freedom and amnesty for the rebel leaders in exchange for peace. French commissioners seriously entertained this unexpected proposal. But black slaves, who were expected to resume servile work on the plantations while their chiefs enjoyed the freedom secured by their subordinates' blood, were less than enthusiastic, as were the most extremist white planters. The deal fell through. Jean-François and Biassou's willingness to maintain the slave system may seem surprising to us, but they had grown up in African and Creole worlds in which slavery was common and practiced by white and black owners alike. It would be at least another year before the slave revolt, which had begun as a simple protest for better working conditions, would turn into an actual campaign for emancipation.

Eager to capitalize on divisions within the population of color, the French formed some battalions of loyal slaves and, in a crucial move, allied themselves with free people of color. The mulattoes had much in common with their white brethren: wealth, education, a father, and, most importantly, slave ownership. After decades of deriding mulattoes as the bastard sons of Africa, planters thus promised them legal equality in exchange for manning the frontlines of the counterinsurgency campaign, where they fought with distinction. By late 1792, the white-mulatto alliance had stemmed the revolt. Most slaves were back on plantations or hiding in the hills. The slaves had benefited from the element of surprise, the rallying cry of freedom, and overwhelming numerical superiority, but their divided, indecisive leadership had snatched defeat from the jaws of victory.

The Foreign Invasion (1793–1798)

Events in faraway Europe gave the slaves a second opportunity to free themselves. In 1793, the French Revolution took a more radical turn, a tribunal sent Louis XVI to the guillotine, and most of the conservative monarchies of Europe declared war on France. For Saint-Domingue's black population, general war meant two things: France would have few troops to spare for colonial duty, and the revolution's leftist turn might finally bring to the fore politicians sincerely dedicated to freedom and the rights of man.

The repercussions of the new European war were soon felt across the Atlantic as England and Spain, France's European enemies and the other two main colonial powers in the Caribbean, invaded Saint-Domingue. The British navy landed troops in most of the colony's major ports, while the Spaniards, operating from their colony of Santo Domingo, attacked by land. As slave-owning powers, neither Spain nor England had any intention of freeing the people of Saint-Domingue. France, on the other hand, chose as its new commissioner Léger-Félicité Sonthonax, a closet idealist who had previously published antislavery articles in

Parisian newspapers. Faced with pockets of continuing slave resistance, a conservative white population aghast at the French Revolution's extremism, and an invasion by two of Europe's greatest powers, he concluded that his hopeless situation called for drastic measures: in a dramatic shift from a century of French policy, he announced the immediate emancipation of the slaves of Saint-Domingue in exchange for their military help (Paris later ratified his decision and extended it to other colonies like Guadeloupe, making France the first European power to free its slaves).

Sonthonax's decree of emancipation runs contrary to the common view that all French colonial officials were racist advocates of slavery. That the entire population of color rose in support of emancipation is also a popular misconstruction. Black and mulatto revolutionary leaders were a diverse lot. Free people of color (many of whom had owned slaves before the revolution) often rallied to the British in the ports they controlled. Prominent black rebel leaders, including Biassou, Jean-François, and Toussaint Louverture—a man destined to play a leading role in Haitian politics—fought for Spain. England and Spain stood for monarchy, colonialism, racism, and slavery, while in 1793 France offered emancipation, racial equality, and the promise of radical social change. Yet despite what France had to offer, Louverture stayed in Spanish service until April 1794, eight months after Sonthonax abolished slavery, and it is still unclear whether his ultimate switch to the French side had anything to do with the law of emancipation. As for Jean-François and Biassou, they never abandoned their Spanish patrons and finished their lives fighting obscure conflicts in Honduras and Florida under the Spanish uniform.

The support of various segments of Saint-Domingue's population allowed England and Spain to occupy parts of the colony until 1798, when white, black, and mulatto supporters of emancipation finally defeated the partisans of slavery. Burdened with a continuing war in Europe, France thereafter kept a token white military presence in Saint-Domingue, where the vast majority of "French" troops were former black slaves, often African-born. This gave an opening to ambitious and capable leaders of color eager to advance in the ranks of the French army—particularly the senior black officer in Saint-Domingue, Toussaint Louverture.

Toussaint Louverture's Reign (1798–1802)

Toussaint Louverture is Haiti's most recognizable revolutionary figure and, arguably, the most notable black individual in world history. Famous, intriguing, and decisive he was; one-dimensional he was not.

Toussaint Louverture.

Published as the Act directs, July 1 1805, by Ja.t Cundee, Ivy Lane, Paternoster Row.

Figure 2.1 Toussaint Louverture as seen by Marcus Rainsford, a British officer who visited the island in 1799.

Like his two illustrious contemporaries, George Washington and Napoléon Bonaparte, he saw nothing wrong with celebrating freedom while condoning slavery or waging war while longing for peace. The patriotic need for mythmaking has led Haitians to celebrate him as a life-long, idealistic enemy of slavery and the French, but his actual record, as is often the case for Haitian revolutionary leaders, is bafflingly complex.

According to his son, Louverture descended from Gaou-Guinou, a "powerful king of the warlike nation of the Arradas" who had been made prisoner and sold as a slave.[3] If true, this noble past may explain why, in a colony infamous for its appetite for black flesh, Louverture was treated well as a slave. As a coachman on the Bréda plantation, he escaped the extenuating duties of field work, received some education, and, more than a decade before the revolution, was freed by his master. Louverture subsequently rented a few acres of land, along with the thirteen slaves who went with it; started a new life as a planter; and eventually bought slaves of his own. When the slave revolt erupted in 1791, Louverture's first move was to take his former master to safety; only then did he join the rebellion—and even then, covertly at first. Louverture's pro-planter past was common among the free people of color of the period—whose worldview was more French than African—and, for obvious reasons, Louverture would spend the rest of his life hiding the fact that he had exploited slaves for a living. Smart and ambitious, he quickly moved up the ranks, first in the rebel army, then in Spain's army, and finally in France's army.

The departure of the last British troops in 1798 left Louverture as the most important military figure on the island. Political power, however, was in the hands of white commissioners sent from France. They were often sympathetic to the cause of freedom (one of them was Sonthonax, Saint-Domingue's great emancipator), but they checked Louverture's growing authority. He first maneuvered to have Sonthonax elected as deputy of Saint-Domingue (a position that conveniently required his presence in Paris, five thousand miles away); then, in a stunning act of defiance, he put Gabriel d'Hédouville and Julien Raimond, two French representatives, on a ship bound for France. Their successor, Philippe Roume de Saint-Laurent, ended his career locked in a chicken coop when he dared oppose some of Louverture's policies.

Fellow officers of color were another impediment to Louverture's political ambitions. In a ruinous civil war, he moved against André Rigaud, a mulatto general who controlled Saint-Domingue's southern region. These internal conflicts resulted in much death and destruction in a colony already weakened by years of warfare, but they allowed

Louverture to achieve his main goal: by 1800, no officer could possibly challenge his authority anymore. In 1801, he unilaterally implemented a constitution that made him governor general for life and granted him the right to name his successor. He now reigned supreme.

The Spanish colony of Santo Domingo on the eastern side of Hispaniola did not have the military wherewithal to invade Saint-Domingue, nor did it have any intention of doing so. Still, hoping to extend his reign to the entire island of Hispaniola, as well as to deny a safe landing zone to a potential European invader, Louverture invaded Santo Domingo in December 1800. The takeover marked the first time in the island's history that a black ruler and former slave was in charge. Louverture could have used his newfound power to advocate independence and emancipation across the Caribbean; he decided otherwise.

Napoléon Bonaparte and other French leaders hoped that Louverture would turn Saint-Domingue into the centerpiece of a revolutionary French empire in the Americas. With an army of twenty thousand veteran black soldiers, Louverture could have threatened France's enemies in North America, most notably British Jamaica and the United States. But Louverture declined the offer, choosing instead to sign secret treaties of nonaggression and commerce with these two countries in 1799. Offensive wars could have helped spread the ideals of the revolution beyond the shores of Saint-Domingue, but the colony's commercial revival and his political survival were more important in Louverture's eyes.

That same year, the French agent Roume drafted an ambitious plan to use part of Louverture's army to invade British Jamaica. After the landing, Roume predicted, Jamaica's slaves would revolt and join local maroons and Dominguian liberators on a victorious march to Kingston. Dominguian troops would become heralds of freedom, France would acquire a lucrative colony at little cost, and the expedition would deal a mortal blow to British commerce. Louverture acquiesced in public, but in private he notified British and U.S. authorities of Roume's bellicose plans. England subsequently captured France's secret agent in Jamaica, a French Jew named Isaac Sasportas, and the entire venture foundered. Having apparently concluded that an expedition would divert key troops and resources that were needed to secure his power base in Saint-Domingue, Louverture chose to sacrifice the Jamaicans' freedom on the altar of his own ambitions. Jamaican slaves would remain in bondage until 1834.

Louverture's attitude toward his own compatriots' freedom was equally ambiguous. After Sonthonax had emancipated Saint-Domingue's slaves, many had taken over small plots of land on which they practiced small-scale subsistence farming. This unambitious Caribbean yeomanry fulfilled the former slaves' fondest dreams, but dividing plantations into small lots, Louverture rightly reasoned, would sound the death knell for Saint-Domingue's economy. Sugar and coffee exports were required to fill the state's (and Louverture's) coffers, buy weapons, pay the army, and generally return the colony to its prerevolutionary state of splendor. Such crops, particularly sugar, could only be grown on large, heavily capitalized estates. Louverture thus implemented laws requiring all inhabitants to be employed as servants, soldiers, or plantation workers. Refusal to do so was equated with vagrancy and punished with hard labor on public projects. Former slaves, now renamed *cultivateurs,* had to resume their customary hard work in the boiling sun. The policy was unpopular, but Louverture and his inspector of cultivation, the famous black revolutionary general Jean-Jacques Dessalines, treated recalcitrant workers with extreme harshness. When Louverture's nephew Moïse backed an uprising of cultivators who were protesting forced plantation labor in November 1801, Louverture had him executed along with as many as five thousand of his followers.

Even the slave trade resumed. As part of his negotiations with the United States, Louverture offered to pay for the return of the black slaves who had been taken abroad by exiled planters. More controversially, his 1801 constitution called for imports of African laborers to make up for wartime losses. That fall, he sent his diplomatic envoy Joseph Bunel to Jamaica to ask English slave traders to sell some of their ebony cargo in Saint-Domingue (where they would have toiled under the semifree cultivator status).

Louverture was no herald of freedom. He was in Spain's service when slavery was abolished in Saint-Domingue, and after he invaded Santo Domingo, he apparently issued no declaration of emancipation in that colony. Contrary to what most Haitians think, he was no precursor of national independence either. He repeatedly insisted that he had no intention of breaking the colonial bond with France and employed many white Frenchmen in his regime (Bunel, for one, was from Normandy). His closeness to the planter hierarchy should come as no surprise since he largely shared their prerevolutionary agenda: to claim much day-to-day legislative authority and open trading channels with the United States while maintaining a loose bond with France and preserving the plantation system.

For the black majority in Saint-Domingue, ten years of revolutionary upheaval had only changed two things: as cultivators, they now received a fourth of the crop; and plantation owners now included *nouveaux-riches* black army officers, like Dessalines, who received land and workers in exchange for their loyalty to Louverture. Dreams of unfettered freedom, imperial greatness, and antislavery crusades had not materialized. Louverture had aspired to become a black Napoleon, only to seek diplomatic arrangements with France's enemies. He had spoken of becoming a black Spartacus; but his ability to emulate Spartacus was put in question by his strict labor laws and closeness to slave-owning powers. He was, however, the sole master of Saint-Domingue and a large plantation owner—two goals that seem to have been foremost in his mind.

The Leclerc Expedition (1802)

In one eventful lifetime, Louverture had risen from slave to governor general for life of France's largest colony. He had defeated Spain and England, eliminated his rivals, begun to revive the colonial economy, and generally achieved enough to be remembered as one of history's great men. All he now needed was for his contemporaries to acknowledge this. He wrote long letters to Napoléon Bonaparte, the first consul of France, and begged him for a response. But to Bonaparte, the idea of an earthly equal was preposterous. Louverture was merely some "gilded African" who dared compare himself to the great Corsican.[4]

It is often assumed that Bonaparte's antipathy stemmed from his closeness to Caribbean planters exiled in Paris—most notably his wife, Joséphine, the daughter of planters from Martinique—and that his policy regarding Louverture was governed by one single goal: to restore slavery and the old prerevolutionary order. But Bonaparte, whose convoluted views on slavery reflected those of the French intelligentsia at the time, never expressed any intention of restoring slavery in Saint-Domingue. His concerns were more strategic. Louverture, he learned from his agents in the Caribbean, had negotiated with the British enemy, expelled French agents, passed a constitution without even consulting Paris, and seemed to prepare Saint-Domingue for independence. Emancipation was not a pressing issue since Louverture had imposed strict discipline in the colony's plantations; his political ambitions were what frightened Bonaparte.

For years, war with England made plans for a punitive French expedition illusory. The French navy was no match for its British counterpart, and any outbound fleet would likely be intercepted. But in late 1801, a temporary peace with England took effect, and a large armada was able to leave French ports and head for Saint-Domingue. Its size and composition were testament to Saint-Domingue's strategic and economic value in French eyes. Bonaparte's brother-in-law, a promising young general named Victoire Leclerc, headed the force. He took with him his wife—Bonaparte's favorite sister, Pauline—and their four-year-old son, Dermide. Louverture's son Isaac and stepson Placide, who had been studying at a boarding school in Paris, also went along so as to assuage their father. Also on board were mulatto generals deported by Louverture, exiled planters, scores of opportunistic interlopers hoping to make a fortune in Saint-Domingue, and the wives and children of the troops. This was the largest overseas expedition of Bonaparte's reign. In addition to the sailors and civilians, no less than twenty thousand experienced soldiers crossed the Atlantic, followed by another twenty-three thousand over the following eighteen months. Most would never return.

The goal of the expedition, Bonaparte assured the black population of Saint-Domingue, was merely to reinforce the island's garrison, while protecting the sacred decrees of emancipation. Its actual purpose, he instructed Leclerc in private, was to deport all prominent black officers and restore French authority on the island. What would happen to former slaves remained unclear. Bonaparte might restore slavery (as he eventually did in Guadeloupe), or he might content himself with the strict labor regulations prevalent under Louverture.

To Louverture, there was no such ambiguity. "The Whites of France and Saint-Domingue all want to take our freedom away," he wrote one officer. "Their most manifest desire is the restoration of slavery."[5] As soon as French troops landed, he ordered his men to burn to the ground the beautiful city of Cap Français, the Paris of the Caribbean as it was then known. They also torched plantations, refineries, and houses all over the colony in a successful attempt to deny the French expedition food and income.

The first encounters were bloody—particularly the lengthy siege of Crête-à-Pierrot—but by the end of spring, the French were generally victorious on the battlefield. What was more troubling for Louverture, however, was that most of his subordinates had defected to the French side. Finding himself virtually alone, Louverture signed a truce with the French and retired on one of his plantations at Ennery.

Louverture claimed to be done with politics for good, but his secret ambition was to resume the fighting at a more propitious time. To this end, he kept a secret correspondence with his officers and spies to stay informed of the strength of the French expeditionary force. The rainy season, he hoped, would soon bring tropical diseases that would decimate the French ranks, just like they had decimated the British ranks in the 1790s, and he felt confident that he could rely on *la Providence*. The word, in French, means God; but it also happened to be the name of Cap Français' main hospital, where thousands of French troops would die of yellow fever and other tropical diseases over the following months.

Louverture Sent to Exile

Louverture's strategy was astute. It made use of Saint-Domingue's climate and terrain while employing guerrilla tactics that would become famous in the twentieth century. Louverture only made one mistake—possibly the only one in his long, cautious career—when he agreed to meet a French officer under a firm promise that he would be safe. Honesty having always been in short supply in the colony, Louverture should have been watchful not to lower his guard. As he was about to meet the French officer, troops entered the room in which he was waiting and captured him. Louverture, who had used similar deceit for years in his dealings with various rivals, had finally met his match.

The road to exile was a long one. Louverture and his family were taken aboard the *Héros,* a ship of the line (a large military vessel) headed for Brest. There, he and his family were separated, and Louverture was sent to Fort de Joux, a dreary French castle near Pontarlier in the Jura Mountains. Louverture wrote a lengthy memo to Bonaparte claiming that he had been France's most loyal ally and that his capture and exile were one tragic misunderstanding. Bonaparte did not bother to answer, though he sent an aide-de-camp to investigate the one thing that mattered most to Louverture's captors: where had Louverture hidden the gold he surely had amassed as governor of Saint-Domingue? Louverture remained silent, and the location of his alleged treasure, like those belonging to the pirates of Tortuga Island, remains a mystery to this day.

The French hardened the conditions of Louverture's detention after he refused to divulge the location of his riches. His beloved servant, the last link Louverture had with Saint-Domingue, was sent away. Rumors swirled that Louverture was planning an escape, so he was cut off from any contact with anyone save the director of the prison, and his money was taken away so that he could not bribe the guards. Finally, to humiliate the old general, his medals and spurs were taken away. By the time the uprising that would decide the fate of Saint-Domingue entered its climatic phase in the winter of 1802–1803, Louverture was an old, sick man spending the last, lonely months of his life in a frigid cell in eastern France. Cold, loneliness, and hunger slowly took their toll, and on April 7, 1803, the director of the prison found Louverture dead in his cell—as isolated and destitute as he had been sixty years before at the time of his birth. His body was buried in a small chapel, which was later destroyed to make way for new fortifications. His remains, along with those of other prisoners, were strewn pell-mell in the new foundations, where they still remain today.

Louverture may today be considered an advocate of rebellion and independence, but like many contemporary Haitian revolutionaries— white and black alike—he was a man of great complexity. Until the very end of his life, he claimed in his letters to French officials that he had always been loyal to France, even though he had governed Saint-Domingue as a quasi-sovereign ruler. He repeatedly embraced emancipation after 1794, while forcing former slaves to remain on plantations under a cultivator system little different from the slavery of pre-revolutionary times.

Louverture is rightly viewed as a great statesman and national hero in today's Haiti, but intriguingly, he was not liked in his time. When French troops landed in 1802, Louverture called on all Dominguians to rebel. The white planters he had tried so hard to seduce flocked to the French side. Most of his troops of color also betrayed him and joined the French. His capture and exile did not spark any major revolt either, as if Saint-Domingue's population was content to rid itself of a man under whose iron hand it had lived for four years. Though a general uprising took place, it was long after Louverture had reached the prison cell from which he never came out alive.

The War of Independence (November 1802–November 1803)

After Louverture's deportation, fighting temporarily abated as Louverture's most prominent black generals, such as Henri Christophe and Jean-Jacques Dessalines, joined the French side. Black troops were sent against recalcitrant cultivators, many exiled white colonists returned, and French officers began to divvy up plantations among themselves (making a quick fortune, rather than pursuing some racial agenda, was their primary objective).

Over the following months, however, a series of public relations faux pas undermined Leclerc's tenuous hold on the colony. Bonaparte maintained slavery in Martinique, and after he took steps to do the same in Guadeloupe, some white planters publicly boasted that Saint-Domingue would be next. French troops in that colony launched a disarmament campaign, the sole goal of which, the black population whispered, could only be to pave the way for a restoration of slavery. Equally worrisome were mass executions of black colonial troops. By the fall of 1802, a general insurrection was once again under way as Dessalines, Christophe, and other black and mulatto generals—who had fought for France, then against it, then for it—switched sides one last time in response to French atrocities and rumors of a possible restoration of slavery.

The uprising could not have come at a worse time. The summer of 1802 had brought a massive epidemic of the dreaded yellow fever, a poorly understood disease that was variously attributed to noxious smells rising from the soil, sudden changes in temperature, consumption of tropical fruit, or the drunkenness and sexual promiscuity prevalent among the troops. (Yellow fever is actually transmitted by a species of mosquitoes called *Aedes aegypti*.) With no natural immunity against the disease, the French died in droves. Entire army units disappeared; warships went through multiple crews. By the fall of 1802, the once-mighty expeditionary army was reduced to three thousand dispirited survivors. Their commander, General Leclerc, succumbed to the disease in November.

Renewed fighting, defections, and the epidemic put Donatien de Rochambeau, Leclerc's successor at the helm of the expedition, in a difficult spot. With a meager army eaten away by despair and disease, he would probably never have held on as long as he did (one year) had the rebel camp not been weakened by its customary social, racial, and political divisions. Dessalines spent much of the winter of 1802–1803 fighting not the French but rival rebel officers, and until the very end of the war of independence the French army included as many mulatto planters and disaffected black cultivators as it did French soldiers.

It was in the spring of 1803, when England resumed its war with France and British warships began blockading the beleaguered French ports, that Rochambeau's situation became truly desperate. There was an air of disillusioned Epicureanism as the rebel lines tightened their grip on the last French strongholds. Rochambeau and his officers held magnificent parties on French ships, battled over spoils of war, and seduced planters' wives. A bizarre blend of the grotesque and the brutal marked Rochambeau's tenure. In Port-au-Prince, he organized a ball at which elite mulatto women were dined and wined in a room decorated with black crepe and other macabre paraphernalia. When the party was over, Rochambeau led the women to an attendant room in which their husbands' bodies lay in state—they had just attended their loved ones' funeral.

Mass drowning, hanging, burning, crucifixion: the entire gamut of humankind's deadly inventions became Saint-Domingue's daily bread.

Having received a shipment of slave-hunting dogs from Cuba, Rochambeau invited Cap Français' high society for a gruesome spectacle held, with a touch of irony, in a former convent. The excitement was at fever pitch; those dogs, should they prove to be an effective weapon, could fill in French ranks depleted by disease and war and provide a useful tool for counterinsurgency warfare. As in the days of decadent Rome, an arena was built where a cloister once stood, an unfortunate black servant was tied to a pole, and the dogs were unleashed. The dogs initially failed to devour the man—Voodoo charm or lack of appetite?—until they were forcefully prodded into action. Rochambeau later lamented that the expensive dogs had proved a military disappointment and a mere footnote to his campaign, but in Haiti, the French use of man-eating dogs has come to exemplify the viciousness of colonial rule to the present day.

Like Leclerc before him, Rochambeau eventually concluded that nothing short of genocide would keep Saint-Domingue in French hands (the term had not yet been invented, so they wrote of "extermination" instead). The black population, they reasoned, had been spoiled by ten years of revolutionary upheaval; former slaves now knew what freedom tasted like and how to fight to preserve it. France's sole remaining option was to kill all adults above the age of twelve and import a new batch of slaves from Africa. Otherwise, recurrent revolts would forever plague France's richest colony. Similarly, many black rebels came to conclude that they would never be fully free as long as white Frenchmen remained in Saint-Domingue.

Blacks and whites answered rape with torture, and death with massacre, until by November 1803, the last French troops found themselves surrounded by rebel armies on land and British warships at sea. Those French soldiers fit enough to sail tried to sneak through the British blockade, only to end up in dreary British prison ships anchored off Kingston, Jamaica. The rest of the population—sick soldiers, civilians, and the black troops who had remained loyal to the bitter end—found themselves at the mercy of the rebel army. Haiti had been ruled by Tainos, then by Spaniards, then by the French. It was now an independent republic ruled by former slaves.

Did Haiti Save the United States? (1776–1803)

When American policymakers think of Haiti today, misery and revolution are foremost in their mind. Haiti, they fear, is so poor and unstable that it can at any time erupt into political chaos and spark an exodus of refugees to the shores of Florida. Their eighteenth-century forebears—George

Washington, John Adams, and Thomas Jefferson—had a different view. Strength and wealth were Haiti's hallmarks in the last years of French colonial rule, and the founding fathers of the United States expended much time and energy trying to secure the trade of Saint-Domingue and enlist the colony as a military ally.

When the U.S. War of Independence began in 1775, Louis XVI's ministers debated whether to enter the war on the thirteen colonies' behalf. The war, they reasoned, weakened the British enemy, while an Anglo–American reconciliation might result in a joint attack on French and Spanish colonies in the Caribbean, most prominently Saint-Domingue. The 1778 French entry into the war, which proved so decisive in securing the United States' independence, thus resulted in part from a desire to save Saint-Domingue; the Franco–American treaty of alliance specifically mentioned that the United States would help protect France's sugar colonies.

Saint-Domingue also played a notable role during the American Revolution itself. White and mulatto troops from Saint-Domingue fought in the 1779 campaign against British-held Savannah, an episode seldom remembered in the United States. Throughout the war, French *américanophiles* such as Pierre Augustin Caron de Beaumarchais used Saint-Domingue as a major transshipment center for weapons smuggled to U.S. rebels, while the French navy established an important base in Cap Français (the fleet that helped defeat the British squadron near Yorktown in 1781 had sailed from that port).

When the United States became independent in 1783—the first colony to do so in the Western Hemisphere—it found itself rather isolated economically. Other colonies were bound by colonial trade rules that banned commerce with third-party countries; thus, U.S. merchants had nobody to trade with, except for Saint-Domingue. France, unable to satisfy its colony's surging demand for food and timber, introduced some loopholes into its mercantilist regulations, and an active U.S.–Dominguian trade (part legal, part contraband) soon began. By the 1790s, Saint-Domingue was the United States' second-largest trading partner after England.

During 1797–1798, various naval disputes brought the United States and its former French ally to a state of undeclared warfare known as the Quasi-War. No official declaration of hostilities ever took place, but for three years, the Caribbean Sea became a giant battleground in which French and U.S. privateers and frigates harassed the opposing nation's ability to do commerce. As the most prominent military leader in a French colony, Louverture could have played a key role in disrupting

U.S. commerce or even used his large army to attack the United States. He did neither. Instead, he signed a treaty with the United States that opened Saint-Domingue's ports to U.S. ships while closing its ports to French privateers. Much to the relief of southern planters, Louverture also promised that he would not sponsor any slave uprising in the United States, thus indirectly ensuring the survival of the U.S. slave system.

The most important contribution Louverture and his black generals ever made to the young American Republic was their victory against Bonaparte's forces. The Leclerc expedition landed in Saint-Domingue in 1802, the same year a secret treaty under which Spain ceded Louisiana to France became effective. Bonaparte hoped to use Louisiana as a source of foodstuffs for laborers on France's Caribbean plantations and create a French empire stretching from the Great Plains in the north to French Guiana in the south, with Saint-Domingue as its centerpiece, so as to check U.S. ambitions in North America. But the Dominguian rebels' military prowess forced Bonaparte to divert troops intended for garrison duty in Louisiana to the killing fields of Saint-Domingue and to shelve his North American ambitions. In early 1803, shortly after learning that Leclerc had died and that the expeditionary force in Saint-Domingue was in a hopeless situation, Bonaparte sold Louisiana to the United States, in large part because of the difficulties he had experienced in Saint-Domingue. Unwittingly, Saint-Domingue's former slaves had made a crucial contribution to U.S. territorial expansion.

Haitians today tend to harbor anti-American views and often describe the United States as an imperialist behemoth that eradicated its native population, crushed its territorial rivals, and repeatedly invaded its weaker neighbors—Haiti in particular. What they often forget is that Haiti, first as a staging ground for French offensives during the American War of Independence, then as a trading partner during the early years of the Republic, and finally as a rebellious colony of France, greatly contributed to the rise of an economic and military American colossus to the north.

The Haitian Revolution: Lessons Learned

In many ways, the Haitian Revolution was the high-water mark of Haiti's history. Haiti has never been as rich as it was in 1788, the last year before the French Revolution began affecting the colony. Haiti has never been as powerful as it was during 1793–1803, when in rapid succession, it defeated Spain, England, and France, the three largest colonial powers of the time. Haiti has never been as inspiring as it was in 1804, when it proclaimed its independence (the second country in the Western Hemisphere to do so) and secured freedom for its people (the only time in world history a slave revolt had ended successfully). Haitians proudly, and rightly, refer to those days as the proof that their country can achieve deeds unequalled elsewhere.

But Haitians also interpret their revolution in ways that have proved detrimental to their nation-building efforts. The (all-too-real) atrocities of the Leclerc–Rochambeau period have left a deep mark in public consciousness, giving rise to deep suspicion of, even hostility against, white foreigners. Even today, a Frenchman walking his dog through the streets of Port-au-Prince will endure snappy comments about colonialists and their slave-hunting dogs—a puzzling insult for a foreigner more likely than not a humanitarian worker little versed in the intricacies of Rochambeau's two-hundred-year-old tenure. Haitians also often claim that their country never fully recovered from the demographic and economic costs of the war of independence and that French imperialists should be held responsible for the country's less-than-stellar economic record after independence. The atrocities and the devastation were real; but they should not underpin xenophobic statements two centuries later, nor serve as an explanation for Haiti's woes in perpetuity.

Portraying the Haitian Revolution as an event in which black slaves fought white imperialists united in their support for racism and slavery also considerably oversimplifies a conflict marked by great racial and political complexity. Blacks and mulattoes fought on both sides during the Spanish–British invasion—a time when France stood for freedom and racial equality. Many French colonial agents were genuinely committed to emancipation, while many Haitian revolutionary leaders, such as Louverture, were former slave owners. Even after Leclerc landed, unity among the rebels was not the norm. Dessalines, the man who would later declare independence and exterminate much of Haiti's white population, fought on Leclerc's behalf throughout the summer of 1802, as did Alexandre Pétion, Henri Christophe, Jean-Pierre Boyer, and most of the officers celebrated today as heroes of Haiti's independence.

Racial boundaries were often porous—as befitted an age in which the very concept of racism was still in its infancy. Black officers often fought each other over spoils or social policies, as Louverture and his nephew Moïse did in 1801. Many whites could be found on the rebel side— particularly during the closing months of the war of independence, when many liberal white troops in France's employ defected to the rebel army to protest Rochambeau and Bonaparte's reactionary agenda. On the opposite side, thousands of black and mulatto troops fought for France until the end of the war, in part because they remembered Dessalines's brutal treatment of black cultivators during his tenure as Louverture's inspector of cultivation.

Far from being a bitter war between Frenchmen and Haitians, the Haitian Revolution was a conflict in which independence from France was a secondary goal—almost an afterthought. U.S. rebels *began* the American Revolution with a declaration of independence; Haitian rebels declared their independence *after* the last French troops left the colony in November 1803 (and again more formally in January 1804). However strange it may sound today, for much of their revolution, Haiti's founding fathers were inspired by the French model. They fought in the French army and borrowed many ideals and symbols from the French Revolution—the Haitian flag and coat of arms, for example, are directly based on the French tricolor and the letterhead of a French general in the Leclerc expedition. Many were so molded by the prerevolutionary colonial mindset that their main ambition was to become plantation owners.

Louverture and Dessalines's rhetoric may have sounded radical, but first and foremost, they were careful politicians who put their political preservation ahead of harebrained revolutionary idealism. One road not taken was that of general insurrection in the Caribbean area. Louverture chose to limit the slave revolt to the shores of Saint-Domingue rather than exporting it to Jamaica and the United States (he only invaded Santo Domingo, a Caribbean colony whose slave population was small and comparatively well treated; even then, however, he did not emancipate the slaves of that colony). For all the fears that independent Haiti would turn into a hotbed of revolutionary activism, Dessalines and his successors pledged not to incite slaves in other countries to revolt for fear that it would invite foreign retaliation. This careful policy secured Haiti's independence, but it also betrayed the ideal of emancipation and prevented Haiti from turning into a regional power. Louverture and Dessalines could have created a Caribbean empire during 1798–1804; they chose not to. The United States had no such qualms about mixing claims of manifest destiny and territorial aggrandizement and eventually surpassed its once-mighty Caribbean neighbor. National greatness is not preordained. It must be demonstrated and fought for, and one is always left to wonder how the history of the Western Hemisphere would have unfolded had Haiti's revolutionaries chosen to export emancipation to foreign shores.

Haiti's leaders did draw some lessons from the revolutionary years, albeit wrongheaded ones that would plague Haiti's political life for decades.

Military power, they discovered, amounted to political legitimacy. Louverture's rise and fall, as well as France's, had been caused by superior might, not greater right. Political ideals could be brandished—but only to seduce the uneducated masses—and could be discarded when they conflicted with one's financial interests. Leveling accusations of racism at an enemy was the most effective method of political discourse. Planters had been idle masters, so Haitians equated social success with inactivity, and work with domination (to this day, the Creole expression "to sweat" also means "to be stupid"). Dictatorship, political instability, and labor exploitation: such were the true legacy of the revolution, which did nothing to lay the groundwork for a lasting free-market democracy. To this difficult legacy Dessalines was about to add a controversial act of revenge that would do much to ruin the reputation of the new Haitian state.

CHAPTER 3

Missed Opportunities: Haiti after Independence (1804–1915)

Founding Murderers (January–April 1804)

On January 1, 1804, a few weeks after the last French troops left Saint-Domingue, the victorious black and mulatto officers gathered in Gonaïves to declare their nation's independence. This was a time for celebration, but also for revenge. Half of the country's population had died in the previous thirteen years of fighting. The year before, as the war neared its fateful end, Rochambeau had unleashed a whirlwind of tortures and mass executions that had left a vivid imprint in the founding fathers' minds. So strong was the hatred of everything French that the country's name, Saint-Domingue, was abandoned and replaced with its precolonial, Taino forebear: Haiti. The new country's flag consisted of a French tricolor whose central white strip had been torn apart and the blue and red stitched back together. Independent Haiti, symbolically at least, would be a country without whites. One of the officers present, Louis Boisrond-Tonnerre, was so incensed at the French that he dismissed the first draft of the declaration of independence as too mellow, famously erupting that "we should use the skin of a white man as a parchment, his skull as an inkwell, his blood for ink, and a bayonet for a pen."[1] These were words that Haiti's first dictator, Jean-Jacques Dessalines, could understand. In his address to the nation, he lashed at the former colonial power and made public the dreadful plan he had conceived.

> It is not enough to expel from our country the barbarians [the French] that drenched it in blood for two hundred years . . . We must by one last

act of national sovereignty secure for all eternity the reign of liberty in our motherland . . . [Soldiers,] give to all nations a terrible, but just example of the vengeance that must be exacted by a people proud to have found freedom again, and eager to preserve it. Let us frighten all those who would dare to steal our freedom; let us start with the French! May they shudder when they approach our coastline, either because they remember all the exactions they committed, or because of our horrifying pledge to kill every Frenchman who soils the land of freedom with his sacrilegious presence.[2]

The words were not mere rhetoric. Over the following four months, under Dessalines' personal supervision, soldiers rounded up French planters, soldiers, and merchants all over Haiti and slaughtered them. Men were the first to die. Women, children, and infants came next. Few managed to kinder Dessalines' mercy. A few foreign merchants, some moderate black officers, and Dessalines' own wife hid a few French nationals. The rest of the white population, thousands of them, was beheaded, bayoneted, or drowned. Under present-day international law, this willful destruction of a racial group would likely meet the legal definition of a genocide, though given the relatively small number of victims (three to five thousand) the term "massacre" might be more appropriate in that case.

Dessalines made no effort to hide the horrors of the massacre as it unfolded. In Port-au-Prince, whites were paraded all the way to the port, where they were drowned in full view of the crews on foreign merchant ships. In Cap Français, now renamed Cap Haïtien, some wounded soldiers and civilians had stayed behind after the French surrender, trusting Dessalines' word that they would be safe. But all the colonial crimes were revisited in reverse. Masters were put to work by their former slaves; black men raped the daughters of white planters; former victims now exacted unspeakable tortures on their past oppressors. A few Poles and Americans, who had aided the slave revolt, and some priests and doctors, whose skills were deemed irreplaceable for the moment, were spared. Those who failed the triple test of skin, citizenship, and trade were put to the sword.

In April, in another address to the nation, Dessalines exulted that the massacre was now complete. To those doubting the necessity of such drastic measures, he explained that it was every Haitian's duty to avenge the many relatives they had lost to French exploitation. Also, whites all over the Caribbean and Europe were so horrified by the Haitians' decision to kill their former masters that they would contemplate any invasion of Haiti with utter terror. Any hopes that France might still have of launching another expedition would be crushed in their infancy.

Despite all of Dessalines' efforts at rationalization, the 1804 massacre was as inexcusable as they were foolish. After 1492, the Spaniards had eradicated the Taino population, but had done so unintentionally. In 1803, the French had considered killing all blacks, but had fallen short of that goal. Dessalines exceeded the worst of the Spanish and French colonial crimes, combining intent with successful implementation. The 1804 massacre now occupied a prominent spot in the annals of human cruelty. Aside from being morally repellent, the massacre immediately put the young Haitian republic on an ill-fated course. For all their faults, Saint-Domingue's whites had been the most educated faction in the colony. White planters organized labor on the plantations. White engineers designed irrigation projects. White bureaucrats and lawyers administered the colony. White officers manned the top echelons of the army. Even Louverture's secretaries were white. In one blind act of revenge, Dessalines wiped out his country's cadres. For decades thereafter, the vast majority of Haiti's population (Dessalines included) remained illiterate and unskilled, substantially hindering Haitian economic development. Securing one's freedom in an orgy of white blood also set a violent tone for future political discourse. Following Dessalines' example, ambitious generals gained, kept, then lost power through violent means. Only five of the thirty-four founding fathers who had gathered in Gonaïves would die of natural causes. Dessalines would not be one of them.

As a majority black republic born of a slave revolt and a war of independence, Haiti would have been surrounded by wary neighbors in any scenario. The massacre replaced wariness with outright hostility, panic even. Throughout the nineteenth century, and to a lesser extent today, Haiti suffered from a diplomatic isolation that was anything but splendid. Potential trading partners that were vital to the country's economic health stayed away; immigrants that flocked to the New World refused to come to Haiti; European ambassadors chose to negotiate under the protective umbrella of gunboats stationed in the bay of Port-au-Prince; former allies delayed official recognition for decades (the United States only recognized Haiti in 1862). Haitians have been quick to blame racism for other countries' standoffishness. They forget that their country's first diplomatic act was to slaughter most foreigners, leading to lasting, and understandable, prudence.

Because Haiti was the first independent black republic in the world, and the only country born of a slave revolt, it stood out as a symbol of black self-rule. For decades until decolonization reached Africa in the 1950s, Haitian leaders bore on their shoulders not only the dreams of their countrymen, but those of an entire race as well. For black slaves in the United States and Brazil, and later for black subjects of France's and England's African empires, Haiti proved that masters and metropolises could be vanquished. If successful, the Haitian experiment in nation building could have proven all the racists, imperialists, and slavery advocates wrong. Unfortunately, Haiti failed to live up to the hopes its independence had raised. The Haitian government's first act of self-governance could have been to outlaw slavery in the New World, to welcome runaways, or to launch a program to educate its illiterate population: it chose massacre instead. Nineteenth-century American apologists of slavery, such as George Fitzhugh and John C. Calhoun, argued that slavery was a humane institution capable of keeping supposedly savage Africans in check; if unleashed, freedmen would soon wallow in laziness and chaos, or fall victim to the greed of northern capitalists. By killing all whites, Dessalines acted as if he wanted to prove his most racist detractors right. For years, people of African descent paid the price of Dessalines' folly, as their calls for racial equality and self-rule were met by memories of the 1804 massacre.

Racism in Nineteenth-Century Haiti

Slavery and the 1804 massacre were undoubtedly the two worst examples of racism in Haitian history, but other, more subtle forms of racism subsided long after independence. Blacks and mulattoes, who had both been victims of race prejudice in colonial times, now became perpetrators, as long-standing grudges led each group to eye the other, and foreign whites, with hostility. In nineteenth-century Haiti, racism cut all ways.

The Mulattoes' unique place in Haitian society was so well established by the 1780s that Moreau de Saint-Méry, Saint-Domingue's most noted eyewitness of the late colonial era, went as far as dividing the population in 128 racial categories in his Description of the French Part of Saint-Domingue (1797). At each extreme stood pure-blooded Africans and Europeans. The remaining 126 groups represented every possible combination of white and black blood, such as the *sacatra, griffe, marabout, mulâtre, quarteron, métis, mamelouque, quarteronné*, and *sang-mêlé* (from blackest to whitest, respectively). These categories survived after independence in a simplified form. Even though no Haitian law posited inequality based on skin color, it was widely understood that for a light-skinned *sang-mêlé* bride to marry a much darker *griffe* groom would be a misalliance. Each color group intermarried as much as possible to preserve its light complexion, with miscegenation being the exception rather than the rule.

Being a mulatto (some Haitians prefer the term *jaune*, or yellow) had social and cultural implications going far beyond racial traits, and race became as important to one's identity as one's name. Mulattoes prided themselves on their French heritage (they were, after all, the descendants of French planters). They understood Creole but refused to speak it save to their black servants. They were pious Catholics who sneered at Voodoo. More internationally minded than other Haitians, they studied abroad, preferably in Paris, and were well versed in French literature and history. Mulattoes, because they only represented a minority of the population, did not always occupy the country's presidential palace, but they monopolized its businesses. To be a mulatto was to be rich, and wealth was the only factor that could trump skin color. A *gwo neg* (rich black man) was really a mulatto, a Haitian proverb went. Conversely, a poor mulatto was really a *neg*. Not surprisingly, mulattoes viewed their black compatriots, whose origins and cultural references were steadfastly African, with utter contempt. Blacks, to them, amounted to rabble: poor, illiterate, disorderly, and bestial.

Blacks, representing about 90 percent of Haiti's population, stood for everything the mulattoes opposed: Africa, not France, Voodoo, not Catholicism, Creole, not French, and the army and agriculture, not business. Blacks, because they descended from slaves, liked to think of themselves as the only true Haitians, calling themselves *authentiques* (authentic). In his 1805 constitution (Art. 13 and 14), Dessalines even specified that all Haitians were officially black, a circuitous way of saying that only blacks could truly call themselves Haitians. Mulattoes, because their fathers were French and because they had frequently owned slaves before independence, were viewed with deep suspicion. In a way, mulattoes were the Jews of Haiti. Wealthier than their compatriots, they excited envy. Ethnically and religiously separate from the rest of the population, they suffered from the widespread belief that treacherous behavior came easy to them. Accordingly, nineteenth-century revolutions were often accompanied by pogroms. Profiting from the temporary breakdown in law and order, mobs would loot and burn Port-au-Prince businesses, while their mulatto owners fled to foreign legations for protection.

In those conditions, race doubled as a profession of political faith. Historians, when encountering an unfamiliar name in a document, like to know the person's background, friends, and wealth in order to gauge the person's political views. In Haiti, the mystery revolves around a single question: black or yellow? The *jaunes* formed the Liberal party that sought accommodation with the outside world. *Authentiques* tended to be staunch Nationalists. Dessalines was black, and he held a deep hatred of whites and Frenchmen. Jean-Pierre Boyer was yellow, and he signed a treaty of reconciliation with France. President Sténio Vincent, who was yellow, collaborated with American occupiers in the 1920s. Jean Price-Mars, who was a black intellectual, lamented their presence. The same racial taxonomy dogged Haitian foreign relations. Most Haitians were black, Dominicans' skin was much lighter, and Europeans and Americans were generally white, so no lasting friendship could exist between Haiti and its neighbors.

After 1804, white presence in Haiti was negligible, but whites too were viewed, as a group, with an antipathy that amounted to racism. To Haitian nationalists, whites were imperialists, slave owners, and murderers, and should not be allowed to take any lasting foothold on Haitian soil (even today, the word *blan*, or "white man," also means foreigner, and carries a pejorative connotation that *neg*, literally "nigger," does not have). Dessalines' 1805 constitution, and every single other Haitian constitution until the U.S. invasion of 1915, carried a provision banning foreign ownership of land. Whites were literally kept at bay, tolerated on merchant ships but discouraged from establishing permanent residence. Even the small German community that settled in the late nineteenth century had to marry Haitian wives to circumvent the ownership ban, thus joining, within a generation, the mulatto community. Syrians immigrants, whose entrepreneurial spirit also allowed them to claim a substantial number of Haitian shops and businesses at the turn of the century, were not so lucky. A wave of anti-Syrian hysteria that peaked in 1903–1905 led to the forced exile of all Syrians. Preserving the country's racial integrity came at a cost: Syrian shops were burnt, Haiti lost valuable citizens, and Italian fishermen, numerous on Haiti's coast at the time, remained at sea for weeks for fear of being mistaken for Syrians. This presumably did little to improve Haiti's reputation abroad.

Unfortunately, in Haiti, history neither dies nor fades away. Many of these examples of nineteenth-century racism still apply today.

An Economic Dilemma (1804–1820)

Like Louverture before him, the most important decision Dessalines made upon becoming dictator of Haiti was economic. Should he distribute the land to Haitian peasants, on which they would most likely grow subsistence crops? Or should he force peasants to remain on large sugar plantations, a more lucrative, but less popular, option? Following in Louverture's footsteps, Dessalines opted for the latter option. Haiti's power stemmed from its army and commerce, which themselves were reliant on sugar and coffee exports. The public good of the country had to supersede private hopes of land ownership. On a more personal note, now that he had killed or exiled all planters, Dessalines found himself at the head of dozens of profitable estates. He directly benefited from the plantation system, and had little interest in letting his people go.

Under Dessalines' leadership (1804–1806), the Haitian countryside thus bore an eerie resemblance to the colonial landscape. Half of the population had died, and many plantations had been burnt, but work continued as usual on the remaining estates. The Haitian whip, or *cocomacac*, had replaced its French equivalent, and peasants now received one-fourth of the crop: these were the only concessions to modernity. Aside from these, forced labor, monoculture, and social inequality remained the norm. A vast army representing 15 percent of the population enforced order, humiliated mulattoes, and kept the country under a yoke as heavy as Louverture's. Upon hearing that Napoléon intended to be crowned emperor, Dessalines even held his own coronation ceremony, thus becoming Jacques I, emperor of Haiti. Haitian peasants, who had fought a long slave revolt only to find themselves under a slightly modified version of the old *Code Noir*, grumbled. The officers, who suffered from the whims of the aging dictator, had their own reasons to complain. In October 1806, a general uprising broke out, and Dessalines was lynched by his own officers outside Port-au-Prince. Haiti's first dictator had lasted less than two years; its first postindependence constitution, passed in 1805, had lasted even less, for a new one was already in the works. The economic system was once again open for debate.

The 1806 revolution that brought Dessalines' short reign to an end was spearheaded by two men, both of them veterans of the revolutionary wars. One, Henri Christophe, was black. The other, Alexandre Pétion, was mulatto. Under a power-sharing arrangement, Christophe was to be named president of the republic; Pétion would become president of the senate. Pétion immediately arranged to draft a constitution that would strip the president of most of his powers, placing them, predictably, in the hands of the president of the senate. Christophe balked and within months, the revolution of 1806 gave way to the civil war of 1807. War again ravaged Haiti, but no clear winner emerged. When the fighting subsided, Christophe was in control of the rich northern plain; Pétion controlled the western and southern provinces of the country. Hoping to surround their enemy, Pétion arranged for the northwestern region to secede under Lamarre, while Christophe financed two insurrections in Pétion's rear—one under Yayou, another under Jean-Baptiste Perrier (a.k.a. Goman). In 1810, André Rigaud's return from France created yet another breakaway republic in the south. Haiti was now split six ways. All of these insurrections were eventually subdued (Goman's lasting until 1819), but the division between north and south was there to stay, creating two Haitis governed by two strikingly different economic systems.

In the north, Christophe preserved the forced labor system, or *fermage*, that he had inherited from Louverture and Dessalines. Peasants worked five long days on large plantations, from before dawn until dusk, earning one-fourth of the crop and the right to tend their own gardens on Saturdays. Discipline was strict. Soldiers and spies were everywhere, backed by a four-thousand-strong Royal Corps of Dahomey whose members were imported directly from Africa. Once again, republicanism fell victim to personal ambition, and in 1811, Christophe, a former cook at the aptly named colonial inn *La Couronne* (The Crown), was crowned Henri I, king of Haiti.

In the south, Pétion instituted a more lenient, though still dictatorial, form of government. Starting in 1809, he fulfilled every peasant's dream when he started carving out the plantations of the colonial era and dividing them among soldiers. This was the first instance of land redistribution in a region known for skewed land ownership patterns, and it immediately earned Pétion the nickname of *Papa Bon Coeur* (Good-Hearted Daddy). Pétion's rule in the south (1807–1818) marked a rare period of public bliss, during which Haitian peasants lived under the benevolent dictatorship of a man who carried out popular reforms.

Contemporary observers were unanimously struck by the difference between Christophe's north and Pétion's south. In the north, sugar exports funded an extensive police and state apparatus. Christophe built a network of massive fortresses, including the Citadelle La Ferrière that still ranks as the most impressive defensive structure in the Caribbean. Perched atop a precipitous twenty-six-hundred-foot peak and bristling with two hundred cannons, La Ferrière was an architectural wonder made of rock, steel—and blood: thousands of workers died building it. Christophe also built mansions for himself, including the beautiful *Sans Souci* palace in Milot, whose marble floors were cooled by spring water tapped from nearby mountains. In the south, sugar production, which required large capital investments and hard, disciplined work, plummeted immediately after the land distribution decrees. Peasants cultivated small gardens instead, leaving what coffee bushes survived on hillsides as the sole source of exports. In the north, inflation was nonexistent; in the south, currency, printed with the insouciance characteristic of Pétion's rule, was barely worth the paper it was printed on. In the north, Christophe hired British tutors and initiated the first network of public schools in Haitian history; in the south, Pétion created two high schools for the sons and daughters of the elite while the rest of the population remained illiterate (the *Lycée Pétion* still exists today; public education has improved little). Northerners were made happy against their will. Southerners were free and poor.

Much crying followed Pétion's death in 1818, the only tears, it was said, the good man had ever caused. Pétion was replaced by Jean-Pierre Boyer, another mulatto veteran of the revolution who continued his predecessor's policies. The south continued its effortless fall into misery, and northerners continued to vote with their feet by sneaking across the border. Finally, in 1820, the aging Christophe suffered a stroke that left him almost paralyzed. His own troops, now finding enough courage to conspire against the dreaded tyrant, revolted. Seeing that all was lost, Christophe decided that only he should be allowed to end his life and shot himself (according to the legend, with a silver bullet). Haiti was reunited under Boyer's rule. Christophe's palaces were looted, his plantations carved out, and his beloved schools abandoned.

Pétion's 1809 land distribution decrees, extended to the northern part with the reunification of 1820, changed Haiti more than all the revolutions and civil wars of the nineteenth century. From the Spanish colonial days until 1809, agriculture had been dominated by large estates; from that point until today, small-scale farming became the norm (a feeble attempt by Boyer in 1826 to reinstitute *fermage* fell victim to universal opposition). Considering that the vast majority of Haitians, then and today, were peasants, the change was nothing short of revolutionary. Sugar exports ceased altogether for one century, a startling development in a country that was the world's largest exporter of tropical foodstuffs in the 1780s. Coffee, more suited to small-scale agriculture, lingered on.

Subsistence crops now dominated, but even these eventually proved insufficient. In 1804, Haiti's population was probably inferior to three hundred thousand, and there was more than enough land to feed everyone. As years went by, however, the substantial plots of the Pétion era were subdivided between heirs, who then had to feed their family on ever-dwindling parcels. In the U.S. environment, individual ownership of farmland led to a sense of personal responsibility and increased production; but the system was only sustainable during the rapid population growth of the nineteenth century because the supply of arable land was virtually inexhaustible. In Haiti's mountainous terrain, clearing new land only brought under cultivation steep fields whose soil was quickly depleted by water erosion. Today, the population stands at eight million, leaving less than half an acre of arable land per person in rural areas. Forests are a distant memory. By dint of such agricultural choices, Haitians had chosen to be happy and poor. The latter proved more enduring than the former.

The shift from sugar production to subsistence farming during the Pétion presidency and its long-term impact on Haitian development have been well documented. The dangers of monoculture, however, are often overlooked. If Dessalines and Christophe had succeeded in forcing Haitians to remain on plantations, Haiti, like other sugar-producing islands, would eventually have experienced a relative economic decline. In the nineteenth century, new sugarcane producers such as Louisiana and India, not to mention the European countries that adopted sugar beet, caused intense competition that brought the real price of sugar down. Sugar, the oil of the eighteenth century, became an undistinguished commodity from whose cultivation limited profits could be derived. The price of coffee fluctuated from year to year, but, in the long term, the purchasing power of a pound of coffee (what economists dub the "terms of trade") declined steadily.

Alternative paths of development beside sugar and coffee would have given Haitians a more promising future. European countries, much like Haiti, saw a big demographic leap in the nineteenth century, which resulted in rural overpopulation. Their answer was to send landless peasants to cities were they worked in coalmines and textile mills. This exodus enriched the country while preventing the rural overpopulation that plagues Haiti today. Heavy industry—steel, coal, railroads, and rubber—and later services—computer software, entertainment, and medical research—now provided the largest profit margins. An industrial revolution, more than sugar exports, would have allowed Haiti to shift from being an agricultural giant of the eighteenth century to an industrial giant of the nineteenth century. Alas, creating factories was a step no Haitian leader of the time, not even Louverture and Christophe, thought of taking. Haitians continued to trade crops for manufactured products, as if the mercantilist *exclusif* had never been abolished and Colbert still served as finance minister of the French colonial empire. This focus on low-margin foodstuffs, even more than misguided agricultural policies, explains why Haiti today is a nation of peasants eking a meager living off a few acres of bare hillsides.

American Emigration to Haiti

Contemporary American presidents focus much of their attention on preventing Haitian boat people from reaching the shores of Florida, but in the nineteenth century, the flow of immigrants went the other way. For slaves and destitute sharecroppers, Haiti was the promised land where black men and women lived free on their own plot. For white opponents and advocates of slavery alike, emigration provided an outlet for black freedmen who, they feared, could never be integrated into American society. Africa seemed a logical choice for emigration, especially after an American colony was founded in Liberia in 1817, but shipping costs were high. Haiti was closer, cheaper, and, because of the population drop experienced during the revolution, welcoming.

Louverture and Dessalines both offered to buy back the Haitian slaves French planters had brought with them to the United States, but Jean-Pierre Boyer was by far the most active proponent of U.S. emigration to Haiti. Boyer lavished considerable state funds on U.S. organizations that offered free passage to Haiti with the hope of bringing as many as four thousand black Americans. Boyer also made rather objectionable arrangements with U.S. consul in Cayes Ralph Higinston to allow southern planters to buy plantations in Haiti and to export some of their slaves there, where they would work on nine-year indenture contracts. The bans on slavery and white ownership of land, dating back to independence and still nominally on the books, did not seem to bother Boyer. The immigration campaign continued after the end of Boyer's long presidency, but it was hampered by accounts of dictatorial rule under the reign of Faustin Soulouque. It was revived in the 1860s, when President Fabre-Nicolas Geffrard sponsored James Redpath's *Haytian Bureau of Emigration in the United States*.

The debate about emigration rebounded as the American Civil War opened the prospect of general emancipation. White leaders such as Abraham Lincoln, uncertain whether freed slaves could adjust to the requirements of American citizenship, concluded that mass deportation was a sensible way to combine freedom and social harmony. Under an 1862 law, one-fourth of all proceeds from sales of vacant property in the South were deposited in a trust fund earmarked to finance emigration. Panama was briefly considered as a destination for freed slaves, but neither the slaves nor Colombia showed enthusiasm for the project; so Haiti once again became the favored destination. In 1863, five hundred black Americans left for Ile-à-Vache, located on Haiti's southern coast. These should have been the first of many settlers, but they returned after only a year.

Overall, emigration to Haiti never involved more than a few thousand black Americans, many of whom subsequently returned to the United States. These small numbers were not sufficient to limit the growth of the black population in the United States in the first half of the nineteenth century (which quadrupled from one to four million), let alone to reach the more ambitious goal of transferring the entire black population out of the United States. Practical difficulties such as lack of funding and the language barrier were partly to blame. Black Americans' opposition to plans based on the premise that dark skin was incompatible with U.S. citizenship was also a factor. But Haiti's infamous reputation as a breeding ground for poverty, epidemics, and revolutions, already well established by that time, probably played an even greater role in discouraging candidates for emigration. This failure to attract American settlers was one of Haiti's many missed opportunities. Better trained and more educated than the average Haitian of the time, black Americans would have been an invaluable addition to a country still recovering from the demographic cost of the war of independence.

Imperialism: Victim, Perpetrator, or Accomplice? (1821–1844)

Standard histories of Haiti emphasize that 1804 did not mark the final step on the path to independence. Haitians like to point out that their country had to fend off repeated attempts on the part of France, Germany, England, and the United States to curtail Haitian sovereignty; this neocolonialism supposedly siphoned off resources that would have been better used serving Haiti's poor. Under Dessalines, the fear of a foreign invasion verged on paranoia. Scaring away French invaders was one of the reasons invoked for the 1804 massacre. Coasts were depopulated, peasants moved to the interior of the country, and forts built against Napoleonic forces who, it seemed certain, would soon come back. If—when—this happened, Art. 5 of Dessalines' 1805 constitution explained, "at the first shot of the warning gun, the towns shall be destroyed and the nation will rise in arms." Christophe followed in his predecessors' footsteps, dedicating large human and financial resources to defense projects such as the Citadelle La Ferrière. The cost of protecting Haiti against a French invasion, the reasoning goes, bankrupted the young republic. In fact, soldiers were dispatched all over the countryside, which suggests that military expenses served to defend the dictators against their own people rather than against outside powers; at any rate, the French never came back.

In 1825, France finally agreed to recognize Haiti's independence, but she demanded 150 million francs for the privilege (the money was earmarked to indemnify French planters who had lost their fortune in Saint-Domingue). Despite the cost, President Boyer agreed to the terms. This indemnity has been invoked repeatedly to explain the financial difficulties Haitian governments experienced throughout the nineteenth century. Haiti, critics say, found itself incapable of paying the hefty sum and had to resort to external financing provided on ruinous terms. Foreign banks frequently floated Haitian loans at 60 or 70 percent par, which meant that banks only gave 60 or 70 percent of a loan in cash, yet expected to be reimbursed on the full value of the loan plus interest. In the time-honored tradition of muscular "gunboat diplomacy" prevalent in the nineteenth century, every Haitian refusal to pay up brought in European battleships threatening to bomb the capital.

The argument is disingenuous. Haiti never paid the indemnity. The sum was reduced to sixty millions francs in 1838 (payable over thirty years), and even these payments were made haphazardly, stopping altogether in 1852 (by comparison, France was assessed a tribute of five *billion* francs after losing the 1870 Franco-Prussian War, and she actually paid it). Most loans secured in the nineteenth century served to pay high military and civilian expenses, which were caused by an all-Haitian propensity for civil war and graft, not by the French indemnity. Political instability and continuing deficits then led newly installed governments to default on their predecessors' loans. Banks understandably called upon their governments to help collect unpaid debts, but Haitian rulers occasionally succeeded in defaulting altogether (Faustin Soulouque, for example, stood up to a French squadron in 1853). Banks were thereafter wary of loaning additional money to a client with such a poor credit history and insisted on terms that reflected past Haitian defaults more than Western greed.

Haitians bemoan foreign imperialism, while remaining silent about their own imperialism. Haiti shares the island of Hispaniola with the Dominican Republic, a Spanish-speaking country that during the nineteenth century was alternatively an independent country, a French colony, a Spanish colony—and a Haitian colony. The first Haitian invasion of the Dominican Republic took place under Louverture's rule in 1801 (Louverture's troops withdrew with the arrival of the Leclerc expedition a year later). The second invasion, in 1805, was led by Dessalines, and is remembered mostly because of the many exactions Haitian troops committed. Rape, torture, and plunder accompanied the army as it marched on the capital; the pattern was replicated, now accompanied by enslavement of prisoners, after a French–Dominican coalition forced Dessalines and his troops to retreat. In 1821, Haitians (now led by Boyer) finally succeeded in their plans, defeated the Dominicans, and started an occupation that lasted twenty-three years. Haiti, for much of the post-independence era, was an imperial ruler, not a victim of colonialism.

The Dominicans declared their independence in 1844. Unwilling to surrender their colony, Haitians launched a retaliatory campaign later that year. Proponents of the Haitian *destin manifeste* to rule Hispaniola were disappointed, for the expedition was a complete failure. Three later invasions (in 1849, 1850, and 1855), all of them under Faustin Soulouque's reign, succeeded in enlarging the border along Haiti's central plateau but failed in their central goal: turning all of Hispaniola into a Haitian empire. Thereafter, Haiti limited itself to financing various rebellion movements in the eastern part of the island, in 1861 and 1870 notably, then stopped intervening altogether. One would like to think that the long-term shift from occupation (1801–1802, 1821–1844) to invasion (1849, 1850, 1855) to foreign meddling to nonintervention showed that Haitians had finally reneged on their imperial dreams and adopted a more consensual vision of diplomacy. More likely, the plans were revised downward only when Haiti entered a downward economic spiral that turned its once impressive military into a negligible force. Haitians were imperialists when they could; when their army became too puny to invade the Dominican Republic, let alone to defeat France and Spain, they became fervent converts to anti-imperialism. Surely, had Haiti invaded most of North America, Yankee mini-states on the East Coast would be churning out scholarly assessments of the evils of the Haitian hegemon, and their counterparts in Port-au-Prince would be writing glowing accounts of the Haitian Century.

Haitian politicians' denunciations of imperialism in the nineteenth century also sounded insincere at times because they served as accomplices to Western imperialism as often as they fell victim to it. Haitian presidents were well aware that Haiti's strategic location in the middle of the Caribbean Sea became ever more valuable as the years went by. The advent of coal-burning steamships in the mid-nineteenth century created the need for a network of coaling stations, a role the bay of Môle Saint-Nicolas could easily fulfill. French and American attempts to build a Panama Canal, first in the 1880s, then in the 1900s, turned the Windward Passage into one of the busiest sea-lanes in the world. Eager to gain political and military backing, Haitian presidents (or would-be presidents) thus took to the habit of dangling base rights in front of Western diplomats, who more often than not turned down the offer. In 1862, President Fabre-Nicolas Geffrard allowed Union warships to establish a coaling station in Cap Haïtien. In 1865, President Sylvain Salnave offered a permanent naval station to the United States. In 1883, President Lysius Salomon offered Tortuga Island, then Môle Saint-Nicolas, to the United States, only to receive the humiliating response that the United States wanted neither. It remains unclear how serious the offers were (in 1888, President Florvil Hippolyte secretly offered Môle Saint-Nicolas, then backed down when the United States showed interest). But the habit of subordinating Haitian sovereignty to one's political career remained a feature of many later presidencies, including those of self-styled nationalists such as François Duvalier, Raoul Cédras, and Jean-Bertrand Aristide, all three of whom loudly denounced imperialism while secretly requesting American involvement.

Faustin the First, Emperor of Haiti (1849–1859)

In European and American eyes, no Haitian president quite exceeded Faustin Soulouque's pomposity and ridicule. In the nineteenth century, he was a favorite of Western caricaturists and humorists alike, frequently derided as the black emperor of Haiti who aped European courts—the only emperor to serve as his own buffoon. Many of these criticisms, clearly inspired by the racism prevalent at the time, sound offensive today. More importantly, by dismissing Soulouque as a harmless clown, they overlooked the tremendous economic and political cost his rule exacted. For Haitians, living under Soulouque was anything but a joke, as the emperor's grandiose calls for racial pride were used to occult graft, tyranny, and military setbacks.

Like many of his political contemporaries, Soulouque was born in a family of slaves. Too young to fight during the revolution, he later became a professional soldier deemed loyal enough to serve under a variety of presidents (including Pétion and Boyer), even occupying the sensitive position of head of the presidential guard. During those years, Soulouque acquired a reputation for joviality and plainness verging on stupidity. In a country devoured by presidential aspirations, he was the compliant soldier whose obedience one could count on. Ironically, his feigned lack of political ambition eventually earned him the presidency.

In 1847, President Jean-Baptiste Riché absorbed a quantity of aphrodisiacs not quite in keeping with the old man's heart condition and died. The resulting battle for the presidency was intense. The Senate divided itself into two camps, each of them supporting a candidate that was anathema to the other faction. To break the gridlock, the senators turned to the unassuming Soulouque, whose reputation for bonhomie presaged that he would soon turn into a harmless puppet in the hands of the Senate. The story, probably apocryphal, holds that Soulouque was approached by senators while taking a nap in his hammock, grudgingly accepted the position, and went back to sleep.

Throughout his career, European newspapers and the French carica- turists Cham and Honoré Daumier, presumably acting under the assumption that such an emperor should have no clothes, portrayed Soulouque as a simian-looking African clad in outrageous outfits. Victor Hugo more elegantly wrote of Soulouque that he was a black Napoléon (the epithet would have filled Louverture with joy, but it referred to Napoléon III, whom Hugo despised). Soulouque's aristocratic preten- sions played into such prejudices. When he decided to be crowned emperor Faustin I on August 26, 1849, the move was so sudden that all that could be found was a paltry crown of gilded cardboard (a more elab- orate ceremony befitting Faustin's imperial dignity was held three years later). Soulouque then went on to ennoble favorites who, foreigners sneered, shared the emperor's humble background. Bobo, whose sole claim to fame up to that point was his skill as a bandit, was upgraded to Prince de Bobo (childish French for "booboo"). Haiti's colorful place names formed the basis for a nobility that quickly outnumbered that appointed by Christophe thirty years before. Voltaire Castor was thus upgraded to Count of l'Ile à Vache (Castor means "beaver"; Ile à Vache means "cow island"). General Sanon became the Count of Port-à-Piment ("Hot Pepper Harbor"). The list went on.

Soulouque dismissed these criticisms as examples of foreign racism. Years before the *noiriste* movement of Jean Price-Mars, and a century before Stokely Carmichael, Aimé Césaire, and Léopold Sédar Senghor launched Black Power and *négritude*, Soulouque advocated racial pride and black nationalism. Haiti's African heritage had been dismissed by previous mulatto presidents such as Boyer and Pétion, but Soulouque took pride in his black skin. He spoke Creole, only learning French at a late age. He and his wife Adelina were the first Haitian leaders to practice Voodoo openly (this did not preclude his practicing Catholicism as well). He promoted blacks to the higher ranks of government, substituting skin color for competence. He fought against Dominicans, the French, and all those he saw as enemies of Haiti. Dessalines had declared Haiti's political independence in 1804; Pétion had abandoned the colonial plantation system in 1809; Soulouque's reign was a declaration of racial and intellectual independence.

Soulouque's assertiveness was so popular among Haitian blacks that he enjoyed a legitimacy that could have served as a mandate for lasting change. Unfortunately, all too often, Soulouque used racial pride merely as an excuse for greed and dictatorship. His invasions of the Dominican Republic were a case in point. Haiti, he claimed, had to invade its neighbor because the loot would help pay for the French indemnity of 1825. Alternatively, a Haitian occupation would preclude a foreign invasion of the Dominican Republic, thus preventing European imperialists from gaining a foothold in the island. Soulouque offered Haitian imperialism as a remedy against European imperialism. The argument was circuitous and self-serving. Adding insult to injury, the invasions failed.

Soulouque served as president for two years and as emperor for an additional ten years. One hundred and forty-three months of total power brought no reforms of substance. Power for power's sake was his only achievement, dictatorship his only field of expertise. In 1848, he ordered prominent mulattoes to be harassed, arrested, and killed, thus radically altering the racial composition of the ruling class. He also doubled the armed forces with a paramilitary force loyal only to him, which he called *zinglins*. The tactic would inspire many of his successors, who would also rely on paramilitary groups such as Papa Doc's *Tontons Macoutes* for their dirty work. Once in power, however, neither he nor the black officers and *zinglins* he had promoted did anything.

Dictatorship came at a cost. Royal pomp cost a fortune. So did the unsuccessful forays into the Dominican Republic, the profusion of soldiers and *zinglins*, and the routine embezzlement that fed the system. To finance his regime, Soulouque defaulted on foreign loans, extorted funds from Haitians, and printed so much paper money that the value of the Haitian *gourde* continued its fall initiated under Pétion and Boyer. The Spanish silver piaster, which bought one *gourde* in 1820 and five *gourdes* by the time Soulouque took over (1847), was worth a full twenty *gourdes* when he left office (1859). By 1856, a worldwide glut of coffee and cotton greatly affected Haitian exports and sparked a political crisis that cost Soulouque his job.

The revolution followed a familiar pattern. Fabre-Nicolas Geffrard, a disaffected officer, first promised converts a fair share of the spoils of power. He then assembled his troops in Gonaïves, a city north of Port-au-Prince with a well-deserved reputation as a focal point of insurgencies, marched on the capital in January 1859, and put Soulouque on a ship bound for Jamaica and exile. Soulouque only returned to his homeland after Geffrard's fall. Now humbly describing himself as an apolitical retiree, the former emperor of Haiti died in Petit-Goâve on August 6, 1867.

Instability, Tyranny, and Incompetence (1859–1915)

The first half-century of Haitian independent rule was far from peaceful. By the time it was over, twenty-nine of the thirty-four men who had signed the declaration of independence had met a violent end. Haiti was ruled by a Jacques I (Dessalines), a Henri I (Christophe), and a Faustin I (Soulouque), but, revealingly, no royal dynasty ever reached the second generation. Haitians could only find solace in the fact that their dictators were able to fend off most of the many coup attempts, thus maintaining a modicum of stability (Soulouque ruled for twelve years, Christophe fourteen years, and Boyer twenty-five years). Unfortunately, Soulouque's exile marked the beginning of a period of even greater political mayhem that would reach its climax in the 1910s. Revolutions, mutinies, and civil wars erupted with disturbing frequency and proved ever more successful. In one four-year period (1870–1874), which would correspond to a normal campaign cycle in the United States, the presidential palace was blown up in the war that brought Jean-Nicolas Nissage-Saget into office and was destroyed again two years later in a fire. The president faced three coup attempts and only agreed not to extend his term after opponents made it clear that they would overthrow him if he did. These four years were considered peaceful for the age: Nissage-Saget was the only president of the nineteenth century to finish his term (if one excepts those presidents who declared themselves president-for-life and were accordingly killed while still in office).

Because political battles centered on spoils, not deeply held ideals, these recurrent civil wars were less violent than one might expect. By the early twentieth century, presidents were overthrown with such regularity that revolutions had become methodical, almost orderly, affairs. A presidential hopeful would gather mercenaries called *cacos* in northern Haiti, promising to pay them with public funds should the revolution succeed (this immediately put the incumbent at a disadvantage, for he had to pay his own supporters in cash). The "candidate" and his supporters, whose numbers rarely topped a few hundreds, would then march on the capital. Bloody pitched battles were rare, and army units usually switched sides rather than risk their lives. As soon as a president understood that all was lost, he would courteously bow to superior force and make arrangements for his exile, rather than hiding in the mountains to keep on fighting. He no longer held power; but he escaped with his life and, if he was prudent enough, sizable riches. Some, like Soulouque, were even able to return from exile once political passions had cooled down sufficiently. Paradoxically, the period following the revolution was generally bloodier than the revolution itself as the new president executed scores of supporters of the old regime and *cacos* profited from the rampant lawlessness to loot businesses.

Few foreign contemporaries admired the ingenuity and efficiency with which Haitians managed their chaotic political life. To some, constant upheaval in Haiti and elsewhere in the region turned Caribbean politics into a farce that was as entertaining as it was outlandish. Others, troubled by the greed and gore, focused on the few instances in which Haitian presidents failed to leave for exile quickly enough. The fate of Henri Christophe (who killed himself with a silver bullet in 1820) and Jean-Baptiste Riché (overdose of aphrodisiacs, 1847) had already entered the body of international lore on Haiti. The following years only added to Haiti's seamy reputation. In 1870, Albert Salnave was overthrown but chose to carry the fight all the way to San Domingo rather than going into exile. Captured and brought back to Port-au-Prince, he was executed by a firing squad in the presidential palace. In 1912, Cincinnatus Leconte decided to store all his powder in the basement of the presidential palace to deny his opponents access to ammunitions, but the move backfired when a spark sent the palace and its occupants into the stratosphere. In 1913, Tancrède Auguste died of a disease that was attributed either to poisoning or syphilis. The following day, as a solemn funeral was held in the Port-au-Prince cathedral, shots fired from the outside signaled that the next presidential campaign was already under way. Haiti's political life, it seemed, had reached its nadir, but the single most gruesome of these presidential deaths, that of Guillaume Sam in 1915, was yet to come.

These deaths were so grotesque that they tended to obscure the enormous economic and military costs of political instability. Every one of these civil disturbances, which took place every year on average, brought domestic and international business to a halt, sometimes for months. The *cacos'* progress was followed by pillage and fire, particularly in the capital, where property valued at several million dollars went up in flames with each revolution. Haitians and foreigners were understandably wary of investing their money in such conditions, requiring hefty rates of return in order to recoup their investment in months rather than years.

Presidents leaving for exile brought the national treasure with them. Pressed for cash, new presidents defaulted on past loans and contracted new ones on unfavorable terms. Economic growth could not flourish in such conditions.

Instability also fostered poor asset allocation. Schools, roads, factories, and sewer systems were routinely neglected as these were long-term projects whose effects would only be felt long after their initiator had left the presidential palace. Poor water sanitation and an antiquated fire system led to recurrent epidemics and fires whose costs far exceeded the money needed to prevent them. Instead, state revenues rewarded *cacos* and financed an outsized army that fed off, rather than protected, the people. Even the army, on which so many of Haiti's resources were lavished, fell short of fulfilling its two main goals: ensuring internal peace and preventing foreign powers from sending gunboats. Spenser St. John, a British consul to Haiti famous for his virulent account of late-nineteenth-century Haitian life, wrote in *Hayti: or, the Black Republic* (1886) that as of 1867 the Haitian army numbered no less than 6,500 general officers, 7,000 lesser officers, and 6,500 privates. The proliferation of generals only accentuated political ambitions. As for the privates, high-level corruption left them unpaid, unfed, and untrained. Military

Figure 3.1 By the early twentieth century, Port-au-Prince was a run-down capital plagued by incessant fires, epidemics, and revolutions.

service was so unpopular that peasants were rounded up by force when needed, tied up with ropes, and herded to barracks.

A traditional democratic system is designed to select leaders known for being educated, experienced, and inspiring. The free-for-all race for the presidential palace of nineteenth-century Haiti attracted a very different breed of politicians: those who, like Soulouque, knew how to hold on to power but not how to do anything with it. Brutality, covetousness, and lack of scruples were the main prerequisites for the presidency, and accordingly the main attributes of many presidents. Only two presidents of the era were worthy of recognition. Fabre-Nicolas Geffrard (1859–1867) built roads and irrigation ditches, started a steamship company, and inaugurated schools. Lysius Salomon (1879–1888) fostered public education, created a national bank, paid arrears on the national debt, printed Haiti's first stamps, modernized the army, and maintained good relations with the outside world (he had met his wife while studying in France). Within years of their departure, infrastructures had fallen into disrepair. Burning a schoolhouse, it turns out, takes much less time than building one.

During the celebrations that marked Haiti's centennial in 1904, angry Haitian intellectuals such as Dr. Rosalvo Bobo complained that Haiti had squandered one century of independent rule (figure 3.1). Their warning was prescient. Within a few years, Port-au-Prince's shameful political intrigues sparked a foreign invasion that took away the independence Louverture and Dessalines had fought so hard to secure.

CHAPTER 4

Benevolent Imperialism: Haiti during the First U.S. Occupation (1915–1934)

Chronicle of a Death Foretold

On March 4, 1915, Jean Vilbrun Guillaume Sam was inaugurated as president of Haiti. The exact length of his term remained uncertain, as there had been no election to begin with, but Sam's immediate predecessors had generally declared themselves presidents for life, then left for exile within a year. Sam was the sixth man to reach the presidency since Cincinnatus Leconte in 1911; there had been three different presidents in 1914 alone. Sam had replaced his predecessor only by dint of a large force of *cacos*, or mercenaries, and feared, with some justification, that an ambitious rival might quickly overthrow him by dint of an even larger force. Sam, who had had a hand in many of the revolutions that had plagued his predecessors, understood that the rich mulattoes of the capital financed presidential hopefuls in the hope of securing lucrative governmental positions, and that the *cacos* who had brought him to power would soon look for another patron. He accordingly set out to secure his power base by jailing two hundred hostages picked from the most prominent families of Port-au-Prince and gave the warden orders to execute the hostages should a revolution break out.

Events proceeded faster than Sam had anticipated. On July 27, barely four months after he had been sworn in, a small group of revolutionaries marched on the presidential palace in Port-au-Prince, captured the machine gun protecting the grounds, and turned it on the guards. Wounded and shocked, Sam climbed over the fence that separated the palace from the nearby residence of French ambassador Pierre Girard and sought asylum there. Prison guards, upon learning that their president had fled from the palace, entered the cells of the hostages Sam had rounded up a few weeks before. The hostages had failed to safeguard the presidency; so the time had come to carry out Sam's menace. The hostages had to die. The guards, armed with clubs and machetes, made a butchery of it. When all was over, 167 bodies, mangled beyond recognition, lay in the cells.

The funerals, all 167 of them, began at daybreak on July 28. Hostages had been taken from all the prominent families of Port-au-Prince, so everyone had a relative to mourn. Members of the elite buried what body parts they had managed to assemble, then made loud calls for revenge. Soon, an angry mob gathered around the residence of the French ambassador. He and his daughter pleaded for forgiveness, but to no avail. A party climbed over a wall, spread through the residence, opened doors and dressers, and finally found Sam's hiding place in the ambassador's bathroom. Neither diplomatic immunity nor presidential deference mattered anymore. All that remained was a terrified man pleading for his life, the toilet providing an oddly comical setting for this tragedy. The grief-stricken fathers paused for a moment, then decided not to grant mercy. Ignoring the ambassador's pleas, they dragged Sam out of the bathroom kicking and screaming. Blows fell. Sam was half dead by the time he reached the street. The crowd finished the grisly job. By nighttime, nothing but a dismembered heap of human flesh remained of the president of Haiti.

Had Haitian politics followed their normal course, Rosalvo Bobo, an influential mulatto and *caco* patron waiting in Cap Haïtien for the situation to settle down, would likely have been the next occupant of the presidential palace. History, however, unfolded differently. Foreign diplomats all agreed that the latest revolution had exceeded boundaries of acceptable behavior, even by the standards of early-twentieth-century Haitian politics. The grisly prison massacre, reenacted on a smaller scale during the murder of the president, lacked the farcical charm of prior upheavals. Granted, no foreigners had been killed in the fighting, but the violation of the ambassador's residence did not bode well for the future. One could not even blame these grisly events on illiterate *cacos* from the mountains, for the main protagonists belonged to the elite. If the best families of the capital took to dismembering the president in open daylight, Haiti had truly become ungovernable. The American ambassador called on Adm. William Capperton of the U.S. Navy to intervene.

Later that day, sailors from the USS *Washington* came ashore. Some confused fighting ensued as various bands of political rivals fought themselves and the American invaders, but, by nightfall, Americans were in control of the capital. The last European invasion, dating back to Napoléon, had cost fifty thousand French lives. This time around, only two Americans died. Haiti, 111 years after the 1804 declaration of independence, was once again a colony. As if the humiliation were not enough, imperial power was now in the hands of Americans, the descendants of the puny New England upstarts who had once contented themselves with the right to sell dried fish to the slaves of Saint-Domingue in exchange for surpluses of molasses.

Taking Control

Haitians like to think that 1915 was the product of greed, and that American imperialists invaded Haiti to take over its resources. Americans, they point out, temporarily took away the gold stored in Haiti's national bank (officially for safekeeping) and later insisted on the right of American businessmen to own land in Haiti. The reality was less glorious. By 1915, the Haitian economy was but a shadow of its colonial counterpart. Total U.S. investments in Haiti amounted to $4 million, fifty-five times less than in Cuba. No sugar had been exported in the previous hundred years. Public infrastructures were ruined by years of neglect. Yaws and other Caribbean diseases were endemic. The capital was a dump. No industry existed. Economically, Haiti no longer mattered.

To Americans, Haiti's sole asset was its strategic location at the entrance to the Caribbean Sea. Haiti controlled the access to the Windward Passage, the main sea-lane from New York to the Panama Canal (which had opened a year before). Haiti was seven hundred miles from Florida and could serve as a staging ground for a German attack should the United States enter World War I (which had also started in 1914). Had it been strong and stable, the odds of a German takeover of Haiti would have been slim. But, given Haiti's incessant revolutions, it could easily be overtaken by any European power willing to muster a few warships. This the United States could not accept; following the doctrine of U.S. preventive action in Latin America, or "corollary to the Monroe Doctrine," posited by Theodore Roosevelt eleven years before, Woodrow Wilson decided to invade Haiti before somebody else did.

The occupation forces immediately proceeded to secure their control over Haiti, further suggesting that their main objective was strategic and political, not economic. Soldiers in the capital were given ten *gourdes* and told to go home. Weapons searches yielded thousands of weapons. Rosalvo Bobo, who hoped to turn his hold on the *cacos* into presidential gold, was sent into exile. Marines were dispatched throughout the countryside. Martial law was imposed in September 1915 (figure 4.1). In February 1916, a fifteen-hundred-strong Haitian constabulary called the *gendarmerie* appeared. All its officers were white and American. The United States now held a monopoly on violence.

Customs and the treasury were next. U.S. officers took over all the customs houses in Haiti's main ports while U.S. administrators, already manning the national bank, were instructed not to sign a check unless specifically ordered to by U.S., not Haitian, authorities. The goal was not to plunder the Haitian treasury (what money there was did not warrant a nineteen-year occupation), but to deny would-be revolutionaries the monies needed to finance their political ambitions. The treasury and the tariff revenue that fed it were now off-limits.

A U.S.-Haitian treaty replaced sheer force as the main justification for the occupation in the fall of 1915. Under the treaty, Haiti kept a president, but the United States unilaterally designated the officials in

Figure 4.1 Marines formed the backbone of the U.S. military presence in Haiti during 1915–1934.

charge of five key sectors: the *gendarmerie*, customs, finances, public health, and infrastructures. In addition, Haiti could not surrender territory to any foreign power save the United States. U.S. interest in Môle Saint-Nicolas had waned now that Cuba had placed Guantánamo Bay in American hands, but it was essential to keep the Germans out.

In order to offset accusations of colonial rule, the United States kept congressmen in place and selected a Haitian mulatto named Philippe Sudre Dartiguenave as president, but American control of the treasury was designed to prevent any independent thinking on their part. When deputies balked at ratifying the 1915 treaty, U.S. authorities held up their paychecks until they adopted a more conciliatory attitude. The tactic was reused every time the senators showed a similar reluctance, and it rendered equally quick results. For years, the American chain of command remained unclear, partly because the invasion had taken Washington by surprise, partly because the United States took a long time accepting the reality that Haiti was, for all intents and purposes, an American colony. Officials came and went until Washington created a systematic line of command headed by a U.S. proconsul in 1922.

Dartiguenave complained of undemocratic American bullying, but his own political style owed more to the iron hand than to the velvet glove. He first dissolved the senate, then the assembly, before drafting a new constitution (Haiti's fifteenth) that secured his power. The United States' main contribution was to insist that the constitutional ban on foreign ownership of Haitian soil be lifted (Haitian courts retaliated by ruling consistently against white plaintiffs irregardless of the merits of their case; foreign investments in Haiti remained minimal). With both houses disbanded, Dartiguenave and his American backers turned to a plebiscite that ratified the constitution with a suspiciously lopsided vote of 98,225 for, 768 against. Dartiguenave then handpicked friends to form a *Conseil d'Etat* (Council of State), which replaced the disbanded parliament (his friends in the council returned the favor by refusing to grant him a second term in 1922). Legislative elections were not held until 1930.

Sons of 1804: The Caco Insurrection (1918–1920)

The 1915 invasion initially encountered little military resistance. Northern Haiti, where revolutions had been a lucrative industry for the native *cacos*, mounted a feeble uprising that was quickly subdued. President Dartiguenave was a southerner who kept his own region quiet. The situation changed in 1916 with the introduction of the *corvée*.

The *corvée* was a provision of an 1863 Haitian law that called on peasants to help maintain local roads by paying a tax or, alternatively, working for free as a construction worker. The law had long since been forgotten (as were the roads the law was meant to maintain), but U.S. occupation authorities revived it in order to improve the communication network at minimal expense. The law left the peasants little choice. They could theoretically pay the tax; or they could work. But nobody had any money; so all were forced to work. To limit discontent, workers were to be treated well, fed, and entertained. The system was initially ruled a success. Highways jumped from 3 miles in 1915 to 470 in 1918, in which year the road between the capital and Cap Haïtien reopened. The potential for abuse, however, was enormous, and stories quickly leaked of peasants rounded up by soldiers of the *gendarmerie* and led to work tied up with ropes. For Haitians mortified that 1915 had erased 1804, the symbol was too strong. The whites, it seemed, had brought slavery back with them.

What made the *corvée* even more unacceptable to the elite was that it applied to every citizen, including—oh infamy—to affluent Haitians who had inherited a strong dislike for manual labor from their distant planter ancestors. One such victim was Charles Masséna Péralte, a mulatto opponent of Dartiguenave. Convicted of complicity in a robbery case, Péralte was sentenced to five years of hard labor and spent much of 1918 sweeping the streets of Cap Haïtien. In September of that year, Péralte finally succeeded in convincing his guard to let him go, dropped his broomstick, and fled for the hills. There, he organized a resistance movement using popular discontent with the *corvée* as the main rallying cry. Attacks against isolated outposts multiplied, and the new *gendarmerie* was quickly overwhelmed; some *gendarmerie* units had not even been trained in basic marksmanship because of fears that they might turn their guns on their American patrons. The abolition of the reviled *corvée* in October 1918 failed to disband Péralte's growing cohorts. The Marines were called in.

Throughout 1919 the Marines chased Péralte and his men in a classic case of guerrilla warfare. Cleverly using the hilly terrain and his popularity among the peasants, Péralte was everywhere and nowhere. U.S. control of the countryside required a network of barracks; but such barracks were also ideal targets for surprise guerrilla attacks. Pinning down the elusive Péralte for a decisive confrontation seemed impossible.

The American head of the *gendarmerie* concluded that no progress could be made as long as Péralte, the insurrection's intellectual and military leader, was allowed to live. The order he gave his subordinates was simple: "get Charlemagne!" Probably remembering the long, unfruitful search for Pancho Villa in the northern deserts of Mexico a few years before, U.S. officers were less than enthusiastic about being entitled with such a task. The assignment went from hand to hand until it landed on the desk of Capt. Herman H. Hanneken, a twenty-six-year-old Marine sergeant employed as one of the *gendarmerie*'s white officers.

Hanneken understood that the United States' overwhelming supremacy in firepower made the issue of killing Péralte irrelevant. Finding him was the one and only difficulty. He thus ordered black *gendarmes* Jean-Baptiste Conzé and Jean-Edmond François to defect and join Péralte's forces. To assuage any suspicion Péralte might harbor against these two new recruits, Hanneken also arranged for Conzé to attack U.S. forces and win the battle. Hanneken appeared in public with a bandaged arm suitably bloodied with red ink and made public his fear of Conzé. Now that he had ascertained Conzé's credentials, Péralte agreed to lead a joint attack against an American position at Grande Rivière on October 31, 1919. Hanneken's ruse had finally paid off. He knew where and when to "get Charlemagne."

As the battle raged through the night, Hanneken and a fellow white lieutenant, their faces blackened with charcoal, led a small group of black *gendarmes* to *caco* outposts. Conzé's betrayal had provided Hanneken and his men with the secret passwords; they got through. After a nerve-racking nighttime stroll deep behind enemy lines, they finally reached Péralte's own camp. Hanneken lost no time. He gunned down Péralte and miraculously made his way back to his own camp.

Benoît Batraville, Péralte's second-in-command, carried on the fight as best he could for the next few months. In one infamous April 1920 incident, his men captured Marine Lt. Lawrence Muth and he ordered Muth's organs to be taken out and eaten. Muth's brain was also smeared on cartridges and sights to improve their accuracy (the *cacos* were notoriously poor shooters). The gory Voodoo rituals proved no match for Marine machine guns, for Batraville himself was killed in May 1920. The *cacos* were defeated.

The human cost of the *caco* uprising was surprisingly small. Thanks to superior training and marksmanship, Marine losses only amounted to 13 killed. Marines estimated *caco* losses at 2,250 (1,861 in 1919 alone); the number might be inflated, for medal-hungry Marines liked to report a high body count. In American eyes, the deaths of a few thousand lowly *cacos* (labeled "bandits" in the official terminology) seemed an acceptable price to pay to stabilize Haiti. Batraville's cannibalistic murder of Muth, at any rate, was seen as proof of the basic inhumanity of the *cacos*.

Haitian views of the *caco* uprising differ. Haitian estimates, which included civilian losses, topped ten thousand dead, and Marines, not Voodoo-worshipping *cacos*, were the ones accused of committing atrocities. In particular, the Marines' decision to prop up the dead Péralte on a door and to disseminate pictures of his corpse led to the widespread belief that he was crucified like an earlier, more famous martyr. Rumors of "indiscriminate killings" reached the United States in 1920 and received widespread publicity when Republican presidential candidate Warren Harding seized on that issue during this election year. Throughout the 1920s, the magazine *The Nation* unquestioningly reprinted accusations by Haitian opponents of the occupation that Haitians were routinely enslaved, abused, tortured, and killed. Such reports were wildly exaggerated. The alleged crucifixion of Péralte was a myth. Accusations that the Marines used attack dogs were borrowed from the Rochambeau era. Only in one sector, that of Hinche on Haiti's central plateau, was suspected abuse substantiated. There, Maj. Clarke H. Wells retained the *corvée* a few months after it was abolished, allowed subordinates to execute Haitians who refused to work, and ordered *caco* prisoners shot. Wells and his subordinates were dismissed immediately after the scandal erupted.

The most ironic consequence of Péralte's campaign was that it extended, rather than shortened, the U.S. occupation. Wilson briefly considered withdrawing troops after the German defeat in World War I made the strategic rationale for the U.S. occupation irrelevant. The favored option was to withdraw most U.S. Marines, leaving only a small legation guard that would symbolize U.S. support of the current government. The 1918–1919 *caco* uprising undermined all efforts at disengagement. Marine reinforcements were rushed in, and plans for a peaceful departure were quietly shelved. In 1922, Washington finally created the position of high commissioner (essentially a proconsul) and offered it to John Henry Russell. The United States was now in Haiti for the long run.

Benevolent Imperialism

The American colonial rulers of 1915–1934 and their Haitian surrogates had a creative interpretation of what democracy entailed, but so did all the dictators of 1804–1915. Haitians could hardly say that Americans had brought Haiti under an unprecedented period of dictatorship. A positive change was that Yankees, not *cacos*, now made and broke presidents. For the first time since Jean-Pierre Boyer, Haiti experienced nineteen years without a revolution and, for the first time since French colonial times, three peaceful transfers of power in a row. Haitian merchants could now travel to and from Port-au-Prince without fearing any raid by roving bands of *cacos*.

Treaty officials could easily have used their prominent role to exploit Haiti economically, but they decided against it. American officials rejected investments by the Sinclair Oil corporation and the United Fruit Company because these U.S. companies expected economic concessions deemed too onerous to the Haitian government. U.S. authorities even refused to enforce special privileges that previous Haitian presidents had granted to the Haitian–American Sugar Company (HASCO), the largest U.S. investor in Haiti. So-called American imperialists proved less submissive to the forces of international capital than their local predecessors.

Another innovation brought by the U.S. occupation was that absolute power, for once, served to benefit Haitians. Custom fees no longer financed revolutions and acquaintances of the president. Instead, they paid for public works and sanitation facilities, two of the five "treaty services" granted the United States under the 1915 treaty. Corruption had been so common among Haitian bureaucrats that it had become a standard perquisite of public service (much like retirement benefits or a health plan today); strict accounting virtually eliminated it. Political stability also strengthened Haitian credit abroad. When the public debt was consolidated in 1922, National City Bank floated it at a record 92.1 par and 7.9 percent yield on the assumption that the U.S.-controlled treasury would pay back Haiti's debts. The Haitian debt to the United States was entirely repaid well ahead of schedule. Debt payments represented 80 percent of the Haitian budget before 1915, so the reduced load freed up funds for much-needed infrastructure projects.

The results were nothing short of spectacular. By the late 1920s, 210 bridges and 1,000 miles of all-weather roads crisscrossed Haiti. Ports were modernized, lighthouses introduced, and a weekly steamer stopped in Haiti on its way to Panama. Nine major airfields appeared, along with the first airplanes to fly in Haiti. In 1929, a clipper introduced the first regular air service from Haiti to Miami. Telephone lines, already existing but unusable because of poor maintenance, were repaired. A new presidential palace replaced the one that had blown up in 1912. The first radio station opened in 1926. The network of irrigation canals created by the French was renovated and expanded, which allowed renewed exports of cotton and sugar, along with a newcomer, sisal. An agricultural school opened. Running water and 11 modern hospitals considerably improved public health. What was most damning to veteran Haitian politicians was that every single one of these projects was financed with Haitian taxes, not foreign aid. Americans only brought stability and technical expertise, proving that bad leadership, not lack of funds, had been the sole source of Haiti's previous troubles.

Anti-Americanism

Despite all the bridges and hospitals built under U.S. supervision, the foreign occupation was widely perceived as a national humiliation. A few years after celebrating the centennial of their hard-won independence, patriotic Haitians found themselves to be colonial subjects again. The Haitian military record was equally mortifying, for Péralte was no Dessalines, and his *caco* uprising fell far short of its colonial predecessor. Americans were even impolite enough to mount a successful infrastructure program, thus showing Haitians how poorly they had run their own country.

The mulattoes, who had played a central role in Haiti's politics and economy in previous decades, found American racism offensive. Many a prominent mulatto attempted to mingle with American officers, sent his daughter to army balls, and invited Americans to his home, only to be rebuked. The interracial taboo became even more pronounced in 1916 when the white wives of U.S. officers joined their husbands in Haiti. Black waiters aside, the all-white American Club was closed to all colored Haitians, the mulatto president included. In American eyes, there were no mulattoes; all Haitians were black. After a century of carefully planning marriages to keep their skin light, mulattoes viewed this generalization as no less than a personal affront. No mulatto took time to notice that this segregation was merely the American version of the racism mulattoes routinely inflicted on their darker compatriots.

Haiti's majority blacks felt even more insulted than the mulattoes did. Americans did not socialize with mulattoes, but they offered government positions to educated Haitians, who more often than not happened to be mulattoes. Haiti under U.S. occupation thus came to mirror colonial Saint-Domingue. Whites monopolized top governmental echelons, including all officer ranks, the proconsul office, and key financial positions. Mulattoes came next. Dartiguenave, whom the United States selected as president immediately after the 1915 invasion, was a mulatto; so was Joseph Louis Borno, who ruled from 1922 to 1930; Eugène Roy, a provisional president who briefly served in 1930, was also a mulatto; so was his successor Sténio Vincent, who outlived the U.S. occupation. Black Haitians, representing 90 percent of the population, came last.

Most were peasants and servants; a few managed to be hired as privates in the *gendarmerie*.

The U.S. government's single most important mistake in 1915–1934 was its failure to understand the centrality of race and history in Haitian politics. Including African Americans in the U.S. force sent to occupy Haiti might have prevented Haitian references to French colonial times; but Woodrow Wilson never took that step. The U.S. Army was segregated and would remain so until 1948; so all of the officers who served in Haiti were white. The rumor that nigger-hating Southerners were specifically selected for occupation duty in Haiti was unsubstantiated, but the overtly racist attitude of officers such as Col. Littleton W. T. Waller did little to endear the U.S. occupation to Haitians.

Lack of cultural sensitivity carried a heavy political price. Reestablishing the *corvée* was the most obvious case of a misguided policy bound to inflame Haitian public opinion; the *corvée* built roads, but its resemblance to French slavery was obvious to anyone but the American officers who designed it. An anti-Voodoo campaign launched in the 1920s at the behest of President Borno was another powerful symbol. U.S. soldiers destroyed Voodoo temples and drums, while black Haitians murmured that their white masters were trying to stamp out the most visible element of slave culture to impose their European version of Christianity. These missteps explained why occupation authorities, who built more roads and hospitals than all other Haitian presidents combined, met outright revolt in 1918–1920 and sullen mistrust thereafter.

U.S. educational policies were another case in point. U.S. authorities complained that Haitian schools, inspired by the nineteenth-century French *lycées*, were elitist institutions that offered a small minority of Haitians a curriculum heavily biased toward liberal arts and the classics. Haiti thus produced hundreds of lawyers who spoke Latin and could quote Racine and Corneille but did not know how to repair a steam engine. A broader-based, more technical educational system, Americans rightly concluded, would have been more likely to spark an industrial revolution in Haiti. In an effort to develop vocational schools, U.S. officials funded an agricultural school in Damien in 1923, but they promptly found themselves faced with a quandary: should they enroll peasants, who spoke neither French nor English and were largely illiterate? Or should they select children of the elite, who had the required educational background but found manual labor beneath them? They chose the latter, adding generous scholarships to incite affluent families to enroll their children.

By 1929, the school was a disappointment. Students used their scholarship money to hire servants who did the field work that was part of the required practical training. When U.S. authorities banned this practice and reduced scholarships accordingly the students went on strike. Within weeks, sympathy strikes had spread throughout the country. In one bloody incident, Marines killed twelve peasant demonstrators in Cayes and martial law had to be reestablished. The U.S. policy was well intentioned and addressed a real flaw of the Haitian educational system; but it ran afoul of local class prejudices that the Americans did not understand.

After the defeat of Péralte's *caco* rebellion, Haitian patriots desirous to oppose the U.S. occupation fought with pens rather than guns. In the 1920s and 1930s, an influential movement known as *noirisme* after the French word for "black" swept Haitian intellectual circles. *Noiristes* were educated Haitians, most of them black, who concluded that Haiti's dual identity was the source of its political problems. Elite Haitians, *noiristes* said, looked to the former colonial ruler as a model; they spoke perfect French, studied in Paris, and scorned Voodoo. Even lower-class Haitians were conditioned to dismiss African traditions as barbaric. Haiti was a country in denial, ignoring the island's predominantly African origins while embracing a culture that was completely foreign to most of its citizens. By contrast, *noiristes* studied and embraced anything African; they incorporated Creole folk tales in their writings, rehabilitated Voodoo, and fought against the widespread prejudice against black skin.

The acknowledged leader of the *noiriste* school was Jean Price-Mars (1876–1969). The descendant of a prominent black family that included two presidents and a host of revolutionary heroes, Price-Mars studied at an elitist *lycée* of the capital and in Paris. His stay in France, and an 1803 visit to the United States, led him to encounter the "scientific" racism then popular among white ethnologists. The notion that blacks were ape-like creatures was anathema to Price-Mars; he was an erudite man who successively worked as a diplomat, a deputy, and an inspector of Haiti's schools. His pent-up resentment against white racism burst into the open after the U.S. invasion of his home country. In parallel with his career as a history teacher and a country doctor, Price-Mars published a series of articles that culminated in his seminal *Thus Spoke the Uncle* (1928). Elite mulattoes, he argued, were responsible for Haiti's disastrous history; Haiti could only reinvent itself if it ceased to denigrate its African roots and used its unique popular culture as a basis for a colorblind, egalitarian society.

Noirisme, because it emphasized independent thinking rather than an imitation of Western intellectual currents, produced some of the greatest masters of Haitian literature. Most influential was Jacques Roumain's *Masters of the Dew* (1944), a novel whose rural setting and celebration of black peasant life were characteristic of the *noiriste* agenda. Later black writers such as Aimé Césaire of Martinique and Léopold Sédar Senghor of Senegal were deeply influenced by the *noiriste* movement, which they renamed *négritude*.

Noirisme did not consist in shooting at U.S. Marines; so few Americans paid attention to the movement until Stokely Carmichael and other civil rights leaders rediscovered it in the 1960s and refashioned it into Black Power. But the movement touched the very soul of Haitian society. It was widely popular among educated blacks; when translated into a more basic agenda of racial pride, it appealed to illiterate peasants as well. Peasants resented that all of their neighbors were black but that tax collectors and officers were white or mulatto; they could not understand why the local school teacher was a French priest who insisted on teaching in French when their children only spoke Creole; they suffered when their beloved Voodoo gods were dismissed as Satanic or even banned outright. It took thirty years before François Duvalier was able to tap into this groundswell of support for a black revolution—and betray most of its principles in a mad dash for absolute power.

Haitian opposition to the occupation finally convinced Americans to leave. Herbert Hoover announced in 1930 his government's intention to bring U.S. troops home. Franklin D. Roosevelt, his successor, declared in 1933 that the United States would heretofore maintain good neighborly relations with Latin American countries. Roosevelt understood the Latin American opposition to the heavy-handed use of American military power in the region and made nonintervention the centerpiece of his policy. Sténio Vincent visited Washington, DC in 1934; Roosevelt came to Cap Haïtien a few months later. That visit is well remembered in Haiti, for Roosevelt always felt a personal attraction to Haiti and he made an effort to address his interlocutors in French. After a final round of official courtesies and hard private bargaining, the Marines left on August 15, 1934. The time had now come to assess the long-term success or failure of the U.S. occupation.

What Went Wrong?

For nineteen years Haiti was, in fact if not in official rhetoric, an American colony. This brand of colonialism was noticeably benign, especially when compared with its turn-of-the-century equivalents. In 1893–1908, agents of the Belgian king Leopold II thoroughly looted

Congo's natural resources while killing half the population through forced labor and mistreatment. In 1899–1902, U.S. anti-insurgency repression in the Philippines resulted in the death of two hundred thousand Filipinos. In Haiti, casualty lists were shorter, looting was kept to a minimum, and the occupiers made significant improvements to infrastructures and sanitation facilities. Colonialism rarely gets more benevolent than this.

And yet, the occupation fell short of its central objective: turning Haiti into a stable, pro-American, prosperous, and reasonably democratic society. Political reform was the weakest point in the U.S. plan. Wilson posited that Haitians would magically embrace Jeffersonian democracy if taught how to elect "good men"; he then imposed favored candidates through high-handed elections or outright force and waited for the Haitian polity to reform itself. This failed predictably; preaching democracy while practicing military occupation and racism was too odd a combination. In 1938, four years after the last U.S. troops left Haiti, U.S.-supported President Sténio Vincent declared a dictatorship. The standard pattern of coups and repression reasserted itself. The lack of attention paid to democratization was ominous considering that bad governance had always been at the heart of Haiti's troubles.

For Haitians to support a foreign occupation was unlikely, especially when the foreign occupiers were white. But U.S. authorities made a series of political missteps that made the U.S. presence even more intolerable than it already was. Failing to understand Haitians' prickly sense of nationalism and the explosive nature of racial relations were the two most important mistakes. William J. Bryan, Woodrow Wilson's secretary of state, was particularly uninformed. In 1912, he contacted the U.S. banker who headed Haiti's national bank and asked for a refresher course—starting with the crucial point of where Haiti was on the map. A few hours later, a puzzled Bryan erupted: "Dear me, think of it! Niggers speaking French."[1] This mix of ignorance and racism turned away many Haitians. Anti-Americanism grew no matter how many miles of roads the Americans built.

The Haitian economy failed to develop for the same reason its political system failed to change: reforms were imposed from the outside instead of being introduced by locals. However benign the U.S. occupation was, it remained an occupation; a few profiteers and political opportunists aside, Haitians refused to collaborate with U.S. masters desirous of making Haitians happy against their own will. In a strange way, Haitians would have been happy to see the Americans fail; this might have left the country poorer, but it would have vindicated Haitian nationalism. When U.S. officials launched an ambitious cadastral survey in the hope of finally codifying the maze of Haitian property deeds, the building housing negatives of the aerial survey mysteriously burned down. Attempts to encourage Haitians to diversify their exports from coffee to cotton and sisal encountered a silent apathy that was the Haitian peasant's main form of resistance; the monocultural agricultural sector subsequently collapsed along with coffee prices during the Great Depression.

U.S. engineers and officers thus imposed an artificial level of development and stability that did not survive their departure. White administrators generally viewed Haitians as ignorant and incapable of reform, so few took the time to train black recruits who could take over after they left. When Franklin D. Roosevelt decided that a U.S. colony in Haiti was incompatible with the Good Neighbor Policy of nonintervention, U.S. officials quickly selected a number of Haitians, gave them the jobs white outsiders had occupied before, and left. This was no trivial matter; from the Congo to India, the main reason why colonies developed or collapsed after independence was the presence, or absence, of trained local cadres. Unskilled Haitians inherited the infrastructures built by Americans and neglected to maintain them properly. Within two decades, most roads and bridges were a potholed mess impassable during the rainy season and accessible only with all-wheel drive vehicles the rest of the year. Dictator François Duvalier later sneered that "foreigners don't know how to build roads in Haiti." "Foreigners don't know how to train Haitians to build and maintain their own roads" would have been more accurate.

Renewed instability and poverty meant that the long-term strategic goal of turning Haiti into a regional bulwark fell short. A 1937 incident along the border with the Dominican Republic made this reality painfully clear. Haitian–Dominican relations had always been tense because of the nineteenth-century Haitian invasions of the Dominican Republic and the two countries' different racial make-up. In 1937, Dominican dictator Rafael Trujillo decided that persecuting the one hundred thousand Haitian immigrants who worked as cane cutters in the Dominican Republic would be a popular move (bizarrely, Trujillo had a Haitian grandmother). He sent soldiers to the sugar-growing regions with orders to round up all dark-skinned individuals, whether they were Haitian citizens or not. The prevailing story holds that Dominican soldiers asked blacks to say the word *perejil* (parsley); the rolling Rs were difficult for native Creole speakers to pronounce correctly, so getting one's parsley wrong was sufficient proof that one was not a true Dominican. Blacks who failed the test were then sent to the border. Some were lucky enough to make their way to Ouanaminthe on the Haitian side, but an estimated twenty-five thousand were killed in the Dominican Republic, bayoneted on the shores of the aptly named River Massacre, or thrown out to sea to be eaten by sharks. This large-scale pogrom, following in the footsteps of the Spanish extermination of the native Tainos after 1492, Leclerc and Rochambeau's war of extermination against Haitian rebels in 1802–1803, and Dessalines's 1804 massacre of white French planters, was the fourth time in Haitian history that racial groups had been targeted.

A strong government would have avenged such infamy, but 1937 Haiti had neither the means nor the will to do so. Sténio Vincent was a mulatto with little sympathy for the black peasants who had migrated to the Dominican Republic. He promptly negotiated a deal with his good friend Trujillo, asked for a $30 indemnity for each dead Haitian, and obtained it. Relatives of the victims would have been outraged to learn that Haitian life was valued at a good pig's going rate, but they never saw the money. Vincent reduced the $750,000 total to $525,000 to speed up the payment and shared the proceeds with his cronies. After nineteen years of U.S. occupation, Haiti was still a long way from being ruled by "good men."

CHAPTER 5

Hearts of Darkness: The Duvaliers' Black Revolution (1957–1986)

The Election of 1957

On September 22, 1957, Haitians went to the polls to select a new president. President Paul Eugène Magloire had resigned the previous December, and Haiti had since been plagued by an instability unseen since 1915. Six governments had come and gone in a nine-month span; two elections had already been cancelled; Haiti had even gone through a one-day civil war. As always, the Haitian polity was divided in two camps separated by a racial and social line. Mulattoes and the urban middle class rallied behind Louis Déjoie, a light-skinned man who made little secret of the prejudices common to his class. Oblivious to the military's importance in Haitian politics and to the majority black electorate he would face on election day, he announced during the campaign that he would, if elected, destroy the army and send all blacks back where they belonged: the fields. His main opponent, François Duvalier, was a shy black physician whom one candidate dismissed as a "profoundly stupid little man."[1] But Duvalier appealed to poor Blacks, in part because he evoked the legacy of Dumarsais Estimé, a popular black president of the 1940s, and in part because he had spent years fighting tropical diseases such as yaws in the Haitian countryside. Two other candidates, Daniel Fignolé and Clément Jumelle, had a significant constituency, but the campaign was so violent that both dropped out before the voting even began.

Fraud was rampant at the polls, as could be expected in a country that had known few elections in its history, none of them of the free variety. The largely illiterate voters were expected to bring to the polls preprinted ballots provided by their candidate of choice, which left them vulnerable to intimidation by henchmen hired by one of the two candidates. There was no registration list, so poll workers dipped voters' thumbs in ink to prevent multiple voting. Voters then washed their hands thoroughly and moved on to the next polling station, repeating the process as many times as time and skin allowed. Ballot stuffing and army interference were routine. La Gonâve won the prize for creative accounting as the sparsely inhabited island reported 18,841 votes for Duvalier, or more than its total population.

When the day was over, official results showed Duvalier ahead with 679,884 votes; Déjoie followed far behind with 266,993 votes. Close to 10,000 voters had cast a ballot for Jumelle, presumably unaware that he was no longer running. In one ironic twist of the Haitian electoral process, the overall results closely matched actual political divisions in Haiti. Supporters of Déjoie had cheated most effectively in areas where he was popular, such as Port-au-Prince and other urban centers with a large mulatto population. Supporters of Duvalier had done the same in the rural areas where his backers were located. The fraud, in a way, had been democratic. Inauguration day, one month later, brought to the fore Haiti's most fascinating ruler since Faustin Soulouque: François Duvalier, a country doctor better known by the nickname of Papa Doc.

Papa Doc: Black Nationalist

François Duvalier was born on April 14, 1907. He came of age during the U.S. occupation and, like most young men of his generation, interpreted Yankee rule as a national humiliation. He was too young to be affected by the *corvée* and the ensuing *caco* war, but the later *noiriste* movement made a deep imprint on him. Born to a middle-class family of Port-au-Prince, Duvalier received a fine education that culminated in his earning a medical degree. Bookish, dark-skinned, and shy, he failed to transform his position into financial affluence. In a country with an acute shortage of skilled practitioners, Duvalier was probably the only doctor struggling to find enough patients to make a decent living. Instead, he moonlighted as an ethnologist fascinated by Haiti's African roots. Following the example of more prominent *noiristes* such as Jean Price-Mars, Duvalier feverishly studied Haitian folk culture—Voodoo in particular—and wrote articles denouncing the U.S. occupation under the pen name Aberrahman. Black pride always remained a central feature of Duvalier's rhetoric.

The year 1934 brought relief from white rule, but the departing U.S. rulers left a mulatto president in charge, Sténio Vincent, who was succeeded by yet another mulatto president, Elie Lescot (1941–1946). It was during those years that Duvalier made two decisions that strangely contradicted his *noiriste* agenda. In December 1939, he married Simone Ovide, the illegitimate child of a mulatto businessman and a black servant. In 1943, he became the Haitian manager of a medical program run and funded by—of all countries—the United States. His mission was to administrate a clinic in Gressier, south of Port-au-Prince, which would employ the newly discovered penicillin to fight yaws. Yaws was a disease, then endemic in Haiti, carried by the spirochete *Treponema pertenue* under a person's skin; there, it slowly ate into the victim's flesh, with consequences much akin to those of leprosies. Limbs became atrophied; the ears and nose fell off; in some rare cases, the patient died. The penicillin treatment proved highly successful. Soon, Duvalier was operating clinics throughout the country and becoming known to hundreds of thousands of grateful Haitians as their beloved Papa Doc. Few remember today that the United States played an instrumental role in ridding Haiti of this crippling disease and that Papa Doc spent a year at the University of Michigan receiving additional training.

In 1946, black nationalist Dumarsais Estimé reached the presidency and Papa Doc got his first taste of politics as minister of health and labor. The experience was short-lived. Despite his popularity, Estimé was overthrown by Paul Magloire in 1950 and Papa Doc spent much of the following decade in internal exile. He only emerged from hiding in 1957 in time for the election that earned him the presidency. The Estimé debacle offered Papa Doc a lesson he never forgot: black nationalism, however well intentioned, would never succeed unless political opponents and the army were kept in check.

What use Papa Doc would make of presidential power after the 1957 election was anyone's guess. Ideally, he would provide prominent government positions for educated blacks, educational opportunities for the rest, and greater racial equality for all. As promised in the campaign, he would defend the rights of Haitian women whose role had traditionally been to work hard and stay quiet. He would proudly defend Haitian sovereignty abroad while working to eliminate the roots of anti-Haitian prejudices at home. Or—following in the footsteps of Dessalines, his personal hero—he would use black nationalism to legitimate his power while doing little save fighting imaginary plots by mulattoes and foreigners. For the time being, it was difficult to discern Papa Doc's intentions. Always impeccably trimmed in a black suit and hat, cool and distant, his eyes hidden behind thick glasses, Papa Doc was known for being impenetrable.

Papa Doc: Dictator

Days after the September 22 election, supporters of Déjoie launched various demonstrations that culminated in a general strike. Having yet to learn to abide by electoral results, they hoped to prevent Papa Doc's inauguration. The army stood firm and the inauguration proceeded as planned, but the incident confirmed to Papa Doc that terror, more than democratic processes, would guarantee his continued rule. Papa Doc's palace was located in downtown Port-au-Prince, in the heart of the Déjoieist stronghold, which made his position particularly insecure. He immediately went to work. He sent to jail hundreds of political opponents, who retaliated by starting a hunger strike well publicized in the press. In January 1958, Papa Doc's henchmen captured a relative of one of the prisoners, an outspoken journalist named Yvonne Hakime-Rimpel. She was dragged out of her home, taken to an isolated location, gang-raped, gunned, and left for dead in a ditch; she miraculously survived to tell the tale.

In her *Haiti: The Duvaliers and Their Legacy* (1988), Elizabeth Abbott recounted an episode that might owe more to Haiti's prolific rumor mill than to historical fact, but is nevertheless representative of Papa Doc's aura as a ruthless practitioner of Voodoo. According to the story, in March 1958, in the Bel-Air neighborhood of Port-au-Prince that was home to many anti-Duvalier activists, a strange public project got underway. At the intersection of Rue du Peuple and Rue des Ramparts, at the very spot where a large cross and the statue of a rooster provided a popular worshipping spot for followers of Christ and *loas* alike, workers dug a deep, square hole and lined it up with a concrete wall. They then left as mysteriously as they had come. The following night, locals were awakened by the noise of two trucks maneuvering next to the crossroad. Muffled moaning coming from the trucks revealed what the strange cargo was: a heap of political opponents, men and women alike, gagged and roped, praying for mercy. The first truck's back door opened and unloaded its human payload into the hole. The second truck followed suit. Workers then shoveled dirt directly on the swarming mass and started work on a concrete slab. By dawn, the concrete gate to hell was shut tight. Papa Doc had rounded up a most unholy trinity of imprisonment, gang rape, and mass murder.

Papa Doc's regime was not yet secure. In July 1958, Alix "Sonson" Pasquet led a bizarre invasion of Haiti at the head of an eight-man force that included five American adventurers, two Haitian mulattoes, and Pasquet himself. The invading party almost toppled Pap Doc despite its small size. After sailing from Florida onboard a small yacht, the *Molly C*, Pasquet and his men landed in Montrouis and stole an army jeep that quickly broke down. Switching to one of Haiti's brightly painted buses, the invaders reached the capital's main barracks in the middle of the night; the guards were so surprised by the colorful equipage that they let Pasquet in and soon found themselves his prisoners. Had Pasquet then stormed the presidential palace, where Papa Doc kept most of the weapons, his odd venture might have succeeded despite its diminutive size. Instead, he opened negotiations and sent one prisoner outside to buy cigarettes. Papa Doc had initially panicked; when he learned from the released prisoner how few enemies he faced, he ordered a general assault on the barracks. All invaders were killed in the fighting or shortly thereafter.

Instability continued despite the failure of the Pasquet invasion. In August 1959, thirty Cuban rebels landed near Cayes. In April 1963, army colonels plotted a botched coup. Later that year, disgruntled officers launched a series of attacks from the Dominican Republic. Thirteen expatriates calling themselves the *Jeune Haïti* (Young Haiti) movement landed near Jérémie in 1964 in a repeat of the *Molly C* invasion. Fidel Castro's overthrow of Cuban dictator Fulgencio Batista in 1959 and the murder of Dominican dictator Rafael Trujillo in 1961 served as a potent reminder that Caribbean dictators rarely leave office peacefully.

These eventful years set the tone for the rest of Papa Doc's rule, as recurring threats to the regime served as an excuse for unending political repression. Papa Doc staged elections, including one in 1961 that gave him a second six-year term and another in 1964 that made him president for life, but official results showing 100 percent of the vote for Duvalier stretched all statistical probabilities. A few dared protest, but Papa Doc's response was usually swift and always brutal. Not only political opponents but their spouses, children, parents, and friends were targeted for retaliation. When Communists launched an insurrection in the town of Cazales in 1969, revenge killings claimed the lives of dozens of local inhabitants. Many of them were descendents of Polish soldiers who had deserted Leclerc's forces in 1803 and had been allowed to settle in Haiti; the genocidal Dessalines had spared them, but Papa Doc did not. No one was safe from the prevailing terror. Prominent ministers were killed or exiled when they fell out of favor; foreign priests were executed; the son of a Marine adviser to the Haitian army was taken captive; even the husband of Papa Doc's daughter Marie-Denise, Max Dominique, had to flee for his life. What drove Papa Doc to switch from shy, benevolent country doctor to murderous tyrant remains a mystery; like many

Haitian politicians before and after him, he seems to have been corrupted by the odd mix of total power and constant insecurity that characterizes the Haitian presidency.

One popular theory to explain Papa Doc's sudden change blames the heart attack that almost killed him in 1959. American doctors flown in from the U.S. base in Guantánamo Bay eventually saved the dictator's life, but the prolonged coma was said to have affected his sanity (Papa Doc's mother, observers added, was interned when he was still a child). The theory overlooks the fact that repression started the day Duvalier reached office, in October 1957, eighteen months before his heart attack. Some Papa Doc supporters had dismissed him as dimwitted in the 1957 election in their misplaced hope that he would become a harmless puppet; they now turned to insanity as an excuse for his sadism. But Papa Doc, like Soulouque before him, was neither stupid nor mad, and organized his repressive apparatus with an efficiency that was a testament to his evil genius.

At the top of the pyramid stood Papa Doc himself. An ever-changing circle of henchmen and bagmen and bogeymen—Clément Barbot, Luckner Cambronne, Clovis Désinor, Octave Cayard, and many others—came next. Fear and greed underpinned their loyalty; so Papa Doc never trusted them. His suspicions were grounded. In April 1963, Barbot tried to kill Papa Doc's children; in 1970, Cayard shelled the presidential palace from a mutinous Haitian coast guard cutter. Two distinct instruments of repression formed the basis of the pyramid. The Haitian army, about five-thousand-strong, was the heir to the *gendarmerie* created during the U.S. occupation. The soldiers' main duties were to enforce internal order, to defeat rebels attacking from the Dominican border, and to bolster Papa Doc's reputation as a regional anti-Communist bulwark. The army doubled as a police force; units were dispatched throughout Haiti's provinces rather than being housed in large urban barracks. The poorly paid rural policemen were infamous for collecting bribes from their neighbors; their assistants, who stood at the very bottom of the military hierarchy and did not appear on the official payroll, earned the colorful Creole nickname of *souket lawouze* (those who collect the last drops of money). Afraid of the army's penchant for independence, Papa Doc also created a paramilitary force entirely devoted to him; known as *cagoulards* in the early months of the regime, it was renamed *Volontaires de la Sécurité Nationale* (Volunteers for National Security) in 1958. They are better known as the *Tontons Macoutes*: Papa Doc's bogeymen.

Recruiting from the ranks of Haiti's impoverished black majority, the *Macoutes* justified Papa Doc's revolutionary agenda. Easily recognizable with their denim uniform, dark sunglasses, red foulard, and omnipresent gun, they manned roadblocks, spied on neighbors, abducted opponents, and tortured and executed them. Their uniform evoked that of the anti-American *cacos* who had fought for Péralte, thus boosting the regime's nationalist credentials. Promoting poor blacks to positions of power from which they could humiliate wealthy mulattoes also introduced a modicum of upward social mobility, albeit one based on violence and corruption rather than personal merit. In a society where women have traditionally occupied a subservient role, the *Macoutes* were male as well as female; one of them, the ruthless Rosalie Bousquet (a.k.a. Madame Max Adolphe), ran the dreaded Fort Dimanche detention and torture center, then took the head of the entire force. The *Macoutes* eventually numbered three hundred thousand. They were everywhere.

Many *Macoutes* were Voodoo priests, for Papa Doc had also enlisted Haiti's gods in his quest for absolute power. As years passed, Papa Doc's ethnological interest in Voodoo turned into a personal obsession. Rumors swirled that he practiced nocturnal ceremonies on the bodies of his enemies, that he had mastered the art of ubiquity, and that he was an incarnation of the *loa* Baron Samedi, who shared Papa Doc's taste for black suits and cemeteries. Numerology also helped, for Papa Doc was convinced that twenty-two was his magical number and he always staged important events on that day of the month; he even managed to die on April 21, 1971, thus allowing his son to take over on April 22. Papa Doc's murders of disapproving priests earned him a papal excommunication in 1960, but he later signed a concordat in an attempt to gain the support of the Catholic god as well. The concordat left control of the Haitian clergy in the hands of Papa Doc, and churches became yet another tool of domination. Papa Doc was justifiably proud of this achievement and dedicated endless pages of his *Memoirs of a Third World Leader* (1969) to the intricate negotiations he conducted with the Vatican. Catechism took an odd turn. "Our Doc who art in the National Palace for life," the daily prayer now went,

> hallowed be Thy name by present and future generations. Thy will be done in Port-au-Prince as it is in the provinces. Give us this day our new Haiti and never forgive the trespasses of those anti-patriots who spit every day on our country. Let them succumb to temptation, and under the weight of their venom, deliver them not from any evil.[2]

Like Soulouque and Dessalines before him, Papa Doc used racial pride to justify his authoritative rule. He killed and exiled thousands of mulattoes. He changed the national flag from blue and red to black and red. He made stirring references to the black slaves' courage in 1791 and claimed to head a new black revolution. He regularly denounced outside powers for their imperialism; the Dominican Republic was the most likely suspect, but France and the United States regularly took their share of public opprobrium.

This black nationalism was as fake as it was self-serving, for Papa Doc never shied away from privately enlisting the support of those foreign powers he denounced in public. He cleverly manipulated U.S. fears of Communist penetration to maintain the constant flow of U.S. funds and weapons. In 1958, months after accusing the United States of sponsoring Pasquet's *Molly C* filibustering expedition, Papa Doc invited a U.S. Marine training mission in the hope that this foreign presence would bolster international support and modernize his army. The Marines, as any patriotic Haitian knew, had not set a foot in Haiti since the end of the U.S. occupation in 1934. Also in 1958, Papa Doc signed a cooperation treaty with Rafael Trujillo, the Dominican dictator who had killed twenty-five thousand Haitians in the 1937 River Massacre incident. Papa Doc then formalized an agreement under which he would provide Haitian cane cutters to Dominican plantations. The dreadful working conditions Haitians experienced in the Dominican Republic were an eerie reminder of colonial slave plantations; but this cynical trade yielded a yearly $1 million bribe and it continued throughout the Duvalier era. The only positive aspect of the deal was that Dominicans offered $50 for each Haitian cane cutter, $20 more than the indemnity Trujillo had paid in 1937; Haitians were worth more alive than dead. With the exception of *Macoute* thugs, Haiti's blacks, who were supposed to be the prime beneficiaries of the Duvalierist revolution, were poorer when Papa Doc's regime ended than when it began.

Haiti had known many dictators in its long history; but Papa Doc was in a league of his own. Political murders had always been the norm, but Duvalier added excruciating torture sessions and unspeakable detention conditions. Entering the political fray had always been a dangerous occupation, but under Papa Doc being a distant family member of a political enemy was sufficient to warrant death. The regime of terror was such that it sparked the first mass exile in the country's history since the 1804 massacre. Journalists and historians often could not find words strong enough to convey the horrors of Papa Doc's years in the presidential palace; luckily, a novelist with the requisite literary skills visited Haiti in those somber years and delivered Papa Doc the severest blow the dictator ever received. In the introduction to his celebrated account of life under Papa Doc, *The Comedians* (1966), Graham Greene warned that the novel was a work of fiction, but that "poor Haiti itself and the character of Doctor Duvalier's rule are not invented, the latter not even blackened for dramatic effect. *Impossible to deepen that night*."[3] Greene was pleased to hear that Papa Doc had read the book and hated it. The criticisms were probably not very far off the mark.

Thousands lost their lives as Papa Doc betrayed the Hippocratic Oath and his *noiriste* revolution, but the system achieved its one and only goal: keeping the Duvalierist boat afloat even as the rest of Haiti was sinking under it. Surmounting both invasions and heart problems, Papa Doc remained in power for fourteen years until he died of natural causes in 1971 at age sixty-four.

Bébé Doc: A Gentler Duvalier?

Everyone looked at Papa Doc's successor with mocking eyes. Jean-Claude Duvalier became president only because he was François Duvalier's only son and because the dying dictator had organized a sham plebiscite making his son president for life. Jean-Claude had never displayed any taste for politics, preferring to spend time with fast cars and beautiful women (in that order). At eighteen years of age, he was the youngest president in the world; chubby and round-faced, he looked so child-like that he immediately earned the nickname of Bébé Doc (Baby doctor). Soulouque and Papa Doc's examples should have served as stern reminders not to underestimate a Haitian president's staying power. The son, who observers thought would not last a year, ended up ruling Haiti even longer than his father had.

Those mourning Papa Doc's passing were few. After fourteen years of stern "papadocracy," Haitians and foreign governments felt that a weight had finally been lifted off their shoulders. Bébé Doc looked and sounded innocuous, delivering speeches written by collaborators in a droning voice. He offered the promise of political liberalization and economic development. No one knew how long his rule would last, though many surmised his presidency would be short-lived. But Duvalierist terror would surely come to an end.

The Haitian economy quickly felt the consequences of Bébé Doc's international popularity. U.S. aid to Papa Doc, offered as a counterpart for his anti-Communist stand, averaged $3.8 million a year when Bébé Doc took over. By 1975, U.S. aid had jumped to $35.5 million because of a mistaken belief that Bébé Doc would soon abandon his father's repressive policies. Millions were lost through corruption, for the son displayed a greed that had never been a part of his father's capital sins, but some key projects were completed. The road from Port-au-Prince to Cap Haïtien, first built under French colonial rule, then rebuilt during the U.S. occupation, was again rebuilt with foreign help. International interest in Haitian art and tourist forays into Haiti went back to the levels last experienced during the heady years of the Paul Magloire presidency (1950–1956). Many tourists were attracted by the "quickie divorce" offered under the local legal system; the new divorcees could then sample the products offered by the rapidly developing sex industry. By the late 1970s, seventy thousand U.S. tourists (out of a total of one hundred thousand) visited Haiti every year, including such African American celebrities as Cassius Clay (a.k.a. Muhammad Ali) and Arthur Ashe. Haiti even had its own Club Méditerranée in Montrouis, site of the failed *Molly C* invasion. The assembly sector working for the export market soon employed sixty thousand Haitians making everything from T-shirts to electrical products and baseballs, though foreign entrepreneurs contributed little to the Haitian treasury because of extensive tax holidays.

Jimmy Carter's 1976 election made human rights the centerpiece of U.S. policy in the Caribbean and forced the regime to give its human rights record a facelift. International monitors were allowed to inspect prisons that were cleaned and emptied of political prisoners the day of their visit. A legislative election was held in 1979, in which two opponents summoned the courage to run. One, Sylvio Claude, had to flee for his life before the campaign was over; the other, Alexandre Lerouge, won a seat and became the token non-Duvalierist in Bébé Doc's rubber stamp legislature.

Haiti seemed to have turned a corner. But, beneath the surface, nothing had changed. Bébé Doc's liberalization was a clever ploy to increase foreign aid while changing nothing of substance, following the time-honored Haitian tradition of fooling powerful white outsiders by faking submissiveness. When law professor Gérard Gourgue organized a meeting of a human rights' league in 1979, *Macoutes* returned to their usual skull-crushing modus operandi to disband the meeting; being Bébé Doc's former law professor offered no guarantee of protection. Bébé Doc preserved all of his father's repressive architecture, *Macoutes* and torture chambers included, and continued to pay lip service to the black revolution while spending his countrymen's money in endless parties with his mulatto friends.

The Economic Crisis

Haiti's economy was virtually dependent on international charity by the late 1970s. Foreign aid provided 70 percent of the national treasury.

Donated bags of rice and powdered milk fed thousands, particularly in the impoverished northwestern part of the country. Foreigners, not government officials, headed reforestation projects, manned schools, and built bridges. These efforts were inspired by anti-Communism (the Duvaliers, for all their faults, were ramparts against Cuban infiltration) as well as by genuine foreign sympathy inspired by the plight of Haiti's poor. Bébé Doc, in a stroke of genius, discovered that Haiti's poverty could be its main source of wealth. He used starving children to increase aid, then siphoned off many of the funds to foreign bank accounts to maintain his people at an adequate level of misery. Donated funds not only failed to address the main impediment to progress—the rapacious Duvalier dynasty—but propped up the regime instead.

Haiti had become the Third World's Fantine, the most miserable of Victor Hugo's *Les Misérables*, whose heartbreaking descent into poverty forced her to sell her hair, then her teeth, then her virtue. Haitian workers came first, as Bébé Doc continued his father's callous trade in Haitian cane cutters sold for $50 a piece to the Dominican enemy. To this, Luckner Cambronne, the powerful minister of the interior and rumored lover of Papa Doc's widow Simone, added a lucrative trade in body parts. Through his company Hemocaribbean, he exported Haitian blood, plasma, and cadavers to U.S. hospitals and medical schools. Haitian virtue came last, as Port-au-Prince became the brothel of the Caribbean. Tourists with a taste for even the most depraved sexual perversion knew that they could find Haitian children desperate enough to fulfill any fantasy for a few *gourdes*.

Bébé Doc's economic structure was now in place. Foreign aid, exiles' remittances, and whatever cash foreign tourists left in Haiti were the main sources of income; Bébé Doc and his parasitic entourage stole enough to enrich themselves without provoking a revolution or an international backlash; Haiti exported those too poor or too rebellious to continue living in such conditions. The system could have lasted decades had it not been for a series of crises, some of them attributable to bad luck, others more easily blamed on Bébé Doc himself.

By the late 1970s, rural overpopulation had become so bad that a massive population transfer took place as peasants fled their denuded hillsides to start a new life in the urban slums. In Port-au-Prince alone, slums such as La Saline and Cité Soleil soon numbered over one hundred thousand people each. Economic opportunities in the big cities were lacking, however; so hungry peasants started embarking on longer journeys, with Miami, New York, Montréal, or Paris as their final destination. These emigrants were very different from the upper-class people who had flown away during the Papa Doc era. Destitution, not political repression, prompted them to leave. They were poor and illiterate, so obtaining a visa and boarding a plane were not an option. Instead, they sailed illegally across the strait of Florida. The exodus of Haitian boat people had begun.

The boat people's plight elicited little official sympathy. When 112 dehydrated Haitians were found marooned on the deserted Bahamian island of Cayo Lobos in 1980, Bébé Doc refused to come to their rescue and Bahamian authorities had to pay for their repatriation. Instead, Bébé Doc signed a September 1981 agreement with the Reagan administration allowing U.S. Coast Guard vessels to patrol Haiti's coast, intercept all would-be refugees, and send them home. Thanks to the agreement, Bébé Doc gained continued U.S. support for his oppressive regime, while Ronald Reagan prevented a mass migration of Caribbean boat people akin to the Mariel boatlift that had plagued his predecessor. But the agreement failed to address the main reason for the crisis, namely, unhappiness with economic and political conditions in Haiti. Emigration temporarily abated, only to resume with renewed strength during the political and economic crises of the 1990s.

In the late 1970s, the medical community first isolated cases of a strange new disease. Later baptized the Acquired Immunodeficiency Syndrome (AIDS), the virus had a devastating impact on Haiti's society and economy. Young adults were most likely to contract this sexually transmitted disease, leaving children and old dependents destitute after the death of the family's main financial provider. Studies showing a high rate of contamination in Haiti prompted the U.S. Center for Disease Control to include Haitians in the "Four H" list of at-risk groups along with heroin addicts, hemophiliacs, and homosexuals. This made it even more difficult for Haitian emigrants to gain acceptance in their country of destination. They were already stereotyped as hungry, Satan-worshipping drug addicts; they were now branded with the scarlet H as well. The AIDS scare also wiped out sex tourism and the blood and plasma trade in the 1980s. The Haitian Fantine had offered her body and virtue to anyone willing to pay for it, but now found that there were few foreigners interested.

The next blow to hit Haiti was the product of Bébé Doc's own doing. In 1982, against the advice of all his entourage, he married the vivacious Michèle Bennett. Michèle had little to boast aside from her beauty and alleged sexual prowess. Her skin was very light, which exposed the black revolution as a sham. The archbishop of Port-au-Prince Wolff Lingondé, Michèle's cousin and a Duvalier appointee, presided over a grandiose religious ceremony in the capital's cathedral, but she was a divorcée and the mother of two children. Worse, her former husband was Alix Pasquet, son of the Alix "Sonson" Pasquet who had tried to overthrow Papa Doc in 1958. The regime was obviously going soft: Papa Doc had a habit of killing relatives of his enemies, not marrying them. When she gave birth to a François Duvalier in January 1983, Haitians noted that he was named after the grandfather who had killed his stepbrother's own grandfather. The wedding, televised live to a nation of peasants living off $200 a year, was a costly $3 million affair. In later years, Michèle would describe herself as Haiti's Evita Perón, but she lacked the Argentine beauty's social touch. Embezzlement and the cocaine trade provided her with the means to support a luxurious lifestyle centering on a multimillion dollar wardrobe. After the wedding, scales fell off the eyes of even the most pro-Duvalierist Haitian. Graft was now so large and overt as to be endangering the financial health of the state, and *noiriste* slogans could no longer rally the faithful.

Another disaster followed before 1982 was over. Swine fever, a disease that originated in Africa before spreading to the Dominican Republic and Haiti, now threatened to reach the U.S. mainland. To circumscribe the epidemic, the United States offered to donate American pigs in exchange for the eradication of Haiti's native Creole pigs. Americans spearheading the program were convinced that they were doing Haitian peasants a service by introducing a breed that was larger, fatter, and in all ways superior to the scrawny Creole pigs, but peasants concluded otherwise. The Creole pigs were small and ugly, but they required minimal care. They were left to fend for themselves and live off garbage until they were slaughtered to meet a financial emergency (annual school tuition, e.g.,). The American pigs required a concrete pen, imported feed, and regular medical care. Haitian peasants, complaining that the pigs lived better than they did, called them "four-legged princes." Peasants tried to hide their Creole pigs, but to no avail; the Duvalierist police was careful not to offend its largest foreign aid provider and saw to it that virtually all Creole pigs were killed. The new pigs quickly died of inadequate treatment, leaving their owners more destitute than ever. The following fall, school enrollment plummeted, a sure indication of agricultural distress.

Another side effect of the peasants' plight was the increased rate of deforestation. The destruction of Haiti's forests had begun in French colonial times, when planters uprooted the island's ancient trees to make way for plantations. For centuries, deforestation was limited to the plains; the country's mountainous interior remained untouched and provided an impenetrable stronghold for maroons and guerillas. By the mid-twentieth century, overpopulation forced peasants to cut trees in previously untouched areas. Jacques Roumain's *Masters of the Dew* (1944), probably the best novel ever written by this prominent *noiriste*, tells the story of Manuel Délivrance's struggle to the death against deforestation. In the novel, Délivrance returns to his native village of Fonds Rouge, only to discover that all the trees (save the sacred Mapou, home of Papa Legba) have been cut down, that water is in short supply, and that the soil is now depleted. He finds a new spring, negotiates to end the bitter feud dividing the village's population, and sets up a *kombit* (rural work gang) to build an irrigation network. Alas, he runs afoul of a local strongman and gets killed before he can complete his lifelong project. The struggle to survive and official oppression shown in the novel combine to make *Masters of the Dew* the truest depiction of Haiti's rural world.

Bébé Doc, who still did not understand in the 1970s what Roumain had foreseen in the 1940s, did nothing to address this environmental catastrophe. Deforestation, fueled by a dual dynamic, reached an alarming rate under his rule. Overpopulation forced young farmers to clear ever more lands, even those substandard plots on Haiti's steep hills; meanwhile, poverty pushed peasants to cut down trees and sell the charcoal that was Haiti's favorite source of energy. The drought-ridden Northwest first experienced the full consequences of deforestation. After the last trees were cut, the soil turned to a baked crust under the brutal sun; rain became even rarer, for clouds rarely formed over the deserted countryside; when a tropical downpour finally came, it washed away the rich topsoil that was no longer held together by roots. Within years, the Northwest became a desolate landscape of rocky outcrops led bare by water erosion. Other, more prosperous regions would follow suit a few years later.

Anxious to prop up his ailing regime, Bébé Doc invited Pope John Paul II to Haiti in 1983. The dictator spared no expense to welcome the holy pontiff. The Vatican regained the right to name Haitian bishops it had ceded to Papa Doc under the 1966 concordat. Descendants of Bonaparte's Polish soldiers were summoned from the countryside to meet their distant cousin. A lavish banquet was readied. When the Pope finally landed, he walked away from the red carpet, kissed Haiti's soil, neglected the banquet, and went right to business. In a Creole speech delivered on the very tarmac and broadcast live on national television, he attacked the oppression and misery that were Haitians' daily bread. He then told them something they never forgot: *fok sa chanj!* (Things have got to change here!). The regime never recovered.

Early in 1986, demonstrations multiplied, first in restless Gonaïves, then in Jérémie, Cayes, and most ominously Cap Haïtien, the country's second-largest city. Meanwhile, on a U.S. Sunday morning program, Secretary of State George Schultz declared that his administration would gladly welcome a more democratic Haiti. Smelling blood, journalists flocked to Port-au-Prince. After a week of dithering, Bébé Doc finally bowed to domestic and international pressure. On the night of February 7, 1986, fifteen years after he had become Haiti's teenage president, he left in a jet provided by the United States. His wife and family members left with him; they took as many furs and jewels as they could cram under the strict two-suitcases-per-passenger rule imposed by the United States. What they left behind was an impoverished nation ruined by almost three decades of uninterrupted Duvalierism.

The Duvaliers: A Legacy

Some politicians concerned by the image they will leave in the history books draft laws that they hope will stand the test of time; others build monuments; yet others conquer empires. The Duvalierist legacy was less glorious but no less enduring: charred bodies and swollen bellies.

Politically, the Duvaliers hijacked *noirisme* to further their own thirst for power. Father and son spoke of racial pride and nationalism while living off foreign support and marrying into the mulatto class. The ploy allowed them to rule for twenty-nine years, but it further strained black Haitians' tense relations with their foreign partners and mulatto compatriots while providing little of value for the poor blacks it was supposed to serve. Haiti's already bad reputation suffered greatly as the world only heard of Haiti as the birthplace of the murderous *Macoutes*. Papa Doc was the worst offender in that regard. Those tourists who landed at Port-au-Prince airport in 1964 were greeted by the bloated body of Yvan Laraque, a member of the failed *Jeune Haïti* invasion. He had been left to rot outside the terminal as a warning to the populace. An incongruous *Bienvenue en Haïti* (Welcome to Haiti) sign stood nearby. The tourist boom of the 1950s plummeted after the incident and did not revive until the 1970s. Duvalierist violence also left a deep imprint on Haitian politics. A bloody struggle for influence between Duvalierists and anti-Duvalierists, all of whom claimed to embody the true spirit of the black masses, continued long after Bébé Doc left office and is still ongoing today.

The economic damage of the Duvalier era was even more enduring. Papa Doc concluded—quite rightly—that economic development, an educated middle class, and democratization went hand in hand. He thus targeted elite families, educated professionals, and students, even if—or precisely because—this would result in the utter ruin of his country. The result was a mass migration of Haiti's skilled citizenry, a brain drain from which Haiti has not yet recovered but that gave Papa Doc a firm grip on the country. Haitian surgeons educated at great expense left to practice their trade in Miami and Paris; those doctors who stayed were Papa Doc and Interior Minister Dr. Roger Lafontant, both of whom enjoyed torturing opponents more than curing patients. The most bewildering decision of Papa Doc's presidency was his 1969 purge of the *Office National d'Alphabétisation et d'Action Communautaire* (National Bureau of Alphabetization and Communal Action), an association at the forefront of a much-admired literacy campaign. Fearing that some instructors might be anti-Duvalierists (and many were: it was difficult for an intelligent person to like Papa Doc), he disbanded the entire program and condemned his people to illiteracy. Papa Doc chose to rule over a people that was poor, illiterate, and submissive rather than prosperous, informed, and restless.

Bébé Doc's economic legacy was more subtle but no less devastating. Under his rule, corruption, always endemic in Haiti, became so widespread that it bankrupted state finances. Bankrolling a force of three hundred thousand *Macoutes* and five thousand soldiers was already a struggle under Papa Doc. When Bébé Doc added champagne and cocaine parties to the list of necessary expenses, the cost became more than an impoverished country of six million peasants could bear. A callous appetite for funds, at the expense of even the most basic sense of public service, characterized the regime's bloodsuckers. None of them had any qualms about fighting over the IV dripping foreign aid into Haiti's dying body or about sharing the victim's remains before the body was even cold. In the 1910s, Haiti had built at great expense a railroad intended to link Port-au-Prince to Cap Haïtien. The line was never completed, but three separate sections provided service in the plains. The regime ordered the line dismantled between Port-au-Prince and Verrettes, sold the tracks, and pocketed the money. The bank accounts of well-connected cronies grew by a few hundred thousand dollars; meanwhile, Haiti's transportation network moved back half a century. Regime insiders also raided the accounts of state monopolies such as the *régie du tabac* (tobacco company) and were notorious for not paying taxes.

The rapid surge in foreign aid during the 1970s did not end Haiti's downward economic spiral, for it failed to address the main source of poverty: Bébé Doc's incompetence and corruption. Surprisingly, aid even sparked a strong wave of antiforeign sentiment. The dominant conspiracy theory, the "American Plan," held that aid projects were a front for a sinister U.S.-led attempt to destroy Haiti's agriculture and force peasants off their land and into urban slums where they would toil in assembly factories catering to the American market. Far from trying to help Haitians, the theory concluded, the American Plan hoped to make Haitians dependent on U.S. food imports and turn the country into one vast source of cheap labor. Every aid project, however well intentioned, was interpreted through this prism. Peasants even destroyed various foreign-run tree nurseries in the Northwest under the mistaken assumption that foreign trees were designed to deplete the Haitian soil. According to the most extravagant piece of Haitian gossip, AIDS was yet another machination conceived in the Washington headquarters of the U.S. Agency for International Development (USAID).

The claims were fantastic. Foreign aid's major pitfalls lay elsewhere. Donated food, especially rice, had the unexpected effect of driving down local prices as homegrown products could not compete with free imports. Haitian peasants thus reduced their production, aggravating the very shortage that food donations were supposed to alleviate. Similarly, foreign gifts of used clothing undermined the local clothing industry, so much so that Haitians came to call hand-me-downs *kenedis* after the U.S. president who started the program. Also, the omnipresence of foreign advisers underpinned the Haitian myth that local economic conditions were caused by external factors, and that foreign aid (or the evil design of the American Plan) could improve (or worsen) the economic lot of the average peasant. Individual enterprise was deemed useless. For Bébé Doc, aid was a godsend. Foreign funds financed his lifestyle and that of the thuggish *Macoutes*; contraband sale of food and drug donations provided a secondary stream of income; meanwhile, Haitians blamed foreigners instead of the Duvaliers for the appalling poverty.

By the time Bébé Doc left office in 1986, the Haitian Diaspora topped one million. Exiles' remittances and foreign aid were the country's lifelines. Deforestation ravaged the countryside. The AIDS plague devastated an entire generation. Remnants of the *Macoute* order battled with anti-Duvalierists for political control. All the essential components of contemporary Haitian society were in place.

Hundreds of suspected *Macoutes* were lynched after Bébé Doc left, but the army quickly reclaimed its customary spot at the center of Haitian politics and backed a series of short-lived governments, none of them democratically elected. The *Conseil National de Gouvernement*

(National Government Council, February 7, 1986–February 7, 1988) was first, followed by Leslie Manigat (February 7, 1988–June 20, 1988), Henri Namphy (June 21, 1988–September 17, 1988), Prosper Avril (September 17, 1988–March 10, 1990), Hérard Abraham (March 10–13, 1990), and Ertha Pascal Trouillot (March 13, 1990–February 7, 1991). Despite frequent governmental reshuffles, these years were marked by a societal *status quo*: the thugs inherited from the Duvalier era were still in charge. It was not until 1991 that a fundamentally novel form of government emerged.

CHAPTER 6

A Glimmer of Hope: Aristide's Rise to Power (1988–1991)

An Assassination Attempt (September 11, 1988)

On September 11, 1988, a young priest named Jean-Bertrand Aristide approached the altar in his church of St. Jean Bosco, located in one of Port-au-Prince's poorest slums. Aristide's physical appearance was deceptive. He was frail, short, plain looking, balding, and wore eyeglasses so large they covered half his cheeks. His nickname, Titid, seemed more suited for a child than for a leader of national prominence. He was also a black man of rural origin, which placed him squarely in the midst of Haiti's disenfranchised majority. Aristide's political appeal stemmed from his political courage and his oratorical skills. He was known as a priest and a radio preacher who dared speak against Bébé Doc before 1986 and against the remnants of the Duvalierist regime after that date. Death threats poured in regularly: the previous Sunday, armed men had attempted to enter the church. But Aristide courageously continued his fight against the *Macoute* order.

The time had finally come for the sermon. The pews were filled with eight hundred parishioners anxious to hear Haiti's most famous priest. His most devoted followers readied their tape recorders. It was often difficult for uninformed observers to understand what made Aristide so famous, for his sermons sounded strangely innocuous. To protect himself, Aristide criticized the regime but did so indirectly, quoting verses of the Bible ambiguous enough to provide veiled criticisms of contemporary events while offering him plausible deniability. Parishioners understood his oblique references, admired his wit, repeated his every word, answered his questions, and laughed and cried on cue. This was why they loved the unassuming Titid. Like Haiti, he was small and fragile; like Haiti, he was able to defy powerful forces through ingenuity.

But this Sunday differed from others in one important regard. Aristide never got to finish his sermon. As he spoke, a group of hit men, some of them armed with guns, others with machetes, surrounded the building, pelted the windows with rocks, then rushed in through the main door. The panicked churchgoers tried to flee through a tiny door that led to the sacristy, but many did not make it in time. A grisly scene ensued. When it was over, gun-riddled bodies and hacked-off limbs littered the floor. Thirteen parishioners lay dead in a pool of blood; dozens more were wounded. The hit men set the church on fire and left.

In later days, the attackers made the rounds through maternity wards, hoping to finish off a pregnant woman they had injured, but not killed, during the attack (both the mother and her child survived in hiding). They also looked for Aristide, who had miraculously sneaked out of the church alive and hid in a nearby building. They did not find him either. Despite the horrific nature of their crimes, the attackers were never threatened by the existing authorities. They appeared on national television, boasted about the killings, and even got to meet the president, an army general named Henri Namphy. Only the greater forces of nature and politics brought an end to the carnage. Hurricane Gilbert grazed the southern coast of Haiti that week, bringing forth tropical downpours that doused the church fire. A coup on September 17 removed Namphy from power. During the period of instability that ensued, Aristide supporters found several of the St. Jean Bosco hit men, killed them, and symbolically burned their bodies outside the ruins of the church.

In the short term, the attack on the St. Jean Bosco church was a deadly blow for Aristide and his supporters; Aristide was even rumored to experience a bevy of psychiatric problems no doubt induced by the shocking events he had just witnessed. But in the long run, September 11, 1988 acquired as prominent a spot in Aristidian mythology as another September 11 later did in the United States. The *Macoutes'* determination to kill Aristide showed just how dangerous and important they deemed him to be. The attackers' collusion with the authorities made them immune to criminal prosecution, so the incident once again showed that the victims could only expect "justice" if they took it upon themselves to exact vengeance; they never forgot that lesson. In a country where spells and charms play an important political role, Aristide's miraculous escape also proved that God was on his side. Aristide made numerous references to the martyrs and prophets who had willingly sacrificed their lives for a greater cause and hinted that he was one of their descendants. Duvalierists might have made use of their Voodoo charms; but Aristide more than matched their powers with his Jesus-like charisma.

Who Is Aristide?

Before 1988, few foreigners had even heard Aristide's name. His political rise, linked to the illiterate culture of radio talk shows, sermons, and *telediol* (rumors), took place well below political observers' radar. As years went by and Aristide emerged as one of the most forceful Haitian leaders of the twentieth century, foreign diplomats scrambled for what information they could find on the popular priest's past. "Who is Aristide?" was an urgent question; but the answer was far from simple. Like Louverture, Soulouque, and Papa Doc before him, Aristide was a vocal patriot who invited foreign involvement, a Catholic rumored to practice Voodoo, an idealist who excelled at brass-knuckle politics, and a nationalist black priest who later married a mulatto Haitian American. Making matters even more complicated, most of what is known about his past is found in the self-congratulatory autobiographies Aristide wrote in the 1990s. Skeletons probably still remain hidden in his closet.

Aristide's origins were humble. When he was born on July 15, 1953, his family farmed land outside Port-Salut, a small town in southern Haiti. Aristide's father died while he was still an infant, and his mother subsequently raised him and his elder sister in Port-au-Prince. Like many other single Haitian mothers, she earned a modest living as a small-scale merchant who sold goods from the countryside in the capital. Aristide seemed destined for an unassuming life as a member of the lower middle class until a Salesian priest named Gabriel Désir noticed his intelligence and arranged for the order to finance his education. Support from the church gave Aristide an instruction other Haitians could only dream of. He spent parts of the 1970s and 1980s studying abroad, traveling from Israel to Greece and Canada. Along the way, he earned a Master's Degree in psychology and a Ph.D. in theology and wrote a dissertation with the mysterious title of *Névrose vétéro-testamentaire* (literally: Veterinarian-Inheritance Neurosis). Aristide also learned some Spanish, Hebrew, Greek, and English on top of his native French and Creole.

Aristide was ordained a priest in July 1982, but politics always seemed to be his calling. He maneuvered to be sent to a poor parish of the capital rather than to a rural location, presumably to be closer to Haiti's political center of gravity. Showing a concern for Haiti's poor uncommon among Haiti's ruling classes, Aristide opened *Lafanmi Selavi* (Family is Life), a foster for homeless orphans. He also became a popular radio preacher, adroitly mixing exegesis and politics in his sermons. Criticizing the Duvaliers was a dangerous occupation. Bébé Doc had preserved the henchmen, or *Macoutes*, inherited from his father, and political opponents had a habit of meeting gruesome and untimely deaths. Even after Bébé Doc left for exile, his supporters continued to impose a regime of terror in Haiti to prevent any meaningful change in the country's power structure. In 1987, general elections ended in an election-day bloodbath that cost the lives of twenty-two voters in a Port-au-Prince school and brought the voting to an end. Aristide's study abroad trips in the 1980s were a reflection not only of his intellectual abilities but also of his superiors' fears that the turbulent Aristide would soon become a victim of *Macoute* political repression if he stayed in Haiti any longer.

The papal nuncio representing the Vatican in Haiti, Paolo Romero, soon acquired a strong dislike for Aristide. Not only did Aristide sour the Church's relationship with lay authorities, but he also breached a long-standing Vatican policy urging clergy members not to enter the political fray. The conservative, Polish-born John-Paul II was particularly opposed to liberation theology, a leftist interpretation of the gospels advocating a social role for the Church that became popular in Latin America in the 1970s and 1980s. Aristide supported the Haitian version of liberation theology, a movement called *Ti Legliz* (Little Church). His radical political views eventually took their toll. In December 1988, just three months after the St. Jean Bosco massacre, Aristide was expelled from the Salesian order (in order to preserve his aura as a religious figure, Aristide did not formally renounce priesthood until October 1994).

Macoute and Vatican opposition failed to destroy Aristide. He survived one assassination attempt after another, continued preaching despite religious authorities' admonitions, and accumulated a large following in the slums of Port-au-Prince. His sermons, delivered in lively, witty Creole, railed against the United States, moneyed interests, and the *Macoutes*. His leftist economic views were in sync with those of Haiti's urban poor. The slum dwellers shared Aristide's black skin, rural origin, and political discontent. No politician before him had mobilized this constituency. Haiti had always been divided between a vast majority of disenfranchised rural peasants and a small group of urban dwellers, the "Republic of Port-au-Prince," that monopolized political office. When the agricultural crisis of the 1970s and the 1980s forced peasants off their land, the growing slums brought the poor to the epicenter of Haitian politics. By the 1980s, slum-dwellers numbered hundreds of thousands. They were unemployed, had a lot of time on their hands, and were located a mere miles from the presidential palace. All that was needed was a leader who would translate their political potential into actual power. Only one man rose to the occasion; his name was Jean-Bertrand Aristide.

The December 1990 Presidential Election

With strong backing from the international community, Haiti scheduled presidential and legislative elections for December 16, 1990 as a way to escape from the political instability that characterized the post-Duvalier era. Historical precedents formed a discouraging record. In 1916, the United States had organized a constitutional plebiscite, but the vote was far from free and later presidents were selected by a small senate or the occupiers themselves. The 1957 election had been more democratic than any election previously organized in Haiti, but it had brought François Duvalier to power. General elections held in November 1987 had been called off because of election-day violence. Given these precedents, there was little chance that the elections would unfold peacefully and that they would select a popular leader dedicated to the needs of Haiti's poor.

The early weeks of the campaign were equally dispiriting. Aristide made public his misgivings about electioneering and decided not to run. Marc Bazin, a former World Bank economist and candidate for the presidency, was strongly backed by the U.S. State Department, but his association with foreign institutions made him more friends in Washington, DC than in Haiti itself. One strong candidate was Victor Benoît, who had emerged victorious from an internal primary organized by the electoral coalition *Front National pour le Changement et la Démocratie* (National Front for Change and Democracy, FNCD). Prospects for a peaceful election dimmed further with the return of Roger Lafontant, Bébé Doc's former minister of the interior, who had lived in exile after the fall of his patron. Other candidates viewed Lafontant's decision to run for president with alarm. The right-wing extremists and other *Macoutes* nostalgic of the Duvalier years would likely strong-arm voters into supporting Lafontant and stage a coup if a rival was elected anyway.

Reversing himself after Lafontant declared his candidacy, Aristide decided to enter the presidential race. "Stopping the *Macoutes*" became his rallying cry. Aristide replaced Benoît as the FNCD's official candidate and instantly became the front-runner. There was no accurate polling data to prove his popularity, but voters registered en masse when Aristide decided to run and flocked to his rallies. The courage Aristide had shown under Bébé Doc's rule was his main selling point. Voters were also attracted by Aristide's uncanny ability to summon political symbols drawn from Haiti's culture and to put them to use in stirring, though empty, speeches. He called his movement *Lavalas* after the Creole name for flash flood. Like those torrential rivers that flush all the garbage away after a tropical downpour, Aristide would rid Haiti of the layers of corruption and oppression inherited from the country's past. He also used agricultural terms the Haitian peasants could easily understand, such as *rache manyok* (pull out the manioc) and *dechoukaj* (uprooting), both of them a metaphor for the need to clear the political field and start anew. Choosing an appropriate symbol was essential in the election, for the largely illiterate voters would pick a drawing, not a name, on the ballot. Aristide selected the rooster as his icon, an animal beloved in Haiti because of its key role in cockfights and Voodoo sacrifices alike. Other politicians had used these metaphors before; but in Aristide's mouth the words seemed to stir crowds in a way no one else could.

Further raising Aristide's chances, the electoral commission rejected Lafontant's candidacy because the 1987 Constitution (Art. 291) forbade former Duvalierist officials to run for office for a period of ten years. Aristide himself could have been rejected based on another provision of the constitution (Art. 135-d) requiring that candidates own property in Haiti, but the commission ignored this clause. Nothing seemed to be able to stop the powerful *Lavalas* flood, not even a grenade attack launched in downtown Port-au-Prince eleven days before the election was to take place. Young, charismatic, and idealistic, Aristide was the popular choice for all those who wanted a clean break with Haiti's history of dictatorships. What Aristide would actually do once elected, however, remained a mystery. In his public speeches, he limited himself to sharp attacks against the dictatorships of the past, but remained vague about his intentions for the future. Aristide drafted two platforms, *La chance qui passe* ("Today is the day") and *La chance à prendre* ("Seize it") but he neglected to translate them into Creole, the native language of most Haitians. He did not even publish the second platform in time for the election.

The sixteenth of December, 1990 saw a most unusual event in Haitian history: a democratic, mostly peaceful presidential election. On election day, with the exception of U.S. diplomats still hoping for a Bazin upset, everyone prepared for a landslide Aristide victory. Everywhere in Haiti, especially in the urban slums that were Aristide's strongholds, voters proudly lined up to vote at daybreak, impatient to select the rooster symbol on the ballot. Lines stretched for hundreds of yards. Because of widespread disorganization, many polling stations did not open until noon. The cardboard boxes and pictureless IDs used as ballot boxes and voting cards did not inspire confidence either. As the day went on, a rumor started spreading throughout the country. Fraud was rampant, the rumor went; soldiers and *Macoutes* were stuffing ballot boxes and intimidating voters.

Aristide, showing an aspect of his personality that would later plague U.S.-Haitian relations, immediately identified the culprit for these technical glitches: foreign, particularly American, interference. The charge was baseless—the international community had sent hundreds of election observers, former U.S. president Jimmy Carter among them, precisely to ensure that the elections would unfold peacefully. Aristide nevertheless held a meeting with prominent American observers including former defense secretary Robert S. McNamara, former National Security Council (NSC) member Robert Pastor, former House speaker Jim Wright, and former UN ambassador Andrew Young. Concerned that Aristide backers might riot if the election did not turn out their way, American observers asked Aristide to tell his supporters to abide by the electoral results, whatever they might be. For Aristide, the call to lay down arms was the proof that Americans were already plotting his downfall. He cut off their pleas abruptly. "I know who all of you are. But you don't see what's happening. They're stealing the elections. I am not going to restrain my people."[1]

Aristide's fears proved unfounded. One day after the polls closed, the electoral commission released temporary results showing that Aristide had garnered an absolute majority of the vote and that no runoff election was necessary. The official tally, released on December 23, showed Aristide ahead with 67.48 percent of the vote (the decimals seemed superfluous; the commission only counted 40 percent of the ballot, then stopped when it became clear that Aristide was ahead). After he was declared the winner, Aristide apologized to American observers for overreacting on election day, but ill feelings were there to stay. U.S. ambassador Alvin P. Adams ominously quoted the Creole proverb *apre bal, tanbou lou* (after the party, the drums are heavy) to remind Aristide of the many hurdles ahead.

In the meantime, Haitians celebrated. Aristide was a gifted orator and a natural politician; he was also black, educated, idealistic, and dedicated. This was the leader Haitians had dreamed of for years. The international community was wary of Aristide's leftist, populist bent, but it remained supportive of the Haitian experiment with democracy. Haiti, it seemed, had finally embarked on a democratic path. Voters were so overjoyed by Aristide's victory that 80 percent of them forgot to vote in runoff elections organized on January 20, 1991 to select members of parliament.

Aristide's election was a watershed event in Haitian politics not only because of its democratic nature, but also because it radically altered the political structure of the country. Most of Aristide's predecessors in the presidential palace had either been poorly educated black officers or members of the mulatto aristocracy of Port-au-Prince, who looked down on their country's black peasant majority. Aristide's black skin and humble, rural background gave him a legitimacy that no mulatto politician, however well trained, could ever attain. Aristide was also superbly educated and would not turn into a national embarrassment the way some black nationalists such as Faustin Soulouque had. He was a priest and an anti-Duvalier activist who could be counted on to renege on Haiti's elitist, tyrannical past and to finally cater to Haiti's impoverished majority. In the twentieth century, only three other Haitians had matched Aristide's political credentials and education. The first was the *noiriste* intellectual Jean Price-Mars (who never managed to be elected president). The second was working-class darling Daniel Fignolé, who was overthrown in 1957 after a mere nineteen days in office. The last, ominously, was François "Papa Doc" Duvalier. Everyone understood that Aristide's election was the greatest opportunity for change since the U.S. invasion of 1915 and the election of 1957. No one foresaw that the following ten years would be a disappointing roller-coaster ride and that Aristide would fail spectacularly—not once, but three times—to turn Haiti's fortunes around.

The Lafontant Coup (January 6, 1991)

One intriguing aspect of Haitian politics is that revolutions happen more often on Sundays that on any other day of the week. This might be a remnant from slavery times, when slaves used their day off to visit other plantations and conspire with fellow slaves (the Bois Caïman Voodoo ceremony took place on a Sunday); or this might be a practical adaptation to the traffic jams of Port-au-Prince, which tend to be so horrendous on weekdays that they would impede the flow of revolutionaries. The first Sunday of January 1991 was a particularly auspicious time. Ertha Pascal-Trouillot was a lame-duck president now that Aristide had been elected president. Aristide, however, would not be inaugurated until a month later, which opened a power vacuum in the capital. In the Catholic calendar, the first Sunday of the year also marks the Epiphany, the day on which the three Wise Men (called *Rois Mages*, or Magi, in French) met Jesus. On this day, children traditionally eat an almond cake in which a little figurine is hidden; the child who finds the figurine is given a crown and feted as a king. This was a day well suited for would-be kings of Haiti.

That night, Roger Lafontant, the former Duvalierist official who had tried to run for president the month before, appeared on national television. He had just captured the presidential palace, he explained, which made him president of Haiti. The main goal of Lafontant's televised address was to enlist the support of the army, particularly that of the commander in chief Hérard Abraham, but Abraham stood by the president-elect. When pro-Aristide crowds took to the streets, Lafontant backed down. In the following days, followers of Aristide searched for, and often killed, those suspected of supporting the coup. The papal nuncio escaped alive, though he was roughed up and saw his residence sacked. Lafontant also survived, but the headquarters of his party were destroyed and he was sent to prison.

The postcoup repression was a lesson in the colorful Creole vocabulary inherited from the post-Duvalier era. The *Macoute* epithet, initially meaning "knapsack" (and by extension the bogeymen who stole children in such bags), then reserved for the Duvaliers' dreaded militia, now applied to all people suspected of collusion with the old regime. *Dechoukaj* (literally "uprooting") was a metaphor for an anti-*Macoute* purge. "Necklacing" was the torture of choice. A car tire was doused in gasoline, thrown around a victim's neck, then set ablaze. Necklacing was born in South African ghettos, but it became a Haitian specialty during the years following the fall of Bébé Doc and earned the all-Haitian name of *Père Lebrun* after a tire commercial showed a salesman putting his head inside a tire. Overall, necklacing and other forms of lynching killed more than hundred people during the days of postcoup popular unrest, whose ferocity struck all observers. Abraham's refusal to support Lafontant was a sign that Haiti had made much progress on the path to democracy; the violent aftermath to the coup, however, showed that violence had not yet disassociated itself from Haitian politics.

Aristide's Political and Economic Reforms

After he was inaugurated as president of Haiti on February 7, 1991, Aristide faced a familiar political and economic conundrum: how would he get Haitians out of poverty? He was self-admittedly inspired by liberation theology and the Latin American, romantic version of Communism espoused by Ernesto "Che" Guevara and Fidel Castro in

Cuba. If given complete free reign, Aristide would likely have imposed high taxes on the rich, nationalized key industries, created generous welfare programs, and aligned himself with Communist Cuba.

This, however, was impractical. Top–down socialist-style economic management called for an expansive state apparatus that Haiti lacked. The government already could not perform basic missions such as policing the streets and collecting taxes; it could hardly think of collectivizing land and operating steel mills. A few nationalized industries aside, Haiti remained by necessity a free-market economy. Land ownership remained as individual and fragmented as it had been since the Pétion era; any attempt to collectivize farms would likely have met stubborn resistance from the peasants. Another matter of concern was the international community. The Soviet Union was on the verge of financial collapse; so funds for development programs would likely come from Haiti's traditional providers of foreign aid, most prominently France, the United States, Canada, the World Bank, and the International Monetary Fund (IMF). All five were convinced that the failure of centralized development in many Third World countries in the 1970s had proven that free-market reforms were the best stimulant to economic growth. The Cold War would not officially end until the failure of a Communist coup in Russia in August 1991; so any hint of radicalism and pro-Castro sympathies would likely have sparked a U.S. expedition similar to the one in Grenada (1983). However great his misgivings about capitalism were, Aristide had to play the part of the enthusiastic entrepreneur. "The dilemma is, I think, the classic dilemma of the poor; a choice between death and death," Aristide later wrote. "Either we enter a global economic system, in which we cannot survive, or we refuse, and we face death by slow starvation."[2]

Aristide's economic policies were thus a moderate lot that lacked ambition and scope but quelled foreign fears about his radicalism. He did not even speak of eliminating poverty; he hoped, he explained, to allow Haitians to move from misery to poverty with dignity so that they could enjoy one meal a day. In order to assuage international lenders, he dramatically reduced the size of the Haitian government, cut down salaries (his own included), and fired eight thousand public employees. He maintained the low tariffs inherited from the post-Duvalier era, which allowed the poor to fight against *la vie chère* (the high cost of living) but exposed Haiti's local industry and agriculture to devastating foreign competition. He called on Haiti's rich to reverse capital flight and invest locally, but did so in strikingly polite terms. All that remained of Aristide's liberal fire were a 60 percent boost to the minimum wage (from $3 to $4.80 a day), rhetorical attacks against those he called hypocritical racketeers (the IMF), and criticisms of the *patripoche* (the disloyal rich who took their money abroad). The strategy worked. Foreign donors, reassured by Aristide's seeming moderation, increased their contribution to the Haitian budget from $200 million (1990–1991) to $380 million (1991–1992).

Political Tensions

As always, economic development programs, even policies as moderate and limited as the ones put forward by Aristide in 1991, could not succeed without a stable political environment. In the beginning, Aristide's landslide victory seemed to ensure lasting peace. His political constituency was large and included some students and liberal bourgeois in addition to the urban and rural poor. The United States had misgivings about the Aristide regime but chose not to interfere in internal Haitian affairs for the time being. The army had remained neutral during the presidential elections and the Lafontant coup. Aristide's opponents only included three relatively small factions: right-wing extremists, conservative mulatto entrepreneurs, and the Catholic hierarchy.

Aristide's bungling immediately added three names to the list. In a veiled reference to the exploitation of Haitian cane cutters in Dominican sugar plantations, he publicly denounced the Dominican Republic's trade in "bitter sugar." Aristide's criticism was warranted; the condition of migrant workers on sugar plantations had improved little since the Papa Doc era, or even since colonial times. But his attacks worsened relations with Haiti's only neighbor and convinced Dominican dictator Juan Balaguer to expel thousands of Haitians after the *zafra* (sugar harvest) was over. Aristide now had one more enemy and a few more unemployed Haitians on his hands.

The FNCD, the coalition of parties that had selected Aristide as its presidential candidate, would have been a natural ally. Riding on the coattails of Aristide's victory, it gained a majority in both houses of parliament during the December 1990 election and the January 1991 runoffs. But Aristide refused to form a cabinet reflecting the parliamentary majority as is customary in the French semi-parliamentary system that inspired the 1987 constitution. Instead, he picked personal friends as ministers. René Préval, an agronomist and longtime partner in the *Lafanmi Selavi* shelters, became prime minister. Feeling slighted, FNCD deputies opposed Aristide throughout his presidency.

In his inaugural speech, Aristide also fired all senior officers in the army, keeping only Commander in Chief Hérard Abraham. The move was singularly unwise: the army had saved Aristide's presidency just one month before by refusing to support the Lafontant coup. The rank-and-file, in particular, had much in common with Haiti's poor and could easily have been enlisted in a broad-based Aristide coalition. But Aristide viewed democracy through the Haitian prism of "winner-takes-all" politics: a victory at the polls could not be complete unless all rival centers of power were eliminated, even at the risk of planting the seeds of future discontent. He thus encouraged his supporters from the slums to create popular gangs, as if he intended to sidetrack the army and create a force loyal to the president only as had been the case under Papa Doc. On July 28, 1991 (another Sunday), sailors staged a mutiny—quite an achievement considering that the Haitian navy was virtually nonexistent by 1991. Later that month, in a singularly ironic display of poor character judgment, Aristide sacked Hérard Abraham, the commander in chief who had spoken against the Lafontant coup in January, and replaced him with Raoul Cédras, a junior officer who would overthrow Aristide less than two months later.

Payback time also targeted political rivals. Former president Ertha Pascal-Trouillot, who had organized the democratic elections that brought Aristide to power, was arrested on April 4, 1991 on a variety of trumped-up charges; Aristide only backed down and freed her when foreign powers insisted that she be released. Lafontant and twenty-one supporters were brought to trial on July 29. Outside the courtroom, a mob of Aristide supporters chanted, tires and matches in hand, that necklacing would punish recalcitrant jury members. Inside the courtroom, the judge declared that the accused were most certainly guilty while opening the proceedings. The absence of lawyers (all of whom had declined to take up Lafontant's defense because of death threats) made for a short, twenty-four-hour show trial at the end of which the accused received long prison terms. Lafontant was sentenced to a life of forced labor, much more than the maximum of fifteen years allowed under Haitian law, but Aristide later thanked the mob for forcing the jury's hand.

In August, the FNCD-controlled parliament, accusing Aristide of moving toward a dictatorship, called for a vote of nonconfidence against Prime Minister Préval. There was little Aristide could do to safeguard his own power except rely on unconstitutional methods now that the army was squarely in the enemy camp; so Préval refused to go to the parliament to answer criticisms. Instead, a tire-wielding crowd gathered around the building. A few deputies were attacked, one of them narrowly escaping an attempt to necklace him. The vote never took place.

Aristide, like Louverture in 1802, had now eliminated all dissenting voices. But Aristide, again like Louverture in 1802, made a tactical mistake. Haitian presidents very rarely travel abroad for fear of being over-thrown (until 1991, the first and only president to dare visit the United States while in office was Sténio Vincent in 1934, at a time when the U.S. occupation of Haiti acted as a deterrent against revolution). But Aristide, feeling secure enough to leave Haiti, flew for New York and the United Nations in September 1991. His three days there marked the apex of his international popularity. The alarming political maneuverings of the previous seven months were little known outside Haiti; what foreigners saw was a soft-spoken priest who encountered throngs of adoring Haitian Americans wherever he went. Mayor David Dinkins offered Aristide the key to the city of New York. He was invited to speak at the United Nations, where he delivered a one-hour speech that was a masterpiece of victimization, humor, and moderation. He attacked the Dominican Republic for exploiting Haitian migrant workers, called for increased aid, and threw the United Nations' translating system off-kilter when he wittily switched from French to English, Spanish, and Creole. Meanwhile, in Haiti, the army was plotting to overthrow democracy's newfound star.

The September 29, Coup

Aristide's mood was exuberant when he returned from New York via Miami on September 27, 1991. Yet another adoring crowd met him at the airport, dancing to the music of Manno Charlemagne in front of seemingly apathetic soldiers. But the party did not last long; Aristide was informed of rumors that a coup was in the offing. He lost no time. Having sacked all top-ranking officers, he had no professional force at his disposal; the mob would be his sole line of defense. He summoned his supporters from the slums, moved to the Champ de Mars (the vast plaza near the presidential palace), and delivered a speech whose tone was strikingly different from the cheerful words he had used in New York. Aristide's incendiary rhetoric first focused on the bourgeois.

> Today, seven months after 7 February, on a day ending in seven, I give you one last chance. I ask you to take this chance, because you will not have two or three more chances, only one. Otherwise, it will not be good for you. . . . If I speak to you this way, it does not mean that I am unaware of my power to unleash public vindication, in the name of justice, against all thieves, in an attempt to recover from them what is not theirs. A word to the wise is enough.

The anti-rich rhetoric and numerological references were sure to please the lower-class, Voodoo-worshipping throngs. The multitude assembled in front of Aristide cheered and applauded. Some held tires, a stark reminder of the horrible penalty of necklacing that would surely be inflicted on any enemy of Aristide. Raoul Cédras, the new commander in chief of the army and a prime suspect in any coup attempt, stood a few feet behind Aristide, looking uneasy. Aristide continued.

> If you catch someone who does not deserve to be where he is, do not fail to give him what he deserves. Do not fail to give him what he deserves! Do not fail to give him what he deserves! Do not fail to give him what he deserves! . . . Macoutes are excluded from the political game. Macoutes are excluded from the political game. Do not fail to give them what they deserve. Do not fail to give them what they deserve . . .
>
> If we catch one, do not fail to give him what he deserves. What a nice tool! What a nice instrument! What a nice device! It is a pretty one. It is elegant, attractive, splendorous, graceful, and dazzling. It smells good. Wherever you go, you feel like smelling it. It is provided for by the Constitution, which bans Macoutes from the political scene. Whatever happens to them is their problem.[3]

Aristide never overtly called on his supporters to use necklacing against political opponents, though his calls to give Macoutes "what they deserved" and to make good use of a tool that "smelled good" in the name of "public vindication" left little room for doubt. In the two days that followed, a series of anxious phone conversations took place between Aristide and Cédras. Cédras demanded that Aristide come out strongly against mob violence. Aristide, unwilling to give away the one trump card in his hand, asked Cédras for assurances that no coup was under way. Cédras swore that he had no knowledge of any conspiracy. Aristide did not believe him.

The army cut the Gordian knot the following Sunday, September 29, when Port-au-Prince police chief Michel François convinced soldiers of the Frère barracks to mutiny (there is traditionally no distinction between the police and the army in Haiti). Soon, soldiers surrounded Aristide's private residence in Tabarre. He only managed to sneak out when the French ambassador offered to take him in his armored car. Aristide's plan was to reach the presidential palace, summon loyal soldiers and supporters, and fight. But the revolutionaries remained one step ahead of him. When Aristide arrived at the palace on September 30, a party of soldiers was waiting for him. The soldiers immediately arrested him and took him across the street to the army headquarters, where yet another surprise awaited him. Cédras, the man Aristide had appointed as commander in chief and who had reaffirmed his loyalty on the phone just hours before, was there. He had joined the rebels.

Tense hours ensued. Soldiers beat and killed companions of Aristide and pledged to do the same with him. Aristide thought that his last hour had come. Some versions even have Aristide going through one of the mental breakdowns that he had experienced during previous stressful times, imploring his captors, crying, even defecating. Cédras, despite his men's calls for revenge, was wavering. Murdering a constitutional president, he thought, might enrage the international community. When the French, U.S., and Venezuelan ambassadors proposed to arrange for Aristide's exile, Cédras finally acceded to their demand. Aristide left the army headquarters unharmed and immediately fled on an American plane bound for Caracas.

The measure of mercy that saved Aristide's life was atypical, for Haiti became engulfed in a bloody struggle for supremacy after his overthrow. Lafontant was murdered in his Port-au-Prince cell the day of the coup. Meanwhile, in the southern city of Cayes, Sylvio Claude, a two-time presidential candidate, Protestant minister, anti-Duvalier activist, and prominent Aristide critic, was necklaced. In both cases, it seems likely that Aristide supporters killed political opponents after learning that a coup was under way. In most other cases, Aristide supporters were the victims. Students and slum-dwellers, Aristide's most vocal supporters, were popular targets, as were all institutions associated with the exiled president—not even his *Lafanmi Selavi* shelter for homeless children was considered a safe haven. Within weeks, several hundred men and women had died. Over the following three years, political repression would claim an estimated three thousand lives.

Raoul Cédras, the new master of Haiti, was a shadowy figure. Light-skinned and affluent, he belonged to a social class far removed from the slums that were Aristide's main recruiting grounds. His family had supported the Duvalier family faithfully, and he had enjoyed numerous promotions under Bébé Doc. He had served as an instructor in the elite Leopards unit, and earned a coveted spot in training missions in the United States. But he also owed his promotion to interim commander in chief to Aristide himself and resisted calls to disrupt Aristide's election and inauguration in late 1990 and early 1991.

After the coup, Cédras continued to follow a devious course. He became the head of a military triumvirate that also included Lt. Col. Michel François and Lt. Col. Philippe Biamby and became the de facto dictator of Haiti. But the junta appointed Joseph Nérette as president and Jean-Jacques Honorat as prime minister in an effort to give a civilian face to the military dictatorship. The junta relied on paramilitary groups, or *attachés*, for the most unsavory elements of the repression, which allowed Cédras to claim that he was not directly responsible for the many human rights violations committed under his watch. Hoping to hide the magnitude of the repression, soldiers did their best to finish off the wounded and to harass family members trying to claim the bodies of deceased relatives. Corpses were then dumped in a landfill located at Ti Tanyen, ten miles north of the capital. Radio journalist Jacques Gary Simeon was killed, others were deluged with death threats, while Cédras stayed away from the Haitian and foreign media. He hoped that keeping a low profile and restricting the flow of information about the number of victims would prevent an international backlash. Time, along with the natural antipathy of the Bush administration for the leftist Aristide, would eventually erase all memories of the September 1991 coup. If all worked well, Aristide would soon become one of Haiti's many ousted presidents—none of whom had ever returned from exile to reclaim office—while the mulatto businessmen who financed Cédras's coup would replace black slum-dwellers as the cornerstone of political power.

The First Aristide Presidency: An Assessment

Aristide's economic policies, when compared with the immense expectations that greeted his inauguration on February 7, 1991, were surprisingly modest. Aristide, it seemed, only hoped to introduce a few welfare measures to soften the plight of the Haitian poor, reduce inefficiencies in the Haitian bureaucracy, and rely on foreign donors to finance health and infrastructure projects. Given the vagueness of his campaign platform, it is difficult to know what else, if anything, he would have done if given a chance to finish his five-year term. These policies, however humble, could have worked. Haiti's main burden had always been graft, incompetence, and instability—political, not economic, problems. An honest, modest government could very well have provided the framework within which to unleash Haiti's economic potential.

Unfortunately, Haiti's political demons were never far away. The Haitian passion for the presidency and the habit of monopolizing power once one reaches the presidential palace bore the brunt of the blame. In 1991 Haiti, it seemed, everyone wanted to be president. The list included priests such as Aristide, former Duvalierist officials such as Roger Lafontant, soldiers such as Cédras, and Supreme Court justices such as Nérette. As for the powers of the presidency, these were defined more by the Haitian tradition of absolute personal power than by articles of the 1987 constitution. Aristide refused to share any ounce of power with any rival. His political allies of the FNCD had a legitimate claim to

cabinet posts; he disregarded them. Deputies tried to exert their governmental oversight duties; he sent a mob to threaten them. Top army
officers had soldiers at their disposal; he fired them. Hérard Abraham
and Ertha Pascal-Trouillot had once occupied the presidential seat; they
too became victims of presidential wrath. Lafontant had launched a
botched attempt to seize power; he was jailed, and possibly murdered, by
Aristide's acolytes. Aristide feared that *Macoutes* might engineer a new
Duvalierist regime; he called on his supporters to burn them to death.
Haiti had adopted the rule by majority championed by Jean-Jacques
Rousseau, but it still had much to learn from Montesquieu's doctrine on
the separation of powers.

Aristide's enemies were equally unwilling to share power. Aristide
hoped to reduce public spending when he fired public servants, but he
also sought to make room for party loyalists. This left a large mass of
discontented office seekers, accustomed to getting a share of the national
treasury in exchange for minimal work, who promptly backed any
candidate willing to redistribute the spoils of power. Aristide's popularity among the poor also worried the bourgeoisie, who interpreted his
election as a revolution that might endanger the centuries-old social
hierarchy on the island (business owners, in particular, saw the higher
minimum wage as a personal assault on their financial well-being). The
army could not agree to abandon its monopoly on power by letting
lower-class vigilantes settle scores for past crimes. Aristide's rise to power,
combined with his and his opponents' determination not to share any of
it, set the stage for a violent political and social confrontation that once
again threw Haiti into a ruinous political maelstrom.

In later years, Aristide and his supporters would blame foreign
powers, the United States in particular, for masterminding the
September 1991 coup d'état. The criticism ignored all of Aristide's own
mistakes—his decision to name Raoul Cédras as interim commander in
chief in particular. It also disregarded the major, positive role foreigners
played in 1990–1991. The international community pressured the army
into letting the 1990 presidential elections proceed peacefully. It provided observers to guarantee a result untainted by electoral fraud. It
funded Aristide's development programs. It gave him a hero's welcome at
the United Nations. Foreign ambassadors even saved Aristide's life during the coup. But none of that mattered to Aristide. He concluded that
the revolution, far from being a homegrown backlash against his own
irresponsible political speeches, was secretly engineered by outsiders,
especially by U.S. ambassador Alvin P. Adams. This belief later became
central to the *Lavalas* credo and justified Aristide's demands that he be

reinstated with the help of a U.S. intervention. The United States, in his view, had a moral duty to give him back the presidency it had taken away from him.

This conspiracy theory is intriguing. The United States later intervened to bring Aristide back to Haiti (1994), then supported a coup that sent him again in exile (2004); should Aristide's accusations be warranted, the United States would have helped take Aristide in and out of power three times in thirteen years. Declassification might one day demonstrate Ambassador Adams's role; documents currently available, however, only prove that the Central Intelligence Agency paid some of Cédras's paramilitaries as informants in 1993–1994, not that it financed a coup in 1991. More generally, the claim that the Bush administration overthrew Aristide tends to exaggerates Haiti's importance for the United States in 1991. In a year marked by the first Gulf War and the breakdown of the Soviet Union, the election of Aristide was the least of George H. W. Bush's concerns. Far from congratulating Cédras for overthrowing Aristide, the Bush administration lamented the failure of the democratic transition and imposed strict economic sanctions on the new regime. This economic embargo, designed to force the junta to allow Aristide to return to Haiti, remained in place, on and off, for the following three years.

CHAPTER 7

The Haitian Invasion of the United States: Haitian Boat People (October 1991–October 1993)

Sea Wanderers

The 1991 coup marked a sharp upsurge in the number of boat people leaving Haiti. Although their plight received intense media coverage in the United States, hard information about boat people was difficult to come by. The emigrants intercepted by the U.S. Coast Guard told harrowing stories of oppression on land and ordeal at sea, but the immigration officials who interviewed them claimed that these were elaborate fabrications designed to gain refugee status. Little reliable information was coming from the military junta either, with Prime Minister Honorat asserting quite implausibly that there were no human rights violations in Haiti and thus no cause for a Haitian exodus. As for the refugees whose boat capsized at sea—half of all those who left, according to U.S. authorities—they left behind no testimony of who they were, why they left, and what they hoped to achieve. Their story will never be told.

The best available witness account was that of Sygma photographer Patrick Chauvel. A Frenchman accustomed to covering war zones, Chauvel took a simple and dangerous step. He went to Gonâve Island west of Port-au-Prince and paid the required fee to the captain and bribes to the myriad local strongmen. He then boarded a skiff leaving for the coast of Florida. He was not alone; forty-two other passengers joined him on the small, rickety embarkation. According to Chauvel's account, the following night and day saw much hunger and seasickness, two cases of drowning, and one pirate attack that was successfully fended off with machetes. All these sacrifices were for naught; the boat people encountered an incoming storm, the captain turned around, and the skiff hit a reef not far from its point of departure.

Chauvel and those refugees who survived the voyage waddled ashore, hid from the local police trying to exact more money, and looked for another ship. Chauvel soon found what he was looking for: a thirty-foot ship, larger than the one he had previously embarked on but unfortunately loaded with no fewer than 140 men, women, and children. Some were told to lie on the keel to prevent capsizing, and the ship went underway. The refugees made little headway in the days to come. Three days after leaving Haiti, the ship was still at least twenty days' sailing time from Miami and food was running short. Still, the mood remained upbeat as Haitians called on Agwe, the god of the sea, to come to their rescue. Agwe never appeared, but one of the Coast Guard cutters patrolling off the coast of Haiti did. The refugees were transferred aboard the cutter and their ship was scuttled. Chauvel went on to publish his story and proceed to his next assignment in a thirty-five-year career spent covering all of the world's hot spots. As for the Haitians, they made their way to the U.S. base in Guantánamo Bay, Cuba, and likely repatriation.

The Roots of Despair: Repression and the Embargo

What is it that convinced Haitians to sell all their belongings, abandon their beloved *Haïti chérie*, often leaving relatives behind, and risk it all on some far-flung dream of exile? The odds of successfully emigrating to Florida were small in 1991–1994. Because of limited funds and the local authorities' constant demands for bribes, Haitians rarely invested more than a few hundred dollars in their plan of exile. This amount bought a few square inches on a small, unsound ship devoid of supplies and overloaded with passengers. Haitians then had to evade the cordon of Coast Guard and Navy vessels that surrounded Haiti, navigate the treacherous Windward Passage, and fight contrary currents in the Straights of Florida. A successful trip required nothing short of a miracle; in fact, miracles did not always suffice, for the many Voodoo *loas* invoked during the journey proved no match for ten-foot waves and the U.S. military. Those boat people who survived typically ended in Guantánamo, where they just as typically spent a few weeks before being sent back to their country of origin. Only 54 Haitian refugees were legally admitted into the United States in 1992, compared with 3,720 for Cuba alone. What, then, convinced Haitians to leave anyway?

The exact causes of the Haitian exodus were the subject of a passionate debate in 1991–1994. Some blamed oppressive political conditions in Haiti; others asserted that most refugees were motivated by a lack of economic opportunities in Haiti. The answer had important legal implications; proving that one faced immediate physical danger in Haiti was sufficient ground to win refugee status, while someone merely looking for a job could be sent home. The Haitians' rationale, however, rarely fit into neat legal categories. Political oppression *and* misery combined in 1991–1994 to create the immigration equivalent of a perfect storm.

Cédras's brutal rule was an important factor. The poor had been Aristide's most fervent supporters during his presidency, so they became the most likely candidates for postcoup repression. Some Aristide supporters fought back, hoping for a repeat of the successful uprising that undid the Lafontant coup. But the army prevailed and imposed a reign of terror that claimed about three thousand victims in three years, including three hundred during the month that followed the coup. Borrowing a page from Papa Doc's book, Cédras's military junta used soldiers and paramilitaries (or *attachés*) to harass opponents and their families. As months passed, the regime became bolder. Instead of hiding the bodies of their victims, regime thugs disfigured and mutilated the corpses, then dumped them in the streets as a warning to would-be opponents. Fearing for their lives, an estimated three hundred thousand Haitians associated with Aristide went into internal exile. For those Haitians whose relatives could no longer shelter them, only two options remained: certain death at home or possible success as a boat people. They chose the latter.

Economic despair also increased noticeably when the Cédras coup quashed the hope, born during the Aristide presidency, that political reforms and increased aid would finally foster development in Haiti. After the coup, the Organization of American States (OAS) imposed a trade embargo in October 1991, followed by the United States a few days later and the United Nations in June 1993. The embargo never accomplished its two main objectives—hitting Haitian elites in their pocketbook and weakening Cédras's resolve—but it destroyed what little remained of Haiti's economy. Foreign aid dwindled as financial sanctions took effect. Oil was on the list of banned imports, so the cost of public transportation skyrocketed while peasants cut down their last trees in a desperate search for alternative sources of energy. Rich Haitians had the resources to pay for their basic needs; some even enriched themselves through contraband. The rest of the population suffered immensely. A 1993 Harvard study showed that an additional one thousand

Haitian children died each month as a result of the food shortages caused by the embargo—a number even larger than the number of victims of political repression. Despite its fundamental purpose, the embargo turned out to be a very effective way of increasing the number of boat people aimed for Florida.

Misinformation also boosted Haitians' hopes of success. The few success stories of Haitians who were granted asylum, not horror stories of capsized ships, were the ones that received wide coverage in Haiti. Those who were denied asylum merely went back and started gathering funds for another attempt. As for the Haitians who never wrote home, the assumption was that they had become so rich in the United States that they had forgotten everything about their suffering brothers back home. Little did their relatives know that the would-be exiles had in fact joined their distant ancestors thrown overboard from slave ships into the watery grave surrounding Hispaniola.

Describing the boat people tragedy as a U.S.-manufactured catastrophe, Aristide accused the United States of destroying the Haitian economy through the embargo while denying access to Haitian boat people. The U.S. refugee policy, he declared, amounted to setting a house on fire, then "throwing people [trying to flee] back into the house."[1] But Aristide's criticism overlooked his own role in the embargo. Far from opposing economic sanctions on humanitarian grounds, he lobbied to expand them and to enforce them more strictly. Speaking from his comfortable American exile, living off $50 million of Haitian government funds that were taken away from the junta because of the financial sanctions, Aristide never shied away from bankrupting his people for a chance to resume his political career as president of Haiti.

Criticisms of the embargo's inability to affect the junta were more to the point. Cédras and his acolytes, accustomed to waddling knee-deep in their opponents' blood, were unlikely to leave office simply because their fellow countrymen went to bed hungry. If anything, foreign opposition only hardened the junta's stand. Contemporary embargoes aimed at Saddam Hussein of Iraq, Muhammar Qadhafi of Libya, Fidel Castro of Cuba, Jiang Zemin of China, and Slobodan Milosevic of Serbia failed just as spectacularly. The Bush administration, and later the Clinton administration, only persisted with this ineffective policy because Aristide insisted on it and because they had no acceptable alternative for the time being. The embargo thus continued even though many doubted it would ever work. Caught between an exiled president asking for sanctions and a dictator who paid no attention to them, the Haitian people suffered for three long years, and consequently kept leaving.

Haitian Women under the Junta's Rule

Politicians such as Aristide like to describe Haitian women as the *poto mitan* of Haitian society after the central pole, or *poto mitan*, that holds the roof of Voodoo temples. The compliment is designed to attract the female vote, but it also is an accurate description of the central role Haitian women play in Haiti's society, economy, and, increasingly, politics. In Haiti, women do everything. They cook, wash, mend clothes, fetch water and wood, and generally perform all the arduous housekeeping labor associated with raising four–five children without the comforts of modern appliances and running water. Their husbands' main duty is to earn cash for household needs, but the high unemployment rate means that most Haitian men find little or no work. Instead, they kill time watching soccer games on television or playing endless games of domino; some even run away from the household altogether when they find a younger and more appealing partner. Nuclear families are a rarity in Haiti. *Plasaj*, or common law marriage with no right to alimony or inheritance, is frequent, and even women who are officially married often end up as single mothers raising half a dozen children from three or more different fathers.

Because fathers provide so little financial help, mothers must earn money on top of their onerous household duties. In the countryside, they help on the fields and sell surplus produce at the market. Haiti's most recognizable icons are the *revendeuses* or *Mesdames Sarah* (figure 7.1), female merchants who can be seen balancing fifty pounds or more of goods on their heads as they travel dozens of miles on mountain trails to profit from minute price differences between rural areas and regional centers. In large cities, women can be hired out as servants to rich families, or find jobs as seamstresses in one of the heavily feminized port factories catering to the export market. This "side job" is anything but; it is estimated that every female worker supports five persons on average. And yet, they receive little gratitude for all their hard work. Husbands, when they are present, consider domestic violence to be a birthright. Male employers expect sexual gratification in exchange for the privilege of working twelve-hour days for fifteen cents an hour. Haitian gender norms are a time capsule from the 1950s, without the meatloaf dinner and the working father yelling "honey, I'm home."

For centuries, the sole privilege bestowed on the overworked Haitian women was immunity from political repression. With few exceptions, politics was a male monopoly, as were civil wars and political murders. Women were to follow the example of the *loa* Erzulie Dantó (usually

Figure 7.1 Selling goods in local markets is one of Haitian women's many tasks.

depicted as the black Madonna of Czestochowa), a single mother of the Voodoo pantheon who was deceived, raped, and beaten by her male partners. According to the legend, Erzulie's tongue was cut off by fellow Haitians during the war of independence so that she would not talk under torture. Revealingly, the symbol of Haitian womanhood was a hard-working Cinderella who could not speak.

Things started to change in the 1950s. Women finally earned the right to vote and played a growing role as both tools and victims of political oppression. Papa Doc's most famous victim, Yvonne Hakime-Rimpel, and his most dreaded *Macoute*, Rosalie Bousquet (a.k.a. Madame Max Adolphe), were both women. Women were active participants in the grassroots movements that emerged in the late 1980s and supported Aristide's rise to power. The 1990s saw Haiti's first female president (Ertha Pascal-Trouillot) and first female prime minister (Claudette Werleigh). In 1991–1994, women organized *bat teneb* ("hitting darkness"), a form of nightly protest constituting in hitting pots and pans with ladles.

This long-term shift in women's roles carried a heavy price tag in 1991–1994, for Cédras's henchmen targeted men and women indiscriminately. It was slightly easier for men to escape unharmed, for they had no children to take care of and could more easily find a place in hiding or a spot on a boat. Female opponents burdened with family obligations and wives and mothers of Aristide supporters thus became a primary target of political retribution, and the female inhabitants of pro-Aristide slums gained the dubious honor of becoming the most exploited half of the most oppressed group in the poorest country in the Western Hemisphere. One such victim was Alerte Belance, a *revendeuse*, Aristide convert, and mother of three who was captured by the paramilitary group FRAPH (Front Révolutionnaire Armé pour le Progrès d'Haïti) on October 15, 1993 and taken to the mass grave at Ti Tanyen. There, according to her testimony, she was beaten with machetes, which left her with severed fingers, ear, arm, and tongue. She was then left for dead. She survived her wounds, fled to the United States, and became a *cause célèbre* as she appeared in one Aristide rally after another.

In 1991–1994, murders, torture, and arbitrary prison time—the daily bread of Haitian politics—were joined by the use of rape as an instrument of terror. Cédras and his thugs far surpassed their mentor Papa Doc in that regard. Interviews conducted by the *Commission Nationale de Vérité et de Justice* (National Truth and Justice Commission or CNVJ) after Cédras's departure showed that thousands of rapes had taken place; thousands more probably went unreported out of shame. The political intent was clear. Women were selected based on their association with the Aristide regime, gang-raped by *attachés*, often in full view of family members, and warned that this was the price to pay for opposing Cédras. The youngest victim of political rape was one year old.

One can only wonder what would happen if Haitian women finally gained the respect and equality they deserve. Politicians might pay more attention to issues central to the welfare of women in particular and to Haiti in general, including access to contraception, a good educational system, functioning maternity wards, and decent working conditions in the assembly sector. Greater gender equality would also give a prominent spot to the single most courageous and hard-working element in society. Any mother able to work all day for a three-dollar pay while fending off unwelcome advances by a lustful boss and raising six hungry children in a one-room tin-roofed hut—all of this on one meal a day or less—can only be described as resourceful. Tapping, rather than beating, this valuable resource would be Haiti's first step on the path to economic development.

U.S. Attempts to Stem the Flow of Boat People during the Bush Administration

When the coup took place in September 1991, the 1981 Reagan–Duvalier agreement on repatriations was still in effect. It had proved its value over the years. From 1981 to 1991, the United States had intercepted twenty-three thousand Haitian boat people, all but twenty-eight of whom had been denied asylum. Despite the agreement's effectiveness, Aristide's overthrow convinced U.S. president George H. W. Bush to halt forced repatriations in October 1991. One could hardly justify, Bush thought, sending Haitians back to a country racked by political violence. His argument was morally sound but politically flawed. As soon as Haitians learned of the more lenient policy, they boarded ships and left for the United States. A first boat carrying nineteen people was intercepted on October 28. Five days later, there were two hundred Haitians onboard Coast Guard cutters. By mid-November, the number had risen to twelve hundred and American ambassadors were frantically asking governments of the region to accept Haitians. All of them declined the offer, and Bush resumed the traditional U.S. policy of forced repatriations.

The decision immediately sparked a political and legal maelstrom. Legal advocates of the boat people argued that turning away black Haitians while welcoming lighter Cubans was racist, that repatriating Haitians without a thorough evaluation of their claims for asylum was illegal, and that claiming that Haitians could safely return home was illogical considering that the United States refused to recognize the Cédras regime precisely because of its brutality. And yet, the AIDS/poverty/drugs/Voodoo stigma attached to Haitians was so well entrenched in American public opinion by 1991 that allowing Haitian boat people in Florida one year before a presidential election was virtual political suicide for Bush. When one hundred Haitians drowned as their boat capsized off Cuba on November 19, Bush justified his policy reversal on the grounds that he was doing Haitians a service by turning them away. Should he let boat people in, more would take to the seas and die. That same day, a Miami judge declared that the U.S. policy was inconsistent with international treaties governing asylum seekers. The boat people conundrum was insoluble.

Not knowing what to do with boat people kept onboard cutters, yet unwilling to admit them on U.S. soil, Bush finally decided to send Haitians to the U.S. base in Guantánamo Bay, Cuba. The base was conveniently located close to Haiti and far from Florida. It was heavily guarded, in U.S. hands, yet officially a part of Cuba, which put Haitians in a legal vacuum that left them vulnerable to expulsion. But a host of sanitation problems appeared as the Haitian population at the base quickly grew to nine thousand and Bush started looking for legal ways to empty the refugee camps. When a U.S. court concluded on January 31, 1992 that it was legal to assess asylum claims in Guantánamo rather than in the United States, forced repatriations resumed. A pattern emerged. For the following two months, those boat people who did not drown were intercepted and taken to Cuba; immigration officials assessed their claims there; Haitians were then sent to the United States if they proved that they had a reasonable claim to asylum status, or sent back to Haiti when they did not.

The policy had two drawbacks in Bush's eyes: it still allowed too many Haitians inside the United States, and led to negative media coverage showing boat people herded in large concentration camps while waiting for their case to be settled. The immigration policy was thus further refined in May 1992. Haitians were now told to apply for asylum in Haiti itself, under the watchful eye of the very tyrants trying to kill them. Should they decide to take to the seas in violation of that policy, they would be repatriated without even the benefit of a hearing. The policy was markedly unfair for those in real need of protection, but it continued until the very end of the Bush administration.

Not in My Backyard: The Haitian Diaspora in the United States

Haitians who reached the United States in 1991–1994 joined a Haitian American community that was already one million strong (another one million Haitians lived in the Dominican Republic, Canada, France, Cuba, Venezuela, and the Bahamas). These Haitian immigrants were very different from John Audubon, Moreau de Saint-Méry, and the thousands of white planters who fled to Charleston, Philadelphia, and New Orleans in the 1790s and 1800s. Most Haitian Americans were black and lived in Southern Florida, New York, and Boston, where they were far from welcome. Like many other immigrants, Haitians were willing to work at any rate, thus giving rise to accusations that they worsened the difficult job market of the early 1990s. Cultural assimilation was difficult, as the cramped New York apartments did not lend themselves to the all-night drumming and chanting required by Voodoo rituals. Rumors that Haitians dabbled in drugs, worshipped Satan, and suffered from AIDS put them among the least desirable of all immigrants. Not even the Haitian community was united in its support of the boat people. In New York, the wealthy, educated immigrants of the Papa Doc era, who lived in Queens and Manhattan, looked down on the newly arrived poor who flocked to the more popular Brooklyn borough.

Because of the hostile conditions in which they arrived, Haitian Americans kept closer ties to their home country than is typically the case among other immigrants. They preserved their cultural traditions; spent a small fortune calling their relatives at home. They also sent workers' remittances that dwarfed the level of foreign aid, and continued to do so even after foreign lenders resumed aid in 1994. It was not rare when traveling in Haiti to encounter villages where neither roads nor telephones lines nor the electrical grid were functional because of the complete collapse of public infrastructures during the embargo, but where a bright yellow and black sign advertised the presence of a Western Union office, allowing exiled relatives to wire money easily.

Haitians who arrived in 1991–1994 and those who preceded them proved highly successful abroad despite all the stereotypes arraigned against them, thus disproving all racist theories of intellectual inferiority. Jean-Michel Basquiat, the son of a Haitian exile, became famous in art circles for his innovative use of graffiti and political slogans. The rap group *The Fugees*, named after the New Jersey slang term for Haitian refugees, became a national sensation in 1996 with their hit *The Score*. Another Haitian musical sensation was Richard Morse, son of Haitian singer Emerante de Pradine and founder of the band RAM; his song *Ibo Lele (Dreams Come True)* gained recognition when it appeared on the soundtrack of Jonathan Demme's 1993 blockbuster *Philadelphia*. In 1995, Edwige Danticat was a finalist for the National Book Award for *Krik? Krak!*, a collection of short stories inspired by Haiti's oral culture. Danticat's *Breath, Eyes, and Memory* (1994) earned the publishing equivalent of the Holy Grail when it was featured on Oprah's book club selection. *Dew Breaker* (2004) explored the life of a Haitian American obsessed with her father's past as a Papa Doc prison guard. These and many other Haitian Americans were Haiti's best and brightest. The exodus was bleeding Haiti white.

Bill Clinton and the Haitian Lobby during the 1992 Presidential Campaign

The most famous addition to the ranks of the Haitian American community during the period 1991–1994 was no less than president-in-exile Jean-Bertrand Aristide, who moved to the posh Washington neighborhood of Georgetown in 1992. The decision to emigrate to the very heart of the American empire was surprising considering Aristide's leftist views and his belief that the United States had supported Cédras's takeover, but it was politically astute. Aristide settled at the epicenter of American politics, a short flight away from the large Haitian American communities of New York and Miami who had financed his 1990 presidential run. His strategy was simple. He would exploit his popularity among Haitian exiles to put pressure on the Congressional Black Caucus, then use this leverage to orient U.S. policy in a direction conducive to his own interests. The Black Caucus' membership was virtually all Democratic; so Aristide's cause became associated with that of Bill Clinton during the 1992 presidential campaign.

Aristide's outward political profile changed overnight when he settled in the United States. The fiery rhetoric he had used in his September 27, 1991 "necklacing speech" did not play well with American audiences, so he polished his image as a saintly priest of the poor and as a friend of the United States. He stayed away from Fidel Castro, attended Nelson Mandela's inauguration instead, stopped making anti-American comments, toned down his calls to give the *Macoutes* "what they deserved," and spoke of "justice" and "reconciliation" instead. His early interviews were almost comical as the newly arrived Aristide, who still spoke little English, stuck to his talking points and answered "what the world needs now is love" to each and every question.[2] He refused to endorse his supporters' calls for an armed uprising against Cédras and insisted on a peaceful solution to the political crisis: strengthening the embargo, forcing Cédras to negotiate, and welcoming the victims of the embargo by abandoning the U.S. policy of forced repatriations.

Aristide's sudden conversion to the virtues of American free-market democracy was highly suspicious, but the ploy worked. Because of his prodding, Haitian Americans denounced the U.S. refugee policy as racist during two mass demonstrations held in New York on April 26 and September 30, 1992. Black and liberal Congressmen took up the cause of the Haitian boat people, and Clinton announced that he would end Bush's policy of forced repatriations if elected. The promise gained him 90 percent of the African American vote, including most of the Haitian American vote, and raised great hopes in Haiti.

Haitians celebrated Clinton's election to the presidency in November 1992 by starting work on a large number of new ships. According to contemporary U.S. intelligence estimates, up to 200,000 Haitians prepared to set sail with the expectation that the U.S. refugee policy would soon be loosened. When Clinton was inaugurated on January 20, 1993, a boat loaded with 163 Haitians was the first to test the new president's promise of hospitality. The boat people were intercepted and sent home. Electoral promises notwithstanding, Bush's discriminatory refugee policy continued under Bill Clinton. Americans had only gotten "half the message," Clinton said.[3] He did not explain what the "other half" was, but fears of a large-scale refugee crisis similar to the 1980 Mariel boatlift probably ranked high.

Disappointment related to Clinton's change of heart on the boat people issue did not diminish Aristide's public courting of the president. Aristide had his back to the wall. After the coup, he had successively asked the OAS, France, and the United Nations to help restore him to power; all three had answered that they refused to move beyond the ineffective embargo already in effect. Clinton was the only person who proved responsive and might be convinced to use threats of military intervention on Aristide's behalf. Aristide could not afford to lose the president's friendship, however wavering it might be. U.S. intercession was his only hope of ever being reinstated as president of Haiti.

Clinton's First Attempts to Restore Aristide: From the Governor's Island Agreement to the Harlan County Incident (July–October 1993)

Bill Clinton—motivated by a genuine desire to help Aristide or by fears of a refugee crisis' political repercussions—immediately got down to work. He used the United States' prominent spot as a permanent member of the UN Security Council to push for the deployment of a group of United Nations human rights observers, then to obtain a tightening of the embargo. Among other things, UN Resolution 841 (June 16, 1993) froze the assets of the members of the junta and that of its most prominent supporters. Cédras, who had refused to blink when his people died by the thousands because of the embargo, reacted immediately when his financial well being was affected. A mere two weeks after the UN resolution was passed, he traveled to Governors' Island, New York, to negotiate.

The negotiations, which took place over the Fourth of July weekend, were complicated by Cédras's and Aristide's mutual antipathy. Both of them refused to meet face to face, or to negotiate directly, or even to live near one another. As a result, Aristide commandeered entire floors of two New York luxury hotels while Cédras slept on Governors' Island itself. U.S. and UN-OAS special envoys Lawrence Pezzullo and Dante Caputo spent days shuttling between the two camps, and even then failed to secure a deal acceptable to both sides. Journalists and government officials watched anxiously as their extended weekend slipped by with nothing to show for it. A ruse finally carried the day. Pezzullo and Caputo drafted an agreement acceptable to Cédras, got him to sign it, put him on a plane to Port-au-Prince, and told Aristide that time had now run out. Faced with a *fait accompli*, Aristide grudgingly signed. The resulting Governors' Island agreement promised that Aristide would return to Haiti as president on October 30, 1993. In exchange, the financial sanctions would be lifted and Cédras would obtain an amnesty for the crimes committed during his rule. A UN police force and an Aristide-appointed prime minister would oversee the transition (Robert Malval was later selected for the prime ministership).

The United Nations lifted sanctions on August 27. Cédras's bank statements are not public record, but one may surmise that he and his friends promptly repatriated funds held overseas during the following two weeks; by mid-September, the repression was again in full swing. The most prominent murder took place on September 11—the fifth anniversary of the attack on St. Jean Bosco—when armed men dragged Antoine Izméry out of a Port-au-Prince church and shot him. Izméry had been a key financier of Aristide's 1990 presidential run and one of his closest friends. Killing him in broad daylight, in the capital, and in the presence of UN observers was a clear signal that the junta feared no one. Junta member Michel François publicly declared that Aristide would never come back to Haiti alive.

The *Front Révolutionnaire Armé pour le Progrès d'Haïti*, or FRAPH, emerged as the junta's main tool of repression during this period. Headed by Emmanuel Constant and Louis-Jodel Chamblain, the FRAPH was officially a youth organization claiming three hundred thousand adherents. Clean, wholesome fun was not the FRAPH's main line of business, however. Like the *Tontons Macoutes* before it, FRAPH used the youth organization charade as a front for a paramilitary force designed to carry out Cédras's worst crimes. The FRAPH's French name meant "armed revolutionary front"; its acronym sounded inauspiciously like the French verb *frapper*, "to strike or hit." FRAPH members' main duty was to abduct Aristide sympathizers, torture them, and dump their body in front of the Montana Hotel, where many foreign journalists and UN employees lived. Their Port-au-Prince office was virtually bare, save for files on the ongoing repression and trophy pictures of their victims.

Still hoping for a peaceful transition despite all signs to the contrary, the United States sent 225 U.S. and Canadian troops on board the USS tank landing ship *Harlan County*. Under the Governors' Island agreement, their mission was to carry out a few construction projects, train the Haitian army, and oversee Aristide's peaceful return to the presidential palace. The *Harlan County* arrived in Port-au-Prince harbor on October 11, 1993. Despite previous assurances, no berth was available for it to dock, and the troops were quickly treated to a crash course in the subtleties of the French language. On the dock stood Vicky Huddleston, an assistant employed by the U.S. Embassy, known as *attaché* in diplomatic parlance. Nearby stood Cédras's own version of official envoys, a group of paramilitaries known as *attachés* in local slang. FRAPH members were present as well, headed by Constant himself. Their behavior was far from diplomatic. They brandished machetes, threatened Huddleston, and chanted slogans hostile to the United States. "Remember Somalia" was a crowd favorite, for the United States had just lost 18 Rangers and Delta Force members in a Mogadishu firefight the previous week. Officially, Cédras announced that allowing foreign troops armed with M-16s on Haitian soil was an affront to his country's sovereignty; officiously, he had seen on CNN the American soul-searching regarding the U.S. mission in Somalia and understood that he might remain in power if he convinced Clinton that enforcing the Governors' Island agreement would cost his administration several American lives.

Had this been the nineteenth century, the captain of the *Harlan County* would probably have ordered his men to bomb the capital and to avenge this affront to his country's honor. This being the twentieth century, he radioed back to the Pentagon to ask for guidance, and Secretary of Defense Les Aspin rushed to the White House for an emergency meeting. The mood was somber. Should the United States back down because of a few machete-wielding thugs, the episode would go down in history as the worst national humiliation since the Iranian hostage crisis of 1979–1981. For the first time since 1915, the United States seriously considered invading Haiti.

Rumors of impending war mobilized an odd coalition of CIA analysts, Republican Congressmen, junta members, and shadowy figures united by a common hatred of Aristide. Lynn Garrison, a mysterious Canadian working as consul in the Cédras regime, played a central role as he passed anti-Aristide information to his contacts in the U.S. intelligence community. Based on this source and other biased information, CIA national intelligence officer for Latin America Brian S. Latell testified in Congress that Aristide was a manic depressive psychopath who had been treated for mental problems in a Canadian hospital and who had condoned necklacing whilst president of Haiti. Both allegations (the first one unsubstantiated) featured prominently in anti-Aristide speeches that Sen. Jesse Helms (R-NC), the outspoken chair of the Senate's foreign affairs committee, delivered on October 20. The junta's rumor-mongering paid off. Aristide's reputation as a democratic saint was seriously dented, and the short-lived war fever of October 1993 subsided. Its hands full with the Somalia debacle, the White House decided not to confront FRAPH for the time being. The *Harlan County* turned tail.

Audiences around the world were thus treated to television footage of the FRAPH demonstration that forced the mighty U.S. Navy to go home, while Cédras burnished his credentials as a Haitian nationalist by winning his high noon showdown with the Yankee sheriff of the Caribbean. The most bizarre twist of the crisis, however, did not become public until months later, when Constant, the FRAPH leader and organizer of the October 11 demonstration, revealed that he was on the CIA payroll as a U.S. informant at the time of the *Harlan County* incident. Being paid as an informant technically does not imply U.S. support, but the fact remained that the CIA gave cash to the man who opposed the landing of U.S. troops and was the main hit man of a regime denounced by the United States for its human rights violations. Worse, Constant informed his CIA patrons during the *Harlan County* crisis that he had no intention of fighting the United States and that the demonstration was just for show. The CIA nevertheless informed Clinton that there was a great danger in landing U.S. troops, thus implying that backing down was the safest policy. The explanation for the CIA's bizarre double-dealing was probably some pro-Cédras CIA bias that pushed local station chiefs to emphasize the risk of civil strife in order to derail Aristide's return. This complex maneuvering boiled down to a simple truth: U.S. taxpayers financed the very man who humiliated the United States.

The *Harlan County* incident was a turning point in the Haitian crisis of 1991–1994. It proved that peaceful negotiations would never bring Aristide back to Haiti. The embargo was imposed again, but it was unlikely to work now that Cédras had had an opportunity to repatriate his funds. The Haitian crisis, a low priority before October 1993, took center stage as Congress and the press made biting remarks that Clinton was a weak-kneed president mired in international crises with no clear vision of how to deal with the post–Cold War disorder. Restoring his and his country's honor—contemporary U.S. policymakers prefer the term "credibility"—became paramount objectives for Bill Clinton. Clinton almost invaded Haiti in October 1993. He eventually decided against it, but the taboo was broken: force was a credible option. Down in the bowels of the U.S. Atlantic Command in Norfolk, Virginia, a small task force received the order to begin precise contingency planning for a U.S. invasion of Haiti. Code name: Dragon's Blood.

Conclusion: The Brain Drain

The dramatic events of 1991–1994 made for fascinating history. Priest-turned-president, gruesome mob lynching, coups d'état, embargo, boat people, and CIA treachery: as always, Haitian history was anything but dull. It would be easy, however, to become so enthralled by day-to-day events as to forget the most significant development of the era: Haiti, the hemisphere's poorest country, saw its economy shrink by 20–30 percent. The Cédras dictatorship was another station in Haiti's five-hundred-year-old Calvary.

The embargo was the most damaging development in the short term. Haiti was not economically self-sufficient; so any disruption to the importation of foodstuffs and the arrival of the foreign aid that financed it immediately created severe shortages. Contrary to what one might think, life in Haiti is anything but cheap. Most food is imported at prevailing world prices plus transportation and distribution costs. Because of high port fees, a lack of roads, and a labor-intensive retail sector, the end price of a bag of rice on a Haitian market is often higher than it would be in the United States. From 1991 to 1994, basic necessities such as oil and medicine became even costlier because of the embargo. To use Haitian expressions, *la vie chère* (the high cost of living) made *la misère* (the prevailing poverty) very hard to bear. The embargo also affected the assembly sector, whose eighty-thousand-employee payroll declined to zero after three years of sanctions. For the women who held the vast majority of these jobs, the everyday struggle to feed their dependents became that much harder. This was the price Haiti paid for Aristide's and Cédras's stubborn ambitions.

The exodus of young Haitians, which started decades before the 1990s but increased during Cédras's rule, was a case study in the long-term causes of, and solutions to, Haitian underdevelopment. Haitians who had starved under the rule of rapacious Haitian dictators suddenly flourished in foreign countries that offered basic infrastructure, security, education, and health care. There was no clearer indictment of the Haitian government's failure to make the most of its people. The Haitians' success abroad proved that misrule, not laziness, held them back in Haiti. Unfortunately for Haiti, the Diaspora also deprived the country of two million of its most energetic citizens. Papa Doc's war on educated Haitians and subsequent waves of emigration sent so many doctors and teachers into exile that the number of Haitian surgeons in Montréal surpassed that of Haitian surgeons in Port-au-Prince itself. Haiti gained a steady flow of workers' remittances, but the country also lost irreplaceable human capital. Those who stayed behind were crooks associated with the Cédras regime, the old and the very young, those lacking ambition, and those too poor to pay for a visa or a smuggler's fee (typically illiterate slum dwellers and peasants). Those who left were Haiti's best and brightest. The boat people's exodus was a hemorrhage Haiti could not afford to bear. Haiti would be much better off today if its rulers had not scared away the likes of Danticat and Basquiat.

The brain drain and its impact on economic development have been well studied in Haiti and elsewhere. The leaders of underdeveloped countries like to criticize rich countries for a "pick and choose" immigration policy that welcomes educated migrants while turning away the illiterate poor (for rich countries to do any differently would be injudicious). But one must emphasize that the brain drain is voluntary; Haitian surgeons and teachers leave their country because they are unpaid and mistreated there, not because rich countries abduct them. The uprooting that accompanies emigration is a painful process; so it would be easy to incite educated Haitians to return home by offering them a future devoid of political terror and economic spoliation. Instead, the Diaspora is treated as a piggy bank that has no political right save wiring money. Haitian politicians' prickly nationalism has led them to denounce expatriates as traitors and to deny them voting rights in the country they do so much to keep alive. They also like to spread rumors that their political opponents hold dual U.S.-Haitian citizenship (the assumption being that a Haitian American is unfit to rule Haiti). Haitians must understand that expatriates have capital and skills and would immensely benefit their country of origin if they came back. This needs to be done now, for Haitian Americans become less Haitian and more American as years pass; second- and third-generation immigrants will be unlikely to wire money to distant relatives, let alone seriously consider "returning" to Haiti. If Haiti is to ever recover its lost splendor, it needs to welcome its prodigal sons and daughters back home today—especially since the Haitian parent, contrary to his biblical counterpart, is the one who dilapidated the family fortune.

CHAPTER 8

Invasion on Demand: The Second U.S. Invasion of Haiti (October 1993–October 1994)

The Best Friends Money Can Buy (October 1993–May 1994)

The embargo imposed immense financial hardships on Haitians after it was resumed in October 1993 in the aftermath of the *Harlan County* incident, but Aristide continued to live comfortably in his Washington exile. With the exception of the Vatican, the international community refused to recognize the Cédras regime; so Aristide had access to the Haitian government's overseas assets that were frozen after the 1991 coup, to which were added all debts owed his country and ATT offsets from international phone calls to Haiti. Taiwan, which has been locked in a diplomatic war with Communist China since 1949, also wrote million dollar checks in exchange for Haiti's continued support at the United Nations. Finally, Aristide received substantial cash donations from members of the Diaspora and received royalties on his many books. The total amount exceeded $50 million.

That money did not sit idly. The *Wall Street Journal* estimated in 1994 that Aristide spent about $2 million a month from the Haitian government fund alone. The fund paid the salaries of Haitian diplomats who had remained loyal to Aristide. It also paid for Aristide's opulent lifestyle in exile, his multiple trips worldwide, and the large entourage that accompanied him wherever he went. The fund also financed Aristide's intimate life as his mistress, Haitian American lawyer Mildred Trouillot, received between $3,000 and $15,000 a month from January 1993 to February 1996 for unspecified services (Aristide did not formally renounce priesthood until October 1994). Love, like God, works in mysterious ways; Aristide, whose struggle against Cédras owed much to the fact that he was a penniless black nationalist priest and Cédras an affluent mulatto in league with the CIA, had picked a mulatto lawyer with a U.S. passport as the woman of his life.

Last and most importantly, the money paid for the most expensive lobbying campaign ever mounted by a Haitian president. Aside from Trouillot (officially registered as a lobbyist), Aristide hired a legal A-team whose main role was to give him unparalleled access to top U.S. officials. First and foremost was Michael D. Barnes, a former Maryland Congressman, and partner at the law firms of Arent and Fox and Hogan and Hartson. Burton V. Wides, also a partner at Arent and Fox and a former assistant to Sen. Paul S. Sarbanes (D-MD) of the Senate Foreign Relations Committee, came second. Ira J. Kurzban, a Florida immigration lawyer who often testified on television against the U.S. boat people policy, came third, followed by a host of lesser-known public relations specialists. Barnes's and Wides's extensive connections in Democratic circles and generous donations to Democratic causes allowed them to defend Aristide's case in numerous private conversations with key U.S. officials, Bill Clinton included. These lobbyists' Rolodexes were worth their weight in gold, which incidentally corresponded to the amount they charged for their services. Barnes's retainer was $55,000 a month plus expenses; Wides's was $10,000; Kurzban's was $30,000.

While these lawyers worked their White House, State Department, and Black Caucus contacts on a daily basis, Aristide's more famous friends orchestrated a public relations campaign aimed at the general public. Religious leaders such as Jesse Jackson demonstrated in the middle of Fifth Avenue and wrote open letters to the president. Susan Sarandon used her allotted time at the Academy Award ceremony to attack the U.S. refugee policy. If not a *cause célèbre*, Haitian refugees were a *cause du jour* among Hollywood liberals whose Southern California mansions were located three thousand miles away from the shores of Florida.

After the *Harlan County* incident, it became clear to Aristide that he was unlikely to return to power peacefully. Using his lawyers to ask Bill Clinton to use force was the next logical move, but Aristide was reluctant to take this fateful step. Calling for a U.S. invasion of his own country was treason; Aristide's nationalist, anti-American supporters would never forgive him. So he dropped hints instead. Asked on PBS whether a U.S. intervention was now necessary, Aristide tiptoed around the issue. "As the head of it [the Haitian state], if I ask for military intervention,

I will be impeached by my constitution, so I fully—that if at the same time I see the folks [military junta] out of the country tonight or even more today, right now, I will feel happy because all of us want life."[1] He made the same point again at a November 9, 1993 press conference and at a January 14–17, 1994 conference in Miami: Haitians would welcome a U.S. invasion, but Aristide was constitutionally barred from asking for one himself.

No one reacted to Aristide's comments; so he applied more political pressure on the Clinton administration. By the spring of 1994, the campaign to support Aristide made headlines everywhere. A full-page ad asking for a "colorblind" refugee policy appeared in the March 23 *New York Times*. On April 6, 1994, Aristide labeled the U.S. refugee policy "racist" and announced that the 1981 Reagan–Duvalier treaty on repatriation would lapse in six months; in other words, Clinton would face a large wave of boat people whom he could not repatriate legally if Aristide was not restored by October 1994.[2] Six Democratic Congressmen (including Joseph P. Kennedy II) were arrested while demonstrating in front of the White House on April 21. Randall Robinson, the head of TransAfrica, started a hunger strike on April 13 (Aristide later hired his wife Hazel Ross-Robinson as one of his lobbyists). Katherine Dunham, a U.S. dancer and long-time friend of Haiti, also went on hunger strike despite her frail health.

Clinton bowed to pressure—slightly. He again allowed Haitians to apply for asylum outside Haiti and replaced Lawrence Pezzullo, the U.S. special envoy to Haiti, with William Gray III, president of the United Negro Fund and an Aristide supporter. Clinton also started an extensive review of the U.S. policy on Haiti. All means to restore Aristide to power would be seriously examined, Clinton announced on May 2—even the use of force. Aristide understood that his lengthy lobbying campaign was beginning to bear fruit, and that all that was needed for Clinton to follow a more forceful policy was a little nudge. It was about time. Aristide's funds were getting so low that he had to cut several key lobbyists' salaries. After twenty months in exile, he feared that his five-year term would expire before he could return to Haiti. He had to take a dramatic step—even if that meant high treason.

Please Invade My Country—But Keep it Quiet (June–August 1994)

According to the Gospels, St. Peter betrayed Jesus not once, but three times. Like his Biblical counterpart, Aristide betrayed his nationalist principles a total of three times in June 1994: first on June 2, then on June 3, and finally on June 6, when he called for a "surgical action" and "swift and determined action" on the part of his new American friend. Referring to the 1989 U.S. invasion of Panama as a template, he added: "Haiti is not the first case. When things were like that in another country, something was done. Why not in Haiti?"[3] Aristide never used the word "invasion" in his three allocutions, nor did he explicitly ask the United States to intervene, but the overall message was clear: economic sanctions and peaceful negotiations were no longer enough. Aristide used nearly identical phrasing at all three venues at which he was invited to speak, suggesting that his words were carefully calibrated to elicit an American response without formally asking for an invasion.

Aristide's friends in the Clinton administration, National Security Adviser Anthony Lake and Secretary of State Warren Christopher in particular, pressured him for a clearer statement; did Aristide truly mean that the United States should invade Haiti? But Aristide, just as he had done in his September 1991 speech advocating necklacing in vague terms, preferred to cultivate plausible deniability. Cédras's supporters, including a female lawyer named Mireille Durocher-Bertin, filed a suit in Haiti charging Aristide with high treason, and Aristide publicly denied having ever implied that he favored a U.S. invasion—while asking for exactly this in his private conversations with U.S. officials.

Events unfolded rapidly during the summer of 1994. The number of boat people rose again after Clinton suspended the policy forcing Haitians to apply for asylum in Haiti. Meanwhile, Fidel Castro expelled thousands of Cubans and negotiations to settle some Haitian refugees in Panama fell through. Fearing a massive exodus of Caribbean boat people, Clinton again tightened the U.S. refugee policy on July 5. This was the seventh time the policy had been modified in three years. It was by then becoming obvious that the only way to bring this endless dithering to an end was to sponsor a U.S. invasion that would stem the flow of refugees at the source.

Because of domestic and Latin American opposition to a U.S. invasion, Clinton turned to the United Nations for diplomatic support. Informed of Aristide's reputation as a slippery partner, UN secretary general Boutros Boutros-Ghali insisted that Aristide endorse an invasion in writing before any UN resolution authorizing the use of force could be passed. Aristide fired back a vague letter of support for UN policies that fell short of unequivocally backing an invasion. Boutros-Ghali insisted again that he needed a written endorsement. Aristide thus turned to his ambassador to the United Nations who wrote a laconic note on Aristide's behalf and, on July 31, 1994, UN Resolution 940 gave the United States the right to use "all necessary means" to restore Aristide to power. Despite months of private lobbying, there is no written document signed by Aristide in which he plainly states his support for a U.S. military intervention.

The last details were economic. The international community was willing to intervene militarily and to commit substantial funds to ensure the success of the democratic transition. But, anxious not to see the aid squandered as it had been during the Bébé Doc era, donors insisted that Aristide would have to agree in advance to a specific set of reforms. State-owned companies—traditionally a prime source of graft—would have to be privatized. The already low tariffs would have to be further diminished. The Haitian bureaucracy would have to be downsized, and aid would be channeled through nongovernmental organizations rather than through the Haitian government. Aristide yielded to all these demands except for one: he insisted that his ministers, not he, sign the final document. He was undoubtedly planning ahead for the days when the foreign presence in Haiti would become unpopular and when he would have to reassert his credentials as an anti-American, anti-IMF, anti-imperialist populist. Aristide was preparing for the invasion's failure before it even began.

Eyeball to Eyeball (September 15–18, 1994)

By September 1994, the Clinton administration had sent unmistakable signals that it was on the verge of invading Haiti. Administration officials were publicly discussing war as the last remaining option. The United States had sought and obtained a UN resolution allowing the use of force. The U.S. armed forces had staged an ambitious war game rehearsing the invasion of a Caribbean island. All the contingency plans for an invasion of Haiti—down to the list of targets and name of units involved in the operation—were voluntarily leaked to the press to scare off the junta. According to the U.S. plan, now called OPLAN 2370, no less than twenty thousand men and two aircraft carriers would be involved in the assault. Haiti would witness the largest parachute drop since Operation Market Garden in World War II Holland. Haiti's seven thousand ill-equipped troops would be no match for the world's most powerful military. The military overkill was designed to limit U.S. and Haitian casualties by following Colin Powell's Doctrine that overwhelming U.S. force made for short wars. Finally, on September 15, 1994, Clinton delivered a televised address to the nation in which he announced his intention to remove Cédras by force. He explained that ships had already left their homeports and would reach Haiti within days. Clinton's message to Cédras: leave now or you will feel the full wrath of the Eighty-second Airborne Division.

Cédras was unimpressed by the saber rattling. He announced his intention to fight to the death and invited the U.S. media to observe the local militia as it labored through its morning drill. Meanwhile, some of his supporters drew magical signs on the sidewalk near the U.S. Embassy in Port-au-Prince, warned that Haitians would make use of dangerous poison powders, and predicted that an army of invisible *zombies* would soon push the American invaders back to the sea. To Clinton, still trying to recover from the humiliation of the *Harlan County* incident, such scenes of Voodoo priests and untrained soldiers standing up to the U.S. military colossus were anything but comical. He had banked his country's credibility on threats to remove Cédras from power, and now had to invade Haiti or look hopelessly weak.

As always, the decisive events took place on a Sunday—September 18, 1994. With U.S. paratroopers already in the air and due to drop after nightfall, Clinton asked his team of negotiators in Haiti to make a last-minute push for a negotiated settlement to the crisis. In charge of this dangerous mission were former president Jimmy Carter, former chairman of the joint chiefs of staff Colin Powell, and chairman of the Senate Armed Forces Committee Sam Nunn. Carter was the "good cop" who begged Cédras to avoid a bloodbath and negotiate; Powell was the "bad cop" who gleefully recited the list of powerful weapons platforms that Cédras would face if he persisted in opposing Aristide's return. Cédras held firm, confident that the United States was not serious about invading Haiti. With a mere one hour to go before the first paratroopers were due to jump, Clinton implored Carter to leave. If the fighting broke out, the junta might be tempted to take a former president of the United States hostage and use him as a human shield. Carter courageously stayed put, hoping to broker a last-minute deal.

Junta member Philippe Biamby finally broke the deadlock. Upon learning through private channels that U.S. airplanes had indeed left from Pope Air Force Base near Fort Bragg, North Carolina, he burst into the negotiating room and told Cédras that U.S. threats of invasion were no bluff. Cédras immediately agreed to negotiate, and did so very effectively considering that he was minutes away from being overwhelmed by a twenty-thousand-strong U.S. invading force. He merely promised what he had already promised at Governors' Island, namely, that Aristide could return to Haiti as president (the date was now set for October 15,

1994). In exchange, Cédras earned political immunity for the many crimes he had committed in office and was told that he was free to stay in Haiti if he wished to. As a last-minute concession, Cédras also obtained that the agreement be signed by the puppet-president the junta had named to replace Aristide—an eighty-one-year-old jurist and Voodoo priest named Emile Jonassaint. Like Aristide, Cédras was willing to let the Americans in, but not on the record. The Carter–Jonassaint agreement, as it was called, became the legal framework for the U.S. takeover of Haiti. U.S. planes turned around in midair, returned paratroopers home, and picked up peacekeepers instead.

Cédras and Aristide could pride themselves on the fact that the United States never technically invaded Haiti. No major fighting took place, so one could use euphemisms such as "intervention" to soothe hurt Haitian feelings—the official codename was Operation Restore Democracy. But the fact remained that 182 years after the Leclerc expedition and 79 years after the first U.S. invasion, Haiti was once again taken over by foreign troops and occupied. This was a de facto invasion, and an inglorious one at that. In 1802, Haitians had fought the invaders and won. In 1915, they had fought and lost. In 1994, Cédras, who had pledged to fight to the death, surrendered before a shot was even fired. Eyeball to eyeball, he had blinked first.

An Invasion in Search of a Mission
(September 19–October 15, 1994)

The first American to land in Haiti—aside from the numerous television crews who had flocked to Port-au-Prince over the previous week—was Gen. Henry "Hugh" Shelton, a no-nonsense, 6 foot 5 inch tall Vietnam and Gulf War veteran who was put at the head of the multinational force in Haiti (MNF). His enthusiasm for the mission, like that of many other soldiers in Operation Restore Democracy, was limited. Restoring an anti-American radical to the presidency was a rather atypical use of American power in the Caribbean, so Shelton's main goal was to organize as smooth a transition as possible to avoid U.S. and Haitian casualties. His main potential ally for that mission, ironically, was the Haitian military that Shelton had trained for months to defeat. Haitian soldiers were the sole authority capable of keeping order until Aristide's return since there was no distinction between the army and the police. Shelton told Cédras during their September 19 encounter that he would be willing to collaborate with Cédras as long as Haitian troops policed the streets and refrained from attacking American forces. Cédras agreed.

The U.S. invasion was thus anticlimactic. American forces jumped out of their helicopters in full combat mode, took over Port-au-Prince airport, set up their positions, and stayed there. Confusion reigned as the planned-for invasion suddenly shifted to a peaceful occupation, and as the enemy became the main local auxiliary in maintaining order. Soldiers had been given various sets of the rules of engagement and debated whether they should use those intended for operation plans (OPLAN) 2370, 2375, or 2380. American soldiers were told to wear full body armor in the steamy Haitian rainy season in case the junta changed its mind again and fought. Patrols were rare in the first few days; fraternization with Haitians was forbidden.

On September 24, a misunderstanding in Cap Haïtien led to a firefight that left ten Haitian soldiers dead and one American interpreter wounded. The Cap Haïtien incident—the bloodiest of the U.S. invasion—resulted in the complete collapse of the Haitian army–police in this city and forced Americans to take over most law enforcement duties there. Paradoxically, the incident also resulted in closer cooperation between the U.S. and Haitian militaries because it convinced Shelton that disbanding the Haitian army would force the United States to take expansive, casualty-prone police duties (figure 8.1).

Figure 8.1 Raoul Cédras meets with Hugh Shelton (September 27, 1994). According to the original U.S. plan, the two men should have fought each other. After the Carter–Jonassaint agreement, they cooperated closely on law enforcement matters.

Cédras thus effectively ruled Haiti for several weeks after he surrendered to the United States. During that time he got away, quite literally, with murder. His specifically Haitian vision of law enforcement consisted in ordering his men to disband pro-Aristide rallies by beating protesters to death. American troops, unsure of what the rules of engagement were, stood by helplessly while civilians died. Angered by his superiors' lack of dedication to democratic ideals, one American soldier, Capt. Lawrence P. Rockwood, took it upon himself to sneak out of his barrack and to inspect Port-au-Prince's main penitentiary, in which political prisoners were kept in medieval conditions. His one-man human rights crusade never got far. He was arrested and flown home to Fort Drum, New York, to face a court martial for insubordination. Becoming a local subsidiary of Amnesty International was not what Shelton and other U.S. officers had in mind.

On October 3, Shelton also cut a deal with Emmanuel Constant, the head of FRAPH, one of Cédras's most brutal henchmen, and another self-styled nationalist who had pledged to fight Aristide's return to the bitter end. In a stark reversal of his bellicose, preinvasion calls to arms, Constant promised to order his men not to attack U.S. troops if the United States agreed not to arrest him. U.S. troops also seized dozens of thousands of pages of FRAPH documents that purportedly documented CIA funding of Constant and other human rights abusers. The documents were flown to the United States, where they unfortunately remain classified and off-limits to researchers. Finally, U.S. officials arranged for Cédras to leave the country. Ever the great negotiator, Cédras argued that the Carter–Jonassaint agreement never called for his departure and demanded a financial package as a counterpart for his peaceful exile. By the time Cédras flew to a Panama palace on October 12, the perks granted him totaled one million dollars. Standing up to the United States for three years before being invaded paid off quite handsomely.

The Carter–Jonassaint agreement and subsequent arrangements with the junta were morally improper, but they achieved their main goal. The U.S. military did not have to fight its Haitian counterpart, which most likely prevented a series of lopsided bloodbaths similar to the one in Cap Haïtien. The relatively peaceful transition also prevented lynching, for Aristide's supporters would probably have used any breakdown in public authority to necklace the FRAPH members and Haitian soldiers who had abused them for the previous three years. The Faustian bargain struck with the Cédras regime allowed U.S. soldiers to take over all strategic positions without a fight and to prepare the ground for Aristide's planned return on October 15.

Conclusion: A Reluctant Imperialist

The Yankee hegemon described in Aristide's *In the Parish of the Poor* (1990), *Aristide: An Autobiography* (1993), and *Dignity* (1996) bears little resemblance to the U.S. government in 1991–1994. Far from seizing any opportunity to invade its smaller neighbor, the United States patiently waited for the embargo and negotiations to achieve their intended goal. The decision to intervene was taken a full three years after Aristide's overthrow, at a time when Clinton's presidential credibility and his refugee policy had been reduced to tatters by the ongoing crisis. The United States carefully planned to limit not only U.S., but Haitian casualties as well, showing a concern for Haitian lives that had always eluded Aristide and Cédras. The United States could have obtained significant economic concessions and turned Haiti into the compliant source of cheap labor outlined in the "American Plan" conspiracy. Instead, foreign donors prepared yet another aid package for Haiti, merely insisting that the money not finance furs and ruffians as had been the case under Bébé Doc's rule. American racism—an important subtext in the 1915 invasion—was nowhere in sight, and Haitians were surprised to discover that many American soldiers were as black as they were; some of them were Haitian American soldiers employed as linguists who even spoke Creole. U.S. policy regarding Constant and Cédras was murky at best, but the main result of the intervention was to overthrow a particularly bloody regime and replace it with a democratically elected one. Overall, Operation Restore Democracy was a remarkably selfless and reluctant use of American power. The only person in Washington, DC to advocate a U.S. invasion of Haiti to further his own political and financial goals was Aristide himself.

A beloved figure of Haitian folk tales is Ti Malice ("Little Cheat"), a poor but cunning individual who regularly outsmarts his slow-witted Uncle Bouki; the tales often serve as a metaphor for Haiti's relationship with its powerful partners, including Uncle Sam. In 1991–1994, Cédras and Aristide could both proudly say that they had outsmarted and outmaneuvered the United States. The former defied the United States for three years and emerged from the confrontation with one million dollars worth of kickbacks. The latter convinced Bill Clinton to dedicate twenty thousand troops and two billion dollars to an intervention opposed by a majority of his constituents. Aristide's single-minded perseverance finally paid off, but it came at a price. Haiti, a country already suffering from extreme poverty, a brain drain, and a notorious reputation abroad endured three long years of embargo, emigration, and political violence that only added to its existing woes. Cédras's and Aristide's diplomatic feats were yet another example of Haitian politicians using their political genius to serve their own career rather than their own people.

Optimists could point in 1994 to the international community's unprecedented commitment to Haiti's democratic transition. The United States and its allies pledged billions of dollars and thousands of troops for an occupation that ultimately lasted seven years. Other Third World countries could only look in envy as donors lavished such attention on a small country of eight million people, which had already received more than its share of aid in previous years with little to show for it. Haiti was full of promise; migration patterns were even reversed as thousands of Haitian exiles returned home. If the country was ever to recover from its centuries-long decline into misery, 1994 seemed to be the year when it could happen. The sole ominous sign was Aristide's refusal to endorse the military occupation and the economic package in writing. One could not help but think that he already knew that Operation Restore Democracy would fall short of its ambitious goals and that he would soon have to indict foreign countries for selflessly bringing him back to the presidential palace.

CHAPTER 9

Gratitude Is the Heart's (Short-Term) Memory: The Second Aristide Presidency (October 1994–February 1996)

Aristide's Return (October 15, 1994)

On October 15, a few days after Cédras left for exile in Panama, Aristide, his entourage, and a host of U.S. officials boarded three planes at Andrews Air Force Base and took off for Port-au-Prince (figure 9.1). The flight was a joyous one. Aristide had not seen Haiti for 1,111 days; he was about to become the first president in Haitian history to be ousted and then restored to power. Aristide was technically serving the remainder of the five-year presidential term he had begun in 1991, but the hiatus had been so long and the post-1994 environment was so different that his return amounted in practice to a second presidency. In Port-au-Prince, the mood was delirious. Aristide's popularity was higher than ever despite years of embargo and repression. His supporters picked up the mounds of garbage lining the streets, swept the dust away, and covered the dilapidated presidential palace with a fresh coat of paint. Murals—Haitians' favorite form of political commentary—proudly showed an Aristide-headed rooster sitting on an egg. In Haiti's colorful political imagery, the egg-and-rooster metaphor was an oblique reference to the rooster symbol that had been Aristide's in the 1990 elections and to the proverb "a laid egg cannot be placed back in the hen" that Cédras liked to quote to explain that Aristide's overthrow was irrevocable.

Figure 9.1 October 15, 1994: The U.S. invasion allows Jean-Bertrand Aristide to return to Haiti.

Aristide was met by throngs of adoring supporters upon landing at the airport, but two things must have caught his eye during the brief helicopter hop to the presidential palace. First, the slums bordering on the main runway were more ramshackle than ever; he would have to feed the hungry multitude or divert their anger at some other political entity. Second, all the main strategic assets, including the airport, the palace, and the helicopter he traveled in, were in the hands of U.S. and foreign troops; he would have to preserve his own political independence while securing donor nations' financial and military support. The situation called for careful political maneuvering. Luckily, Aristide had learned a lot from the mistakes he had made in 1991.

Aristide remained remarkably quiet during the days that followed his return to Haiti. His silence was due in part to his strategy of not associating himself too closely with the United States in the eyes of Haitian patriots, but he was also genuinely furious that Clinton had called off the night assault and let Cédras slip out of Haiti unscathed. Because of the last-minute twist, U.S. soldiers and Aristide's supporters never got a chance to crush the Haitian army and its paramilitary stooges. Aristide would have to deal with them on his own. Another bothersome neighbor was Prime Minister Smarck Michel (November 1994–October 1995), a neoliberal businessman Aristide had appointed to please his foreign backers but who did not share his leftist economic views. In the long run, foreign troops were the last rivals Aristide would have to sideline. The United States might have intervened on Aristide's behalf in 1994, but he was convinced that the United States had overthrown him in 1991. In his view, the two were now even. Gratitude was not the order of the day.

Who Will Control the Police and the Army?
(October 1994–April 1995)

Aristide finally got down to work. The first objective was to eliminate or control rival centers of power, in particular the remnants of the seven-thousand-strong Haitian army that had served Cédras during Aristide's exile and had been preserved under the Carter–Jonassaint agreement. This was an arduous task, for the United States supported counter powers with the hope that they would limit Aristide's authoritarian tendencies.

Following Constant's and Cédras's demise, the United States created the Interim Public Security Force or IPSF, a temporary force designed to police Haiti while a more lasting national police was trained. Who joined the IPSF immediately became a contentious issue. The United States advocated hiring Haitian army soldiers, who had accumulated law enforcement experience during the junta years and who could be counted on to check Aristide. Aristide opposed the U.S. plan for precisely the same reasons and advocated hiring lower-class Haitians who were not tainted by their association with the Cédras junta and were more likely to support him. The United States won this first round. Half of all Haitian soldiers found a spot in the IPSF after undergoing a perfunctory one-week refresher course on human rights. Aristide merely obtained that those soldiers most notorious for committing human rights violations under Cédras be vetted out from the IPSF and that nine hundred Guantánamo refugees be employed as unarmed IPSF auxiliaries.

The composition and training of the permanent *Police Nationale d'Haïti* (Haitian National Police or HNP) were equally contentious. The United States insisted on a U.S.-trained police force that drew heavily from the Haitian army, but Aristide obtained significant concessions this time. Only fifteen hundred of five thousand policemen were Haitian army veterans. The second half of their four-month training took place inside Haiti, doubtless because of Aristide's concerns that a long stay in the United States would result in CIA contacts (all three members of the deposed junta had trained in the United States during the 1970s and

1980s). The first class of cadets started training in February 1995. Their deployment began the following July, and the IPSF was completely phased out by December 1995.

What to do with the remaining members of the Haitian army was the last outstanding question. Ever the philanthropists, Cédras and other top officers had taken away their men's retirement and health care trust funds upon leaving Haiti, resulting in understandable discontent among the rank-and-file and a brief mutiny that cost four soldiers their lives in December 1994. The United States, which had created the ancestor of the Haitian army during the first U.S. occupation in 1915, was opposed to disbanding the army and argued that disgruntled soldiers might form the nucleus of an underground military opposition. U.S. officials thus suggested that a small, nonpolitical army should remain and that demobilized soldiers should be offered vocational training to facilitate their return to civilian life. Aristide imposed his own views this time. He attributed all army barracks to the new police, refused to pay soldiers their salaries, fired all senior officers, and finally disbanded the entire army in April 1995, save for one unit that was unlikely to unseat Aristide: the presidential band. Aristide, still angry that the September 19, nighttime assault on Cédras's army had been called off, had finally obtained vindication for the 1991 coup d'état. Haiti, once feared as a military power, no longer had any army.

Restoring Haitian "Democracy" (March–October 1995)

By early 1995, all the prominent men associated with the junta, including Cédras, François, Biamby, and Constant, were in exile. Those who stayed in Haiti were the regime's lower-level soldiers, executioners, and bourgeois financiers. Aristide publicly made assurances that they would be treated well. In stark contrast with his loud calls for revenge in 1991, he promised that he would fight for "justice," not "vengeance" and created a truth and justice commission to investigate political crimes in an even-handed manner.[1] Aristide's opponents had learned to take his promises with a grain of salt, however, and rumors soon swirled that he had created a death squad that systematically executed political enemies. Accusations were numerous and poorly substantiated. The best-documented case was that of Mireille Durocher-Bertin.

Durocher-Bertin was an outspoken lawyer and Cédras supporter whose main claim to fame was that she had sued Aristide for high treason after he called for a U.S. invasion in June 1994. She remained in Haiti after Aristide's return and, in the spring of 1995, one Haitian interpreter working for the U.S. occupation force alerted his employers that he had learned of a plot to assassinate Durocher-Bertin. Acting on the tip, U.S. troops arrested the suspected hit man and his accomplices near Durocher-Bertin's house. After their arrest, the men confessed to having been hired by Aristide's minister of the interior Mondésir Beaubrun (the car they were driving when they were arrested indeed belonged to the ministry). Gen. George A. Fisher, the new head of the multinational force, told Aristide and his justice minister to notify Durocher-Bertin of the mortal danger she faced. They never did. A few weeks later, on March 28, 1995, Durocher-Bertin was gunned down in her car as she drove through Port-au-Prince.

FBI agents were immediately sent to Haiti to assist their Haitian counterparts working on the case, but they made little headway. The FBI complained that Aristide systematically obstructed their attempts to interview witnesses without governmental interference. Aristide countered that the Haitian police was still in gestation and could not devote resources to the case, and that his opposition to a full FBI enquiry merely stemmed from sovereignty concerns. After six months of mutual recriminations, the FBI agents left. Smelling blood, the Republican-controlled Congress launched a thorough investigation and accused Aristide of condoning Durocher-Bertin's murder, then conspiring to cover up his implication by hindering the FBI investigation. Aristide blamed the murder on some apolitical, drug-related dispute; his supporters within the Clinton administration, even though they had doubts about his version of events, were unwilling to provide ammunition to their Republican critics. Durocher-Bertin's murder was never elucidated and cast the first shadow on the U.S.-Haitian *entente cordiale*.

While the controversy over the Durocher-Bertin murder raged in Washington, DC, one of the main concerns of the occupation authorities was to elect a new parliament. The process was marred by numerous technical and political difficulties due to the fact that Haiti did not have the means to organize a free and fair election on its own, and that Haitians displayed little interest in the legislative elections anyway. The 1987 constitution had put extensive powers into the hands of the prime minister, who supposedly ruled with the support of parliament, but Haiti had a strong presidential tradition and voters considered the election of deputies to be irrelevant. Aristide, who would lose out if a strong parliament and prime minister emerged, did little to encourage his people to abandon their cult of presidential power. As a result, the elections were largely a foreign affair. Foreign donors paid for all the voting material, international monitors provided the expertise, and, after a seven-month delay, two rounds were held in June and October 1995.

Despite a low turnout, the elections saw the victory of candidates from Aristide's *Lavalas* party. More popular and powerful than ever, Aristide could have used the elections as a political mandate to launch an ambitious program of economic reforms. But little of substance emerged except for further tariff reductions.

Free Trade and the Agricultural Sector

Trade policy was one of the few areas of agreement between Aristide and his foreign backers. The United States was a determined sponsor of free trade under Bill Clinton, particularly in Latin America. Building on the successful ratification of NAFTA, Clinton convened thirty-four Latin American statesmen (including Aristide) at the December 1994 Summit of the Americas in Miami, where they agreed to create a free trade zone for the entire Western Hemisphere (the project subsequently slowed down, but Clinton signed the U.S.-Caribbean Basin Trade Partnership Act in May 2000).

Aristide also advocated free trade because he associated high tariffs with the import licenses of the Bébé Doc era, which had enriched Duvalierist supporters while raising food prices for the rest of the population. In 1994–1995, Aristide thus virtually eliminated the already low tariffs that had been set after the fall of Bébé Doc. Tariffs now averaged 8 percent. Many goods, foodstuffs in particular, entered the country tax-free. Aristide's tariff reductions were popular among Haiti's core constituency—slum dwellers living off imported food—but their overall impact was devastating in the provinces.

Foreign competition was most acute in the agricultural sector. Because of antiquated farming practices, soil erosion, and lack of land, the prices of most crops produced by Haitian peasants exceeded world prices (coffee and cocoa beans were the exception). Haitian rice, in particular, could not compete with its U.S. equivalent, which benefited from efficient use of fertilizers and machinery and generous farming subsidies. The 1996 *Freedom to Farm Act* promised to phase away all U.S. subsidies (including those for rice) within seven years, but it was quickly abandoned and replaced with even more generous farming bills. The combination of high-priced Haitian crops, low tariff barriers, and cheap foreign imports worsened the existing crisis in the Haitian agricultural sector. Few Haitians bought local rice when they could obtain cheaper U.S. rice, or even free rice offered by foreign charities.

Modern economists, starting with David Ricardo in his *Principles of Political Economy and Taxation* (1817), have defended free trade on the grounds that foreign competition forces domestic manufacturers to lower their prices, thus benefiting local consumers. It also encourages national economies to focus on the products they produce most efficiently (economists speak of "comparative advantage") and to import the rest. Free trade policies have indeed fostered higher growth and lower prices in many countries, but they proved completely inadequate in Haiti. Under prevailing economic theories, Haitians should have shifted their focus from the inefficient, overcrowded agricultural sector to a sector in which they enjoyed a significant cost advantage, namely, assembling simple products with cheap unskilled labor. The recommendation ignored the fact that the Haitian assembly sector suffered from an adverse political environment, not from a dearth of laborers. The sector, which employed eighty thousand workers at its peak in the 1980s, had been wiped out by the three-year embargo. Political instability, insecurity, nationalistic laws, and corrupt politicians and judges kept foreigners at bay even after Aristide was restored to power. Recovery was thus slow and incomplete. Only twenty thousand workers regained their jobs. Haitian rice farmers thus lost their livelihood, fled to the big city slums, and found no jobs waiting for them. The tenets of David Ricardo, like those of John Locke and Adam Smith, found the Haitian climate to be rather inhospitable.

Restaveks: Child Slaves of Haiti

The *restaveks*—undoubtedly the most troubling feature of contemporary Haitian society—were a collateral casualty of Aristide's misguided trade policy. The Creole word *restavek*, derived from the French verb *reste avec* ("stays with"), referred to young rural Haitians placed in urban families. Variously described as household servants or distant relatives, the *restavek* should really have been referred to for what they were: the child slaves of Haiti.

Child slavery went back a long way in Haiti. During French colonial times, children of female slaves were legally enslaved at birth and were assigned light menial tasks until they were strong enough for field duty. Slavery was abolished in 1793, then again in 1804, but the habit of employing children as household servants endured. Katherine Dunham, an American who visited Haiti in the 1930s to study Haitian Voodoo and dance, was intrigued by those she called the *ti moun* (little children).

I had seen women coming to town from the hills and plains with small children who might not return to the hills and plains with them. There were child servants at the hotel, usually kept in the back quarters, but doing their share of sweeping and cleaning and scrubbing. There were these *ti moun* in all urban Haitian homes, a regular part of Haitian social structure. But I had not realized or my conscience was not stirred enough to admit that these child servants should be in some institution of learning, have shoes, clothes rather than the rags one usually saw them wear, and their labor have some recompense. . . . The parent bringing the child to town might be given a few *gourdes* or a silk kerchief as a token payment, and the parent would return to the country hoping for shoes, sufficient food and clothing, medical care, and eventually schooling for the child.[2]

Dunham credited President Dumarsais Estimé (who also happened to be her lover) with fighting against this institution in the late 1940s, but she admitted that it did not completely disappear. In the 1980s, during his years as priest of the poor, Aristide also took up the cause of homeless children and created the shelter *Lafanmi Selavi* (Family is Life) for orphans and former *restaveks*. Haiti passed laws specifying that household servants had to be at least twelve years old, properly fed and taken care of, and monitored by social services. Alas, such laws were as routinely ignored as the *Code Noir* was in colonial times. The worsening condition of the peasantry in the wake of tariff reductions and rural overpopulation only reinforced the *restavek* system. Various estimates put the total *restavek* population at one hundred thousand to three hundred thousand in the mid-1990s.

The *restavek* system was built on an otherwise commendable tradition of Haitian hospitality. When parents experience financial difficulties, it is common in the Caribbean for distant relatives to host their children, often for years, and to raise them as their own. Poor peasants of rural Haiti thus considered it normal to give away one of their children (usually a girl) to a wealthier family living in Port-au-Prince, Cap Haïtien, or another large town. Parents hoped that growing up in a more affluent family and in a big city environment would give their child educational opportunities unavailable in the provinces (a gift of money also softened the deal).

The child's actual future, however, rarely lived up to the parents' hopes. The primary role of the *restavek* was menial, not educational. Even then, the system was more closely related to servitude than to normal household service. Children were expected to mop, cook, and take care of children. Hours were long; work started before daytime to give the *restavek* time to prepare breakfast for the family. In addition, young girls were often expected to satisfy the lust of the young men of the household. Wages were a rarity; the host families considered food and lodging to be sufficient compensation, but even these they skimped on. A piece of cardboard or a mat thrown on the living room floor doubled as a bed; meals were composed of leftovers; clothing, if any, consisted of rags and hand-me-downs. Discipline was strict, and unsatisfactory performance was punished by verbal and physical abuse. A few *restaveks* attended school on a part-time basis, but this was far from being the norm. *Restaveks* were ostracized by other children and often stayed at home. Jean-Robert Cadet, a Haitian American and former *restavek*, writes that

> other children taunt [*restaveks*] with the term because they are often seen in the streets running errands barefoot and dressed in rags. *Restavek* are treated worse than slaves, because they don't cost anything and their supply seems inexhaustible. . . . As a *restavek*, I could not interact with Florence [his host mother] on a personal level; I could not talk to her about my needs. In fact, I could not speak until spoken to, except to give her messages third parties had left with me. I also did not dare smile or laugh in her presence, as this would have been considered disrespectful— I was not her son but her *restavek*.[3]

Cadet was actually lucky. He was the illegitimate child of a white father who placed him in host families to save himself the embarrassment of caring for his mixed race offspring. Cadet's light skin and his father's occasional help thus protected him from the worst abuses and eventually allowed him to immigrate to the United States, where he was manumitted. Few *restaveks* had that chance. More typically, when the *restaveks* finally got old enough to fight back, or when they became pregnant, they were kicked out of their adopted home and joined the cohorts of orphaned children who roamed the streets of Port-au-Prince. Isolated, uneducated, psychologically battered, and malnourished, they faced an uncertain future.

This institution was undoubtedly repellent from a moral point of view, but one could not help but wonder what the human and economic costs were as well. *Restaveks* were ostracized by the community they lived in and had limited contacts with anyone but their very owners. Raised by masters who also acted as surrogate parents, they developed a complex love–hate relationship with people who were both providers and abusers. The psychological scars from such a traumatic childhood—difficulty to interact with strangers, inability to distinguish normal behavior from sadism—were lifelong. The *restaveks* also provided a service whose economic value was limited; their masters could easily have washed their own clothes and scrubbed their own floor. Meanwhile, the *restaveks* did not perform the duties expected of children in most societies: go to school, learn valuable skills, and become a productive citizen. The *restavek* system created generation after generation of uneducated, mentally disturbed children who then became a weight on society when they could have succeeded admirably if given a chance. In a way, Haitians were right to claim that their country suffered from the economic legacy of slavery—but the main culprit was contemporary child slavery, not its colonial ancestor abolished in 1793.

A scathing 1995 UNICEF report and Cadet's 1998 autobiography increased awareness about the *restavek* system in the United States. Abolishing the system, however, was a thorny issue. Many Haitian children, *restaveks* or not, were hungry; physical punishment was a widely accepted educational tool; poor children routinely worked at a young age to supplement their family's meager income; thousands of children orphaned by the AIDS scourge had to rely on foster families' charity for survival. Because *restaveks* were not legally enslaved the way their colonial ancestors were, distinguishing them from the legions of battered, hungry Haitian slum children was an arduous task. Many Haitians even disputed the fact that unpaid child labor was a form of slavery, insisting that the exploitation was temporary and that the *restavek* had few alternatives anyway.

This attitude was typical of the Haitian habit of emphasizing age-old forms of foreign oppression (such as colonial slavery) while ignoring much more recent institutions (such as the *restavek* system) for which they, not foreigners, were responsible. The *restaveks* were unpaid, overworked, raped, beaten, uneducated, bought and sold, and generally compelled to provide free labor under the threat of physical punishment. Under any definition of the term, they were slaves. Two centuries after Dessalines' victory over the French, Haiti was still home to hundreds of thousands of slaves. What was even more troubling was that Aristide, who had dedicated himself to the cause of the *restaveks* as a political opponent in the 1980s, did little to address the issue as a president in the 1990s. He denounced the institution in his speeches, ignored it in practice, and focused his attention on the all-consuming struggle for political power—first the police and the army, then the legislative elections, and now sovereignty concerns over the foreign occupation.

Aristide: Born Again Nationalist
(October 1995–November 1995)

By the fall of 1995, the initial honeymoon period that followed the invasion was starting to dissolve (figure 9.2). Nationalist resentment at the

Figure 9.2 The pro-American demonstrations that followed the 1994 U.S. invasion proved short-lived.

presence of foreign troops on Haitian soil and disappointment that foreign aid had not immediately boosted the income of average Haitians combined to spark the first displays of xenophobia. On September 19, 1995, Haitians marked the one-year anniversary of the U.S. invasion by demonstrating against the foreign occupation and foreign demands that Haiti privatize its public companies. When Vice President Al Gore and his wife Tipper traveled to Haiti on October 15 to celebrate the first anniversary of Aristide's return from exile, Tipper's car was pelted with rocks to the sound of "go home Yankees."[4] Aristide got the message; he replaced Prime Minister Michel with the more leftist Claudette Werleigh (October 1995–February 1996), asserted that the privatization plans he had agreed to during his exile were not binding, and declared on television that anyone who dared privatize state property would be "arrested immediately."[5]

The next big crisis erupted in November 1995, when a deputy and Aristide friend named Jean-Hubert Feuillé was shot dead by unknown aggressors. The prevailing conspiracy theory held that former president Prosper Avril had ordered Feuillé killed, that the CIA had known ahead of time of the murder, had done nothing to stop it, and had acted to protect the most likely suspect instead. Avril fled to the Colombian embassy and exile. Because of Feuille's high profile, a large crowd attended his funeral at Port-au-Prince's beautiful National Cathedral. Aristide intended to use his eulogy to direct Haitians' anger at the foreign community, but hesitated to do so overtly for fear that the foreign diplomats attending the ceremony would take offense and cut off foreign aid. Aristide thus resorted to multilingual deception. Constantly switching from French to Creole, he reassured his foreign friends—in French—that "the month of November 1995 must be a month of peace, a month of success. . . . Gratitude is the heart's memory, we said more than once. We are grateful to our friends, to those who helped us restore democracy in Haiti." Foreigners might have concluded that the Creole sections they could not comprehend were merely translations of Aristide's suave comments, but this was far from being the case. "Freedom or death!" he chanted six times in a powerful reminder of Dessalines' revolutionary motto.

> I ask the Haitian people to do the following: do not sit by idly, do not wait; accompany the policemen when they are going to enter the homes of the people who have heavy weapons, do not be afraid of them. When you do that, tell the policemen not to go only to the poor neighborhoods, but to go to the neighborhoods where there are big houses and heavy weapons. . . . [applause]
>
> I am reminding you that until further notice there are not two or three heads of state, but just one. [applause] The head of state has spoken. . . . [applause] I order you to arrest anyone who wants to block this legal, total, and complete disarmament operation if he is a Haitian. [applause] If he is not a Haitian [applause], if he is not Haitian [applause], if he is not Haitian, we will send him back to his country. [applause]

Aristide's French-speaking donors were thoroughly pleased by his calls for reconciliation. His Creole-speaking supporters, however, were spurred by his calls to carry out vigilante operations against the upper class. They spread through the streets and looked for political enemies likely to attack other *Lavalas* deputies. Ten people died in a 1995 repeat of Haiti's 1986 and 1991 *dechoukaj*.

Unfortunately for Aristide, his victorious twelve-month battle to impose his authority over the police and domestic and foreign rivals was for naught. His five-year term, which had begun with his December 1990 election and February 1991 inauguration, was almost due to expire. The 1987 election banned all attempts at reelection; a president could only serve two, nonconsecutive terms. Aristide could not run. He had promised that he would step down on schedule during his Washington exile, but started having second thoughts upon returning to

Haiti. Pro-Aristide demonstrators circulated demands that the three-year period of exile not count as a part of the five-year term and that the presidential election be postponed until December 1998. Aristide approved of their attitude in his usual roundabout rhetoric. "I must acknowledge what you request, listen to what you request, and understand it," he told a crowd imploring him for three more years. "I have seen, I have heard, and I have understood."[6]

The United States pressured Aristide not to follow through on his reelection plans. A mere one year after a controversial intervention to democratize Haiti, the president could hardly extend the length of his term unilaterally. Aristide eventually backed down. One month before the presidential election, he told his supporters that he would not run and that they should vote for his former prime minister and friend René Préval instead. Voters dutifully elected Préval in an 88 percent landslide that left the other thirteen candidates far behind in the total tally. No one could predict, however, how Aristide and his increasingly restless supporters would react to a non-Aristidian presidency backed by foreign troops. The risk that Aristide would act in the shadows to undermine his friend's tenure in office and that Haitian politics would return to their time-honored state of chaos was like a Damocles sword hanging over Préval's head.

The last development of the transition period came as a bad surprise to the Haitian poor. On January 20, 1996, a few days before leaving office, Aristide married his former lawyer and lobbyist Mildred Trouillot in a private ceremony held in his residence at Tabarre. Aristide went out of his way to avoid parallels with Bébé Doc's disastrous nuptial extravaganza with Michèle Bennett, even skipping the wedding cake as a sign of frugality, but his supporters were upset. Aristide was liked because he was saintly, black, patriotic, and honest. By renouncing priesthood and marrying a mulatto Haitian American he had employed with public monies, he betrayed all four principles at the heart of his popular appeal. For the first time, the poor had doubts about their beloved Titid.

Conclusion: The Welfare State

Aristide's return to power was reminiscent of the 1970s, when Bébé Doc's short-lived international popularity sparked a massive upsurge of foreign aid. Learning from their past mistakes, aid agencies made use of local channels to circumvent official fraud and favored training programs over outright donations to reduce dependency. These changes aside, foreign aid resumed its customary spot as a pillar of the Haitian economy. Major donors gave Haiti no less than $625 million in the 1994–1995 fiscal year alone, to which must be added money spent by occupation troops in Haiti, aid distributed by nongovernmental organizations, and workers' remittances sent by the Haitian Diaspora. Aid thus represented the most significant portion of the total Haitian GDP, which the World Bank estimated at about $2.5 billion in the mid-1990s (the size of the informal sector made it difficult to obtain more precise economic statistics; the GDP was slightly larger when taking into account purchasing power parity). Aristide rarely mentioned the size of foreign donations to Haiti in his books, preferring to remind his readers of the gold allegedly stolen by Spanish, French, and American imperialists decades and centuries before.

Foreigners also took over duties normally considered to be a state's most basic ones. International monitors held elections. Former New York City police commissioner Raymond W. Kelly trained Haitian police cadets. Foreign troops defended the country now that the Haitian army was extinct. Financial difficulties virtually destroyed the public school system; instead, those students who could afford it attended foreign-funded parochial schools and local private schools. The Inter-American Development Bank even found the need to create a $1.2 million program to instruct the Haitian Ministry of Cooperation on proper ways to ask for and manage foreign aid!

Aristide's resort to xenophobic populism was particularly damning in this context. Not only did he spend the end of his presidential term fighting subterranean battles for political control at the expense of more urgent problems such as the *restavek* plague, hunger, law and order, judicial reform, and AIDS, but he publicly attacked the very countries that had brought him back to power and then bankrolled his government. "Gratitude is the heart's memory," an expression Aristide used in his Feuillé eulogy, was apparently little more than bold balderdash intended for foreign consumption. "Gratefulness is a form of cowardice," one of Papa Doc's favorite proverbs, would have more aptly described Aristide's attitude toward the international community.

CHAPTER 10

Divide and Founder: The Préval Presidency (1996–2001)

Préval's Inauguration (February 1996)

René Préval's inauguration on February 7, 1996 was a historic event. Haiti had known a few peaceful transfers of power in the twentieth century—the last one in 1971 when Bébé Doc replaced Papa Doc—but 1996 marked the first transition from one democratically elected president to another in Haitian history. The new president was a fifty-three-year-old man of high ideals and education. Préval had lived in Belgium and in the United States after his family left Haiti to flee Papa Doc's repressive rule; there, he had learned perfect French and English in addition to his native Creole; he then came back to Haiti in the 1980s to open a bakery business. Contrary to many other Haitians of affluent birth, he was also a compassionate man who helped Aristide run the *Lafanmi Selavi* shelters. An agronomist by training, he promised to modernize the agricultural sector that employed a majority of Haitians but was traditionally neglected by the oligarchy of Port-au-Prince. He had extensive government experience, having served as Aristide's prime minister in 1991, then as his confident during their years in exile, before heading the patronage machine that rewarded loyal Aristide supporters with jobs. His close association with Aristide earned him the nickname of *marassa* after the twin brothers of the Voodoo pantheon and prompted Haitian voters to grant him an electoral majority greater even than that of Aristide in 1990.

One cloud that marred the inauguration was growing international impatience with the slow pace of economic reforms in Haiti. Aristide had agreed to an ambitious program of privatizations in 1994 but had refused to implement it after his return from exile. Donors were irritated by the delays and warned that aid levels would be reduced unless Préval honored his predecessor's pledge. The United States withdrew most of its troops in 1996, keeping only a small humanitarian operation that renovated schools and provided free health care until their departure in 2000 (non-U.S. peacekeepers remained under a series of UN mandates).

Préval's most serious weakness was that he was not Aristide. The Haitian poor professed a love for Aristide that was as passionate as it was exclusive. They were willing to vote for all candidates running with the *Lavalas* label, Préval included, but their only allegiance was to Aristide himself. Only two hundred people bothered to attend Préval's inauguration, two months after a presidential election in which two-thirds of the eligible voters had opted to stay home. There had been more guests at Aristide's private wedding two weeks before the inauguration. Those who came applauded the outgoing Aristide noticeably louder than they applauded the incoming Préval, and they made a point of chanting slogans asking Aristide to run again in 2000.

In theory, Aristide could use his popularity to bolster Préval's and to facilitate the passage of unpopular economic reforms required by foreign aid donors. Alternatively, he could undermine the new president's authority in order to come back as a savior five years later. A few signs indicated that the latter option was more likely. Hours before leaving office, Aristide reestablished diplomatic relations with Communist Cuba, a move sure to result in American ill will. He later confided to a French weekly that Préval was "closer to zero than to mediocre."[1] The incident was the first sign that internecine battles had resumed within the Port-au-Prince ruling class. During the remainder of Préval's mandate, political rivalries would wreck Haiti's transition to democracy and the Haitian people, as always, would pay the price for their leaders' fractiousness.

The Privatization Controversy (March 1996–April 1997)

Préval appointed a fellow agronomist named Rosny Smarth as prime minister on February 16, 1996. Under the 1987 constitution, Smarth could only push a legislative agenda if he enjoyed the support of deputies and senators, 80 percent of whom were members of the *Lavalas* party and shared Aristide's distrust for neoliberal economic reform and foreign interference. Conflicts between a moderate president and prime minister trying to assuage foreign donors and the more radical *Lavalas* base controlling the parliament were the dominant subtext of the early Préval presidency.

Smarth's first project was the privatization of Haiti's nine main state companies, or parastatals, which Aristide had delayed after his return from exile. These companies controlled such key businesses as the telephone company, power plants, flourmills, cement factories, ports, and airports. They were poorly run and provided bad service at high rates. Reforming them was a necessity if Haiti was to experience its long-awaited economic boom. The capital's port, for example, was infamous for exorbitant port fees that made shipping a container from New York to Port-au-Prince costlier than shipping it to Buenos Aires in distant Argentina. But public companies also provided thousands of sinecures and had enabled Aristide to reward loyal backers with well-paid jobs requiring minimal work when he was president.

Aristide thus refused to support Préval in his battle for privatization, preferring to reestablish his reputation as a virtuous liberal firebrand instead. He founded the Aristide Foundation for Democracy with the goal of creating a radio for children and a cooperative bank. The bank was a positive step, for Haiti's poor frequently resort to loan sharks who demand double-digit interests for a one-month loan. Aristide's continued role at the head of the *Lafanmi Selavi* homeless shelter was more shadowy. He obtained that a $20 million Taiwanese grant intended for road repairs be managed and disbursed through the shelter, but by late 1996 the trust fund carried a mere $7 million balance and not a single road project was yet underway. It was impossible to know where the money went, for Aristide did not publish a list of his personal assets upon leaving the presidential palace as was required under Haitian law. The popular priest of Haiti's poor was no longer a priest nor poor. He also took on a new role as a priest-turned-president-turned-father when his first daughter was born in the fall of 1996.

Foreign demands that companies be privatized prompted aid delays that resulted in acute budgetary shortages. By the summer of 1996, public employees complained that they were owed months of salary arrears. Préval refused to follow Aristide's policy of printing more money and insisted that salaries be disbursed only after parliament acted on a privatization bill. Deputies finally yielded in September 1996 and, the following month, the International Monetary Fund (IMF) granted Haiti a low-interest $130 million loan (after further delays, the flourmill was sold in 1997, followed by the cement factory in 1999; other companies remained in state hands).

The privatization law brought Aristide back in the political spotlight. He cleverly remained silent about the presidential corruption that plagued the companies, preferring instead to frame the debate as a battle to defend Haitian sovereignty. Foreign countries, he argued, were imperialists for insisting that privatization proceed before further aid was disbursed, and Préval was a puny puppet for yielding to their demands. In November 1996, Aristide created the *Lafanmi Lavalas* (Flood Family) movement. The movement was initially described as apolitical, but Aristide formally registered *Lafanmi Lavalas* as an opposition political party in January 1997. His rupture with his old friend Préval was now official.

The Political Crisis (April 1997–October 1997)

Political passions soon shifted from the privatization debate to April 1997 elections held to fill vacant house seats, replace one-third of the senate, and elect numerous local officeholders. Préval supported candidates from Aristide's old party, the *Organisation Politique Lavalas* (now renamed *Organisation du Peuple en Lutte*), while Aristide pushed his new *Lafanmi Lavalas*. The privatization controversy aside, ideological divides were hard to pin down, for three of Préval's own ministers and long-time allies defected, while Aristide oddly recruited some former Haitian army officers as his candidates. More than fifty political murders took place during the weeks that preceded the elections, creating a climate of uncertainty that did nothing to reassure potential investors. Rivaling factions boycotted parliamentary sessions and essential laws failed to be passed for lack of a quorum, resulting in yet another drop in foreign aid.

Probably puzzled by this Byzantine struggle for power, 90 percent of eligible voters stayed home when the elections were held on April 4, 1997. The final tally of the few votes cast showed that Aristide's *Lafanmi Lavalas* had gained a majority in the senate, but Préval's followers kept their control of the chamber of deputies and accused their opponents of electoral fraud. The parliament was now divided in two irreconcilable factions, each of which claimed to represent the Haitian people. Doubts about the fairness and decisiveness of the electoral process pushed political debates to the streets. Aristide fanned the fires, boasting that Haiti was not "indebted to imperialism" and should stand up to foreign demands to sell off public assets.[2] Aristide-engineered strikes convinced Prime Minister Rosny Smarth that he would never be able to carry out his privatization agenda. He resigned on June 9, 1997.

Préval asked Smarth to remain at the head of a caretaker government while waiting for his successor to be named. The procedure is standard in parliamentary systems, where it facilitates everyday business during the few days it takes to form a new cabinet. But the crisis was anything but usual; the days turned into weeks, and then into months. A flurry of candidates declared themselves for the prime ministership, including university rector Hervé Denis, former prime minister Smarck Michel, former minister of agriculture Gerard Mathurin, and former ambassador to the United Nations Jean Casimir. The *Lavalas* splinter groups controlling the two houses of parliament refused to come to terms despite the devastating consequences of this long period of anarchy. No consensual candidate emerged. Smarth finally left office in October 1997. Haiti no longer had a government.

The Economic Crisis (1997–1999)

Aristide's ungrateful attitude and his successful maneuvering to delay economic reforms reduced foreign donors' enthusiasm for Haiti. Many donor nations, aghast at the endless flow of bad news streaming out of Port-au-Prince, were intent on abandoning a nation-building project they thought would likely fail. The political crisis of 1997 provided them with an excuse to do so. The fractious parliament that emerged from the April 1997 election did not vote on a budget for two years in a row. Smarth's resignation and Préval's subsequent failure to find a replacement acceptable to the different *Lavalas* factions left Haiti without a functioning government for a full fifteen months. With nobody to give money to, donor nations simply put their aid on hold. The results were catastrophic. The foreign community had pledged over $3 billion for the 1994–1997 period. Part of that aid was cancelled because of the privatization controversy, but disbursements still totaled a substantial $1.5 billion over a three-year period. The asinine *Lavalas* split of 1997 and the subsequent aid freeze of 1997–1999 thus cost the comatose Haitian economy half-a-billion dollars a year of effortless income, or 20 percent of the country's annual income.

The main indicator of economic wealth in a country is the annual growth rate of the Gross Domestic Product (GDP), which indicates how many more goods and services a country produced than it did the previous year. A 2–3 percent annual growth rate is considered healthy in rich countries, though GDP growth must equal at least 2 percent per year in poor countries such as Haiti just to keep up with rapid population growth (in such countries, it is thus better to measure GDP growth *per capita*). More comprehensive development statistics such as the United Nations' Human Development Index (HDI) include life expectancy, literacy rates, access to health resources, and income distribution in addition to national wealth. By the late 1990s, all these statistical indices—GDP growth, GDP *per capita*, and HDI—showed that Haiti was mired in a poverty that billions of dollars of aid had failed to alleviate. From 1985 to 1995, Haiti's GDP *per capita* fell an average of 5 percent a year; the GDP grew a mere 2–3 percent a year from 1995 to 1999 despite multibillion dollar aid pledges. Haiti's HDI had ranked 137th worldwide in 1990; it sank to the 150th rank in 1998. By that date, Haitians had a life expectancy of fifty-seven and a literacy rate below 50 percent. Three-quarters of the population had no access to vaccines or potable water. A full 80 percent of the nation lived in poverty. Haiti was, by far, the poorest nation in the Western Hemisphere.

Under the development model agreed upon before the intervention, foreign aid should have been gradually phased out as foreign investors seized the economic opportunities created by Aristide's return. But the hoped-for flood of French and American businessmen never took place; the *Lavalas* flood of political ambitions took its place. Aristidian talk of economic imperialism notwithstanding, foreign investments in Haiti remained virtually nonexistent. Many members of the Diaspora who had returned to Haiti in 1994 complained of insecurity, chauvinism, and corruption and left again. The blanket ban on foreign ownership established under Dessalines' 1805 constitution had disappeared during the first U.S. occupation of Haiti, but Art. 55 and 55-2 of the 1987 constitution still prevented foreigners from purchasing a lot larger than 1.29 hectare in urban areas and 6.45 hectares in rural areas. A law stipulated that no foreigner could own land near the Dominican border because of national security concerns, even though Haiti did not have an army to guard this very border. The bans were symbolic of a general hostility toward outsiders, rich ones in particular. Foreign investors complained that Haitian judges typically ruled against foreigners on the grounds that the *blan* (white foreigner) had money while his Haitian opponent did not. Misguided economic nationalism, already the basis for Dessalines' ruinous massacre of white planters in 1804, was alive and well.

The Security Crisis (1997–1999)

Control of the Haitian National Police, which had been the focus of Aristide's attention after he returned from exile in 1994, remained a primary goal after he left office. Starting in 1997, the UN peacekeeping force was reduced to a mere three hundred men with the understanding that the police, equipped and trained at great expense by foreign donors, was now ready to take over. Law enforcement was nominally the police's sole duty, but the failure of standard democratic processes meant that the police was likely to become a key instrument of political power as well. Aristide's goals were simple: turning the police into a body loyal to him only and preventing the emergence of any political rival with police connections.

A series of mysterious assassination attempts proved that the battle for control of the police was anything but civil. Léon Jeune, a former police chief who had entered the political fray as an Aristide opponent, was summarily jailed and mistreated in November 1997—ironically by the very policemen who had once served under him. Jeune's political ambitions were the most likely explanation for his arbitrary detention (foreign intercession secured his release three weeks later). Two years later, Vice Minister for Public Security Robert Manuel became the target of Aristide's verbal attacks, presumably because he insisted in his role as overseer of the police that the force should remain free from political interference. Concluding that Aristide's continued criticisms prevented him from working effectively, Manuel resigned in October 1999. Aristide immediately pushed for a more pliant replacement, but his favored candidate Jean Lamy was shot dead within days of being mentioned as Manuel's successor. Suspicions focused on Manuel himself, but the investigation never went far. The judge assigned to the case became the victim of an assassination attempt himself and Manuel fled for exile. Rumors, following a centuries-old Haitian tradition, swirled that Aristide, or Manuel, or some alternative third party, were responsible for these acts of violence. Haiti confirmed its international reputation as an impenetrable, irretrievable hotbed of political violence.

While politicians and top police officials continued their bloody politicking, Haitians complained of a resurgent climate of insecurity that the police did little to halt. International human rights agencies found numerous cases of policemen known to mistreat suspects, detain them arbitrarily, or even shoot them on sight. The problem was so prevalent that the U.S. government quietly created a compensation fund to indemnify families of victims and finance safe houses. Haitian politicians' failure to reform the judicial system and to pay judges adequately was a chief factor of police abuse. Concluding that suspects would most likely languish for years without trial or bribe a judge to be released, policemen took it upon themselves to punish suspects on the spot. This informal process made it difficult to distinguish between accidental killings, summary justice, and political violence.

Few businesses thrived in this unstable context except for one: drug trafficking. Haiti's strategic location between Colombia and Florida had prompted some drug traffickers to establish contacts with army officers as early as the 1970s, but drug trafficking only took center stage with the political and economic crises of the late 1990s. Little drug production or consumption took place in Haiti itself; it was Haiti's status as a transit area that concerned U.S. officials. In 1995, Haiti joined the list of twenty-eight countries subject to annual U.S. certification to verify whether they actively combated drug trafficking. An estimated forty-six metric tons of cocaine transited through Haiti on its way to Florida in 1997, an amount that grew by an additional ten tons for each of the following two years. By 1999, 14 percent of all the cocaine imported to the United States transited through Haiti.

The Haitian government's complete breakdown was the main reason for the cocaine trade's sudden surge. Haiti had no navy, no army, no air force, and found it difficult to patrol its long coastline with its minuscule coast guard. It was not until 1997 that the *Bureau de Lutte contre le Trafic de Stupéfiants* (antidrug trafficking bureau or BLTS) was created as a unit specifically designed to combating drug trafficking, and even then the United States had to provide the BLTS's entire training and budget. That same year, the United States, Signed a treaty with Haiti allowing Drug Enforcement Agency (DEA) Coast Guard agents to patrol Haiti's waters and conduct searches in Haiti itself. Policing one's borders, a country's most potent symbol of sovereignty, was beyond the Haitian government's ability. Concluding that Haitian officials' inaction was to blame for the surge in cocaine trafficking, the United States only certified Haiti based on national security needs from 1999 on. Should Haiti lose its certification altogether in the years to come, it would become Myanmar's sole companion as a certified narco-state and lose all rights to obtain U.S. aid.

These threats failed to halt cocaine imports. Delays in aid disbursement and the ensuing salary freezes made penniless policemen and local officials an easy prey for the well-financed drug lords. In 1998, the DEA administered a polygraph test to members of the BLTS antidrug unit created with U.S. help the year before. Six out of twenty-four officers lied when asked if they had condoned drug trafficking. Judges were equally unpaid and freed those few traffickers who were caught in exchange for bribes. By the late 1990s, driving a brand-new SUV through the streets of the capital could only mean three things. One could be a foreign aid worker, though these were getting increasingly rare; one could be a government official who had managed to secure bribes; or one could be involved in drug trafficking (the last two were usually related). Standard venues of economic betterment were unknown to the majority of

Haitians. Peasants came to conclude that their sole hope of ever getting rich was to find some wayward drug shipment in their backyard. One small plane that landed in the impoverished northern province of Haiti was even mobbed and burnt in 1999 after a rumor spread that its cargo consisted of cocaine; drug traffickers came to dread such incidents more than the Haitian police. The growing drug traffic brought some cash into Haiti, but it also introduced theft, greed, guns, and insecurity to a country that had previously experienced few crimes other than the endemic political violence.

Election Year: 2000

Concluding that Haiti could not afford to operate without a government any longer, President Préval bypassed the parliament and unilaterally nominated Jacques-Edouard Alexis as prime minister in January 1999. The following day, Préval's sister narrowly escaped an assassination attempt; her driver did not. Foreign aid resumed, though previous pledges put on hold during the crisis were rarely honored in full. Préval then announced that legislative elections would be held in May 2000, followed by run-offs in the summer and the presidential election in November. The political violence associated with this busy electoral season claimed dozens of victims. Among them was Jean-Léopold Dominique, a popular radio commentator and long-time Aristide supporter who was shot dead on April 3, 2000. Préval and Aristide both attended Dominique's mammoth state funeral, which turned into a political rally that unofficially kicked off the presidential campaign when Aristide supporters chanted "Aristide or death" and "elections or not, Aristide is already our president."[3]

The May 2000 legislative elections were held one month later and did little to appease political tensions. The balloting was plagued by disorganization and fraud. When counting the votes, Aristide sympathizers within the electoral commission decided to declare any *Lafanmi Lavalas* candidate the winner of a race when he earned a plurality, rather than the majority, of the votes. Préval's OPL allies and Léon Manus, Haiti's top election official, insisted that in such cases one should hold runoff elections as required by law. Pro-Aristide mobs threatened violence, the OPL candidates were arrested, Manus fled in exile, and the runoffs never took place. *Lafanmi Lavalas'* unconstitutional behavior was as damning as it was useless, for the party would have controlled parliament anyway. But control was not deemed sufficient; only a total, uncompromising domination of both chambers would do. The rewriting of electoral law gave *Lafanmi Lavalas* eighteen out of nineteen senators and seventy-two of eighty-three deputies; it also gave other parties an excuse not to abide by election results and to boycott the presidential election held that fall, which they would likely have lost anyway. When electors were once again summoned to the polls in November 2000, only a handful of candidates competed for their votes. All but one of them were complete unknowns. The one familiar name on the ballot was that of Aristide himself, who could run again now that he had been out of office for five years. He was elected with 92 percent of the vote, eight points short of Duvalier's score in his 1960 reelection.

Foreign countries voted with their feet. Despite Aristide's loud nationalism, he and Préval had relied on the usual combination of off-the-record private letters and highly paid lobbyists to convince a reluctant United Nations to maintain troops in Haiti years past its initial 1996 deadline. International frustration at Haiti's slow progress was such, however, that by 2000 the neologism of "Haiti fatigue" was coined to describe the general consensus that Haiti had missed its chance. The United States, previously a key supporter of the UN mission, withdrew the small humanitarian mission it still maintained in Haiti in January 2000, and other UN members debated whether they should follow suit. The August 2000 murder of a Barbadian peacekeeper was the deciding factor. The UN mandate, set to expire with Aristide's inauguration in February 2001, was not renewed.

Conclusion: A Missed Opportunity

The Préval presidency seemed custom-made to demonstrate that Haiti's misfortunes were a consequence of its rulers' nefarious incompetence rather than foreign exploitation. For a few years, the international community lavished money and attention on the fledgling Haitian democracy, sparing no expense in that endeavor. Members of the Diaspora came back with much-needed capital and expertise. International investors took a serious look at Haiti for the first time in twenty years. Foreign peacekeepers enforced order in Haiti, while law enforcement specialists trained the national police and foreign administrators advised their Haitian counterparts. So many hundreds of millions of dollars of grants poured in that the IMF, when trying to enroll Haiti in the Heavily Indebted Poor Countries program (HIPC), realized that Haiti's public debt was so small that the country did not qualify. Economists debated whether the IMF's cure-all adjustment policies or a more liberal framework were most likely to maximize economic growth, but no one doubted that, with so much money pouring in, Haiti had nowhere to go but up. All that was expected of the professional politicians who formed the Republic of Port-au-Prince was to apportion public positions in an orderly fashion, let the money flow, and cash the checks. They failed.

Exhibit one was the nationalistic posturing that opponents of privatization mistook for love of country. Whether the public sector is best suited for the production of cement and flour than its private equivalent is a matter of debate; but losing hundreds of millions of dollars a year in aid to maintain ownership of companies worth ten times less was obviously not in Haiti's best public interest (the private interest of anti-privatization crusaders hoping to keep their plum job at a public company was another matter). One's patriotic duty was to seize this unique opportunity to collect funds for infrastructures and developments, not to attack those offering such funds. One should have taken pride in Haiti's ability to astound the world by its economic turnaround, not in its ability to disappoint others by its stubborn hostility. Decades later, a self-sufficient Haiti could have afforded to make angry anti-imperialist comments and experience an international backlash. Doing so in the midst of a foreign aid bonanza was sheer irresponsibility.

Exhibit two was political fractiousness. Cédras's demise had given *Lavalas* a monopoly of power. Aristide had the luxury of finishing his interrupted term and handpicking his successor while knowing that Préval could not run for a second consecutive mandate and that the presidency would most likely return to Aristide in 2000. Opposition forces were small and divided; they could not defeat Aristide in a fair election; attempts on their part to overthrow the *Lavalas* order by force could not succeed as long as the UN mission stayed on Haitian soil. With no conceivable enemy to defeat, *Lavalas* split in two and started bickering with itself. *Lafanmi Lavalas* fought the *Organisation Politique Lavalas*. Senators fought deputies. Aristide turned on Préval. Men who had risked their lives for a common ideal during the junta years suddenly claimed that two years were not enough to agree on a prime ministerial nominee. This confused battle between old friends would have been entertaining were it not for the fact that it undermined Préval's reformist potential from the outset and eventually resulted in the utter paralysis of the Haitian government.

Aristide was exhibit number three. His attacks against the alleged imperialist maneuvers of the great powers were nothing new; they merely indicated that the vocal Aristide of 1991, temporarily put on hold during his exile to obtain the military support of the United States, was back in full force. His apologists could claim that his ungratefulness and anti-Americanism were fueled by a fire within that had too long been snuffed out. His patient underground work to sap his friend's presidency, on the other hand, was new. Préval shared Aristide's basic agenda; he was less confrontational when negotiating with outside powers, but he was closer ideologically than any of the Duvalierist thugs Aristide had faced in his career. Breaking away from Préval, in that context, smacked of vanity. Aristide had always derived personal pride from the pomp of state visits to other countries and his ability to speak several languages (hence the Spanish, Creole, French, and English segments in the speech he delivered at the United Nations in September 1991). But by the late 1990s, playful pride had turned to arrogance. Aristide was seemingly unable to accept that any other man, even such a close ally as Préval, could occupy the presidential seat that was rightfully his. The ability to change Haiti was not the main issue at stake, for Aristide had passed surprisingly few laws during his two stays in the presidential palace. Power for power's sake—and, increasingly, the money that came with power—were now Aristide's fix. During the months that followed his controversial 2000 reelection, a fidgety Aristide waited impatiently for his third triumphal return to the presidency.

CHAPTER 11

Boss Titid: The Third Aristide Presidency (2001–2004)

Two Inaugurations and a Withdrawal (February 7, 2001)

On February 7, 2001, ten years to the day after he was first inaugurated as president, Aristide was sworn in as Préval's successor. Major foreign officials were conspicuously absent. Neither U.S. president George W. Bush nor his secretary of state were present, leaving U.S. ambassador Brian Dean Curran as the sole representative of the United States. The heads of states of other countries closely involved in Haitian affairs, such as France, Canada, and Venezuela, had also refused to come, as had UN secretary general Kofi Annan. Joyous Aristide supporters took to the streets, though the absence of any major candidate in the November 2000 election made it impossible to know how popular Aristide really was six-and-a-half years after his return from exile. This was another historical first in his short political life. Aristide, the first president to be democratically elected and the first president to return from exile, was the first president ever to enter the presidential palace for the third time. He was forty-eight years old.

Aiming to revive the spirit of hope that had accompanied his 1991 inauguration, Aristide outlined an ambitious plan whose key components, he announced, would be implemented within one hundred days. Within that time frame, inspired by Franklin D. Roosevelt's first New Deal, Aristide promised that he would give land to the 40 percent of Haitian peasants who had none and that he would see to it that the country was agriculturally self-sufficient again. He would also develop free trade zones, improve public infrastructures, create half-a-million jobs, give urban dwellers round-the-clock electricity, fight illiteracy, fund schools, build hospitals, and increase the annual GDP growth rate to 4 percent. The political laundry list included everything Aristide could think of except for a bill; financial details were handed over to the new prime minister Jean-Marie Chérestal, who promised that his government would fund all these priorities while also reducing public deficits.

Haiti never had a shortage of presidential hopefuls. Accordingly, inauguration day saw not one, but two presidents being sworn in. Before the official ceremony honoring Aristide unfolded at the presidential palace, opposition parties, loosely organized in a coalition called the *Convergence Démocratique* (Democratic Convergence), had inaugurated Gérard Gourgue as their president. Gourgue had been one of the university professors Papa Doc had hired to tutor his son on the intricacies of Haitian law; he had also acquired a reputation for political courage when he called on his former pupil to respect human rights. Leaders of the *Convergence Démocratique*, aware that presidential power was firmly in Aristide's hands, explained that Gourgue's inauguration was merely a reminder that all major parties save *Lafanmi Lavalas* had boycotted the presidential elections. They also hoped that foreign backing and a network of grassroots organizations, unions, and companies known as the *Groupe des 184* would help them challenge Aristide's hold on Haitian politics by peaceful means.

Alfredo Lopes Cabral, the head of the UN peacekeeping mission in Haiti, was one of the few foreign notables to attend Aristide's swearing-in ceremony on February 7, but his presence was not intended as a sign of support. The United Nations had refused to renew the UN mission in Haiti set to expire with the end of Préval's term; so Cabral took a flight to New York later that day. UN employees and their white vehicles, for years a familiar sight at the posh Hotel Montana in Pétionville, became a dim memory; the foreign military presence that had begun with the September 19, 1994 U.S. invasion of Haiti was now over. Aristide could have been expected to celebrate as the foreign imperialists he loudly denounced in his speeches left Haiti. He was, after all, free to set an independent course for his country for the first time since 1991. But diminished foreign interference also took away a favored villain, leaving no scapegoat to blame should his ambitious dreams of rapid development fail again.

The Hundred Days (February 2001–May 2001)

The first important decision Aristide made during his Hundred Days was the composition of Prime Minister Chérestal's cabinet. As could be expected, many nominees were members of Aristide's *Lafanmi Lavalas* party, which had swept the legislative elections the year before, but he also picked a few candidates known for their past association with the Duvalierist regimes. Marc Bazin had briefly served in 1983 as Bébé Doc's finance minister before being forced to resign under the typically Duvalierist charge that he opposed corruption; he had also run for president against Aristide in 1990 and become one of the de facto prime ministers the Cédras junta had appointed during Aristide's 1991–1994 exile. This résumé made him a particularly odd choice for an Aristidian cabinet, but he obtained the all-important position of minister of cooperation, whose main duty was to obtain foreign aid. Stanley Théard, Bazin's new colleague as minister of commerce, had held the same position under Bébé Doc; within weeks of his nomination, stories surfaced that he had been involved in one of many embezzlement scams that had characterized Bébé Doc's administration. Aristide also purged the electoral oversight commission and replaced its members—whose main duty was to ensure that future elections would be free and fair—with a few historic Duvalierists; Dracula's old henchmen were now in charge of the blood bank. Finally, Aristide allowed *Macoute* ideologue Serge Beaulieu to return from exile, then invited him for a private talk at the presidential palace.

Aristide's behavior was most puzzling. He might have chosen Bazin because he was popular with international institutions and could be expected to obtain more foreign aid than a nationalist *Lavalas* die-hard. Théard belonged to the business elite of Port-au-Prince and might convince rich mulattoes not to support an anti-Aristide coup as they had done in 1991. But Aristide supporters found no solace in such hypotheses. They only saw that Aristide—the man for whom they had risked their lives in 1991–1994—had consumed his democratic credentials to secure landslide victories in the 2000 elections, only to give away prominent governmental positions to his bitterest critics shortly after his inauguration. Was this national reconciliation, they asked, or was it a sign that Aristide had sold out to the enemy?

A less surprising move, yet one just as intolerable to his patriotic supporters, was the private letter Aristide sent to Kofi Annan asking for the UN mission to be reestablished, accompanied by a suitable increase in foreign aid. Resorting to the tactic he had used to great effect when he had called for a previous UN takeover in 1994, Aristide financed an expensive lobbying campaign in Washington, DC that cost $50,000 a month for the firm of Patton and Boggs alone. Alas, international subservience yielded little. Annan, by now well aware of Aristide's duplicity, turned down all offers to create a new peacekeeping mission. George W. Bush shared his father's distrust for Aristide and made no effort to shore up his regime either. For the following three years, UN, U.S., and OAS officials limited themselves to frequent—and unsuccessful—visits to Haiti in a vain attempt to solve the political impasse resulting from the May and November 2000 elections. The country's aid lifeline, already interrupted in 1997–1999 during the governmental crisis, then restored when Préval announced new elections in 1999, then cut off because of the electoral controversies of 2000, was put on hold while both parties debated. The total amount of aid pledges waiting to be disbursed was half-a-billion dollars. To supporters of Aristide, one hundred days of presidential power had only yielded two bitter pills—Duvalierist nominations and the demand for another UN mission—and no rewards.

Zero Tolerance (May 2001–January 2002)

To the average Haitian, personal safety was as elusive as economic success. The limitations of the police, when combined with the growing drug trade and the large number of weapons left in circulation when the army and the FRAPH were summarily disbanded in 1994–1995, had set off a crime wave that had already been at the forefront of Haitians' concerns throughout Préval's presidency. Aristide, for whom there was no social problem a good speech could not tackle, offered his solution to insecurity in a June 20, 2001 speech delivered at the national police's headquarters. His "zero tolerance" policy, as he called it, hinted that those *zenglendos* (criminals) caught in the act should be shot on the spot. There was no need for a policeman to bring a robber or a car hijacker to court, he explained, before adding with his trademark double-entendre that "you [policemen] do not need to wait for that *zenglendo* to appear before the judge, you can prevent that murderer from taking action."[1]

Western-style justice carried out by trigger-happy policemen was one pillar of Aristide's law and order campaign. The *chimères* (chimeras) were the other. Named after the part-goat, part-lion, part-dragon fire-breathing monster of Greek mythology, the *chimères* were yet another incarnation of Haiti's many paramilitary groups (the *chimères* were officially known under the more benign name of *organisations populaires*, or "popular organizations"). They were Aristide's brainbeast. Their presence was felt most in the restless slums of the capitals, where they formed gangs that enforced order, collected bribes, and ensured 100 percent support for Haiti's "beloved" president. True to Aristide's favorite political strategy, plausible deniability was their greatest strength; the most gruesome political murders could always be blamed on some loose cannon belonging to an organization that did not officially answer to the president.

Journalists were a primary target of political violence. Dozens died in 2001 as gangs loosely associated with the *Lafanmi Lavalas* hierarchy punished those who condemned the law of the *chimères*. One such victim was Brignol Lindor, a Haitian radio talk show host who received several death threats after he invited Aristide critics on his show. One December day, as Lindor was traveling to his second job as a customs official in Petit Goâve, several *chimères* hijacked his car, dragged him out, stoned him, then finished him off with machetes. The *chimères'* unofficial association with Aristide and their involvement with many nonpolitical illegal activities (such as the drug trade) made it difficult to assess motive and blame.

Even judges investigating the murder of Jean Dominique, the popular mulatto journalist from Radio Haïti Inter who had been killed during the 2000 legislative campaign, found it hard to interrupt Haiti's tradition of political impunity. The first judge assigned to the case resigned after receiving various death threats; the second, Claudy Gassant, received similar threats and complained that Aristide's minister of justice refused to offer protection. Ironically, the only man to receive protection was Dany Toussaint, a senator elected on the *Lafanmi Lavalas* platform who was a prime suspect as a potential employer of the hit men. In 2001, when Senator Toussaint refused to allow Judge Gassant to question him on the case, fellow *Lafanmi Lavalas* senators backed his claim that he was above the law and should not even have to answer a judge's questions. Aristide remained surprisingly silent during the controversy and did little to speed up the investigation into the murder of a journalist who had consistently opposed the same Duvalierist groups Aristide had battled throughout his career. Gassant resigned in April 2001, then resumed his task with new assurances that Toussaint's *Lavalas* friends in government would not impede the investigation. Progress remained slow, however; the preliminary investigation was not completed until March 2003, three years after Dominique's death, at which point Gassant had been replaced by another judge who absolved Toussaint and asked that the suspected hit men be the only ones to be prosecuted.

The belief that elections and court proceedings would never hold Aristide accountable led his most dedicated enemies to resort to violent means. On July 27, 2001, a series of coordinated attacks struck police stations nationwide. The aggressors fled to the Dominican border before they could be apprehended and interrogated, making it difficult to know whether this was some criminals' daring attack on the police or a *bona fide* coup attempt. Opponents of Aristide struck again before the year was over. During the night of Sunday, December 16, a heavily armed group led by Guy Philippe, a former police chief whose once-warm relationship with Aristide had gone sour, came back from their Dominican exile, attacked the presidential palace, blew up the entrance door with a grenade, and entered. They held on throughout the night as policemen loyal to Aristide and thousands of civilians surrounded the palace. Philippe's men, dressed in the khaki uniforms of the disbanded Haitian army, finally forced the cordon of policemen blocking their exit and sped on the road to the Dominican Republic. Like the perpetrators of the July attacks on police stations, they found refuge across the border before they could be apprehended. The failed coup served as a pretext for the *chimères* to pillage and burn the headquarters of the *Convergence Démocratique* and a French cultural center because of unfounded rumors that France and Aristide's democratic opposition were involved in the failed attempt to overthrow Aristide. Opposition members claimed, even though there was no proof for this, that Aristide had engineered both the July 27 and December 16 disturbances to give himself an excuse to crack down on his enemies.

As the year 2001 reached its end, President Aristide had become a man far removed from his origins as an idealist priest of a slum parish. His custom-tailored suits, when combined with the presidential sash, evoked memories of the fancy uniforms favored by nineteenth-century Latin American *caudillos*. He multiplied voyages abroad, always traveling with an entourage of bodyguards and sycophants, to give himself the illusion, though not the reality, of international influence. He rarely stepped out of his glittering white presidential palace or his personal residence at Tabarre to experience the harsh realities of the miserable society struggling to survive under him. Large billboards celebrated his achievements in the streets of the capital while Haiti's television channels scheduled hours of daily programs narrating his every gesture and broadcasting his speeches in full. Rich, oblivious to his countrymen's plight, always mindful of the next attempt to overthrow him, Aristide increasingly resembled the stereotypical dictator of Woody Allen's *Bananas* (1971).

Aristide Development (March 2002–February 2003)

In January 2002, Prime Minister Chérestal fell victim to legislative opposition fed, according to rumors circulating in Port-au-Prince, either by some senators' fears that he would investigate corruption scandals, or by Aristide's desire to blame his prime minister for his first year's disappointing results. Yvon Neptune was selected in March 2002 as Haiti's new head of government. Afraid that his hungry people might ask why they were even more miserable than they were when he was first elected president, Aristide concocted a recipe for economic development that centered on a client network worthy of a nineteenth-century Tammany Hall party boss. Helping himself to funds he had skimmed off the public treasury, Aristide generously distributed envelopes of cash to grateful Haitians from whom he had taken the money in the first place. The handouts echoed a popular "breakfast for the poor" Aristide had held in February 1991, as well as an old tradition of paternalism in the presidential office (Bébé Doc had been known to throw handfuls of cash from his car window when visiting the provinces). Aristide could not cure visitors of scrofula the way some medieval kings used to do; but he could allow his most loyal subjects to stave off hunger pangs for a few days. The *petits projets de la présidence* (little presidential projects), as this form of clientage was called, endeared Aristide to relief recipients but were of no use for long-term development.

The only significant infrastructure projects to see completion were small meeting rooms designed to foster communal friendship; the bridges and hospitals and schools Aristide had promised in his inaugural speech remained on the drawing board. What little money Haiti had had been spent on lobbyists' fees in Washington, DC in fruitless attempt to obtain the resumption of the aid flow. Despite the cash crisis, Aristide's own residence at Tabarre grew ever more luxurious as Haiti foundered around it. Many a Haitian child, obliged to walk for miles in search of potable water for her family, must have looked with envy at the large pool the president had built for his two daughters.

One project mentioned in the inaugural speech that did see completion was the establishment of free trade zones in which foreign investors could exploit Haiti's abundant manpower free of tax. Following a parliamentary vote authorizing the creation of up to fourteen trade zones in late 2001, Aristide signed a preliminary agreement to set aside over fifteen thousand hectares of land in the Ouanaminthe region near the Dominican border for U.S. and Dominican investors in January 2002. Zoning operations began the following spring. The trade zone policy could have succeeded in creating thousands of jobs (albeit the low-paid, unskilled kind), but it was singularly at odds with Aristide's leftist economic tradition and sparked widespread opposition. Local peasants complained that they were expected to give away some of Haiti's most fertile land without even being consulted on the matter. Nationalists added that the trade zones were strategically located along the Dominican border, would benefit investors from traditional enemies such as the United States and the Dominican Republic, and would be patrolled by Dominican security guards. There was little to explain why Aristide was resorting to this most unpatriotic policy, so critics immediately whispered that the $40 million earmarked to finance the trade zone would finance the *Lafanmi Lavalas* regime rather than compensate expropriated peasants.

The cooperative scandal was the most damaging blow ever to hit Aristide when it exploded in 2002. Cooperatives were communal banks designed to pool together the resources of local Haitians to finance low-cost loans and infrastructure projects. To induce investors to contribute funds, the cooperatives' promoters promised a munificent 12 percent monthly interest and noted that Aristide was personally vaunting the cooperatives as a safe investment. The uneducated poor, but also members of the middle class who should have known better, invested all their meager savings in the hope of doubling their investment in less than a year. Some sold their houses; some even borrowed money to invest more than they owned. The cooperatives were a classic pyramid scheme in which new funds were used to pay the interest of previous investors, but the presidential seal of approval convinced many Haitians to fall for it. After a few months of rapid growth, the banks imploded in the spring of 2002. The funds mysteriously disappeared, as did the promoters who had collected them, and Haitians found themselves $170 million poorer than they already had been. Aristide promised to prosecute the culprits, but the head of the victims' association was the only one to ever spend time in jail.

The most egregious spin-off of the cooperative craze was *Poun nou tout* ("For All of Us"), a subsidiary of the Aristide Foundation for Democracy, which was given a license to import seventy thousand metric tons of donated "peace rice." Few benefited from this cooperative scheme except the prominent *Lafanmi Lavalas* parliamentarians who were allotted quotas of rice, ostensibly to buy support by distributing free food to supporters of the regime. By donating rice, the deputies ruined the rice farmers from their own districts who could not compete against subsidized imports. Taxpayers were flouted of much-needed tariff income because the cooperative enjoyed a tax concession. Even the recipients of the peace rice lost out when the deputies decided that they should not give away rice they could sell for a profit. Old, idealistic *Lafanmi Lavalas* supporters denounced the scandal and ceased to support an Aristide presidency that now amounted to a form of organized crime living off bribery and sustained by handouts and the fear of the *chimères*.

The drug trade was another prominent supplier of bribes. Knowing who partook in the trade was a closely guarded state secret, but a stunning February 6, 2003 incident hinted that local officials in remote rural provinces were not the only ones to be implicated. On that date, officers of the BLTS police unit (ironically created by the United States to combat drug trafficking) sealed off Highway Nine near the Cité Soleil slum on the north end of the capital so that a Colombian plane could unload its one-ton cargo of cocaine more easily. The operation's brazenness most likely required complicity at the highest level of government. Aristide's opponents did not shy away from claiming that the growth of the drug traffic and that of the president's personal wealth were two related phenomena, but the secretive nature of the business made it impossible to prove such accusations.

Haitians often complain that their country is the only one with a last name, as every American newscast on Haitian events inevitably begins with the words "Haiti, the poorest country in the Western Hemisphere." The venality of Aristide's regime finally allowed his country to appear on an international ranking as a world leader. Haiti was included in Transparency International's annual survey of the world's most corrupt countries for the first time in 2002, when it ranked eleventh. Haiti moved up to the third spot in 2003 (behind Bangladesh and Nigeria), then finally secured the top spot in time for the country's bicentennial in 2004. Almost two hundred years after defeating the soldiers of Bonaparte, this was an achievement in which few Haitians could find pride.

Bicentennial Fever (January 2003–November 2003)

Economic setbacks, insecurity, and corruption threatened to undermine Aristide's popularity, forcing the experienced politician to pull yet another ace from his sleeve. The year 2003 marked the official countdown to the bicentennial of Haiti's independence. Celebrating the achievements of an earlier, prouder generation of Haitians was an agenda likely to be consensual; bicentennial fever would also make it easy to draw parallels between the very real past oppression of the slaves and the current, alleged foreign exploitation of Haiti and thus blame Western powers for Aristide's own incompetence.

The year 2003 started with the independence day speech that Haitian presidents traditionally deliver in Gonaïves, where the country's independence was declared in 1804. Aristide attacked the "international sanctions" imposed on Haiti in his January 2003 speech (the term implied that Haiti was hit by an embargo similar to the one imposed in 1991–1994, when in reality foreign donors had merely halted a generous foreign aid program; no sanctions were in place).[2] Aristide added that the national currency's plunge from twenty-three *gourdes* to the dollar when he took office in 2001 to forty-five *gourdes* to the dollar by early 2003, which had doubled the price of imported food, was due to a foreign "economic destabilization" conspiracy (large public deficits and private markets' lack of faith in Aristide were the real culprits). However inaccurate, the charges served to explain why Aristide's previous promises of infrastructural development had not yet materialized five hundred days after the end of his fabled one hundred days. Aristide immediately added fourteen new promises to the list—presumably paid for with funds from the aforementioned foreign imperialists— which included a high school in Gonaïves, better roads and streets, a new drainage system, and the customary pledge to deliver electricity twenty-four hours a day.

The next historic anniversary—the bicentennial of Toussaint Louverture's death on April 7, 2003—gave Aristide the opportunity to resort to a most ingenious idea to shore up his flagging popularity. The main cause of Haiti's current financial crisis, he explained, was the indemnity of 150 million francs awarded to France in 1825 in exchange for diplomatic recognition. Failing to mention that Haiti had never fully paid the indemnity, and that it had received many times that amount in foreign aid in recent decades, Aristide demanded that France reimburse the money, complete with penalties. "Restitution and reparations for us, victims of slavery!" he demanded. "Yes it is necessary! Because slavery is a crime against humanity, we need (1) restitution (2) reparation (3) celebration of the bicentennial of our independence."[3] The updated amount, which made extensive use of compounding interests and adjustments for inflation, was meticulously assessed at $21,685,155,571.48 (Aristide's reluctance to drop the last 48 cents was motivated, a popular joke explained, by his desire to have something left to donate to his people after he had taken his share).

France immediately rejected the $21 billion claim, which represented more than ten times its worldwide foreign aid budget for that year, but this did not seem to bother Aristide. He spent the rest of the year elaborating on the twin themes of past foreign exploitation and future foreign aid (or "restitution"). On November 18, as he visited Cap Haïtien to celebrate Dessalines' 1803 victory in nearby Vertières against

Rochambeau's forces, Aristide explained that "today's misery is a result of a 200-year-old conspiracy . . . This plot, this embargo are genocidal in nature," then listed all the great things $21 billion could buy.[4] Some Haitians, following their leader in his illusory world, dreamed of free schools, new roads, generous welfare subsidies, and round-the-clock electricity, all of which would be paid for by the former colonial ruler. Others understood that the hopeless indemnity claim was a ploy to divert economic discontent away from the regime and the very real chimeras who defended it and grumbled that Aristide's sole qualification was for the Neverland presidency. This they cautiously whispered, for Aristide's lost boys had a most fearsome reputation.

Gonaïves: A Bicentennial to Remember

As 2003 drew to a close, the government of Jean-Bertrand Aristide made careful preparations to celebrate the bicentennial of Haiti's declaration of independence with a pomp befitting a nationalist regime looking for renewed public support. Gonaïves, known as the *cité de l'indépendance* in Haiti because Dessalines proclaimed the colony's independence in that city, was to be at the center of festivities. The year indeed turned out to be one of the most eventful in Gonaïves' turbulent history; alas, few of those events unfolded according to plan.

The crisis began innocuously in the fall of 2003 when foreign backers of the Aristide regime, the United States in particular, repeated their long-standing demand that Aristide disband the armed bands of *chimères*, which were blamed for dozens of political assassinations. The most violent of these *chimères* gangs was a group headquartered in Gonaïves and led by Amiot Métayer, (a.k.a. *Kiben*, "the Cuban"). Métayer had spent six months in prison in 2002 before his men freed him and 158 other prisoners in a daring August 2002 attack on Gonaïves' prison. The political agenda of Métayer's group need not be detailed; suffice it to say that it called itself *armée cannibale* ("cannibal army"). U.S. criticisms of Métayer initially met no success as he refused to bow to international pressure and reform his unique interpretation of the democratic discourse—until a mysterious murder brought his political career to an abrupt end on September 23, 2003. The murder was never elucidated, but the dominant rumor held that President Aristide himself was behind it. He had allegedly rid himself of his turbulent ally to assuage the increasingly hostile international community.

The most fervent supporter of the conspiracy theory was Amiot Métayer's brother Buteur, who promptly took the reins of the *armée cannibale* and declared himself in open rebellion with Aristide's government in Port-au-Prince. Buteur then went on to enlist two powerful allies. One, Louis-Jodel Chamblain, had led the FRAPH with Emmanuel Constant in 1993–1994; the other, Guy Philippe, was the former police chief who had participated in the coup attempt against Aristide in 2001. The group's platform was thin. In public, they attacked Aristide for his dictatorial government style and for his poor economic record; in private, they insisted that Aristide's decision to disband the army in 1995 had been unconstitutional and that soldiers were owed nine years of salary arrears. All three were also rumored to battle for control of Haiti's police and customs so that they could increase their stake in the cocaine business.

Meanwhile, in Port-au-Prince, policemen and *chimères* killed dozens of political opponents in a series of crackdowns, including one aimed at university students on December 5, 2003, and demonstrations against Aristide's rule reached a size unseen in Haiti since the 1985 strikes that led to Bébé Doc's downfall. Aristide officially condemned his henchmen's violence but did nothing to stop it; several cabinet members resigned, claiming that Aristide had now turned into a fascist thug. As a result, the capital was in a state of chaos when the bicentennial celebrations began with a large Aristide rally in front of his palace on January 1, 2004. The once-hailed president was now radioactive matter. The only foreign head of state who dared appear next to Aristide during this historic commemoration was President Thabo Mbeki of South Africa. Mbeki also provided an aid package to pay for the festivities, but he got little for his efforts. A helicopter preparing his visit to Gonaïves was shot at from the ground, and Mbeki returned to South Africa under a torrent of criticisms for associating with Aristide. Oblivious to the ongoing mayhem, Aristide made elaborate plans to explain how the French "restitution" package would be spent when he visited Gonaïves to deliver his bicentennial address. "Instead of a 21 gun salute, my bicentennial proclamation has 21 points. Yes, a 21-point proclamation while waiting for the 21 billions of the restitution."[5] By 2015, Aristide would use French money to eliminate illiteracy, reduce the poverty rate from 56 to 28 percent, lay two thousand kilometers of new roads, build ten thousand public housing units, and perform seventeen other economic miracles. He was less specific when addressing his plan's two main prerequisites: that France would foot the bill and, what was even more improbable, that he would remain in power another eleven years.

As Aristide spoke, he had already lost control of the sectors of Gonaïves in the hands of the *armée cannibale*, such as the beachfront slum of Raboteau. The rebellion progressed rapidly in subsequent weeks. On February 5, the rebels, now calling themselves National Revolutionary Front for the Liberation of Haiti, took control of the main police station, which Aristide's police failed to retake in a later counteroffensive. Rebels captured Hinche on the Dominican border on February 17, thus allowing Philippe and Chamblain to return from exile along with many former soldiers. By February 24, rebel control had expanded from Gonaïves to include most of Haiti's northern towns, including Cap Haïtien and Port-de-Paix. Rebel leaders then announced their intention to move south at the head of thousands of troops. Their actual strength probably came closer to a few hundred men, but this number included many of the soldiers who had been demobilized when the army was disbanded in 1995.

The United States and France abandoned Aristide to his fate. Ten years after the massive military intervention to "restore democracy," Aristide's most fervent international backers concluded that he was undemocratic as a president and unreliable as a partner. In the last week of February, the French and American ambassadors met Aristide privately and told him that they could not ensure his safety if the rebels overtook the capital and that it would be better for him to leave for exile before it was too late. Aristide hesitated, then, faced with the very likely probability that the *armée cannibale* would kill him after deposing him, he bowed down. As required by Haiti's political tradition, he left at dawn the following Sunday; in a nod to the many Haitian adepts of numerology, this Sunday also happened to be the magical February 29 of leap year fame. Aristide, the first Haitian president to return to power after being overthrown, now became the first president to be overthrown twice.

France had welcomed Bébé Doc in 1986 and the United States had done the same with Aristide during his previous exile, but Aristide was now an international pariah. Neither France nor the United States, nor traditional friends of Haiti such as Canada and Venezuela, extended their welcome. Even Thabo Mbeki closed his door, explaining that he was in the midst of a reelection campaign and that Aristide's visit would be too disruptive. After many negotiations, U.S. troops arranged for Aristide to leave for Antigua, then for the Central African Republic.

Neither France nor the United States intended to let Métayer and his thugs reach the national palace. Their brutality, cocaine connections, and links to the *chimères* and FRAPH disqualified them from the outset. Instead, Canadian, Chilean, French, and American troops rushed to Haiti to maintain order in the capital and keep Philippe's men away.

They promptly backed a provisional government composed of members of the *Convergence Démocratique* and the *Groupe des 184* who had welcomed, but not fought in, the rebellion. Gérard Latortue became prime minister. The choice was singularly unwise. Latortue was a business consultant living in Boca Raton, Florida, who had to be flown in to assume the leadership of the country he had abandoned decades before; so nationalists were quick to exploit Haitian prejudices against Haitian Americans and accuse Latortue of being a treacherous puppet subservient to the forces of Yankee capitalism. André Apaid, Latortue's main backer within the *Groupe des 184*, was equally suspect on account of his wealth and very light skin. As for the French and U.S. troops, their presence on Haitian soil a mere two months after Haiti celebrated its independence was a national humiliation. To paraphrase Gabriel García Marquez, the much-anticipated bicentennial had come to symbolize Haiti's two hundred years of decrepitude.

Haiti's troubles were not over. Latortue's supporters were known as a "convergence" and a "group of 184" because they belonged to a myriad political parties and nongovernmental organizations; they accordingly spent much time bickering amongst themselves. To stabilize the situation and relieve the emergency force sent by France and the United States, the United Nations created yet another peacekeeping force, set to take over on June 1 with eight thousand men, but few countries expressed their enthusiasm for the task. Gen. Augusto Pereira of Brazil eventually took the head of thirty-two hundred French, U.S., and Latin American troops who were not numerous enough to patrol the capital effectively, let alone impose security throughout the provinces (another eleven Brazilians visited Port-au-Prince on August 18; they belonged to the *selecçao*, Brazil's illustrious soccer team, and promptly defeated the Haitian selection in a six–zero friendly at Sylvio Cator stadium in Port-au-Prince). The rest of Haiti was a political patchwork ruled by local *chefs de guerre*, Aristide devotees, remnants of the army, or, in the case of Gonaïves, *chimères* warlords. Because of a general breakdown of law and order, traveling from Port-au-Prince to Cap Haïtien, the country's two largest cities, was impossible. The road, already in poor condition, was intersected by roadblocks manned by local gangs who insisted on bribes and shot on sight. There was no more potent symbol of Haiti's long decline than the mayhem bisecting the country's main thoroughfare. These were probably not the bicentennial celebrations Dessalines had hoped for when he had declared his country's independence on January 1, 1804.

Aristide was as persistent in 2004 as he had been in 1991–1994. Shortly after arriving in the Central African Republic, he declared that the French and American ambassadors who had facilitated his departure and saved his life had in fact kidnapped him and that he had become for the second time in his life the victim of a coup d'état engineered by a President Bush. He even claimed, quite implausibly, that the Central African soldiers attending his press conference were prison wardens whose role was to prevent his return to his homeland. The charges were inaccurate, but they resonated with his supporters in the heated post-coup environment. Aristide had funds to back his words; looters who sacked his Tabarre mansion after his departure found thousands of dollars he had forgotten during his hasty departure. With a combination of populist rhetoric and financial prodding, Aristide could manipulate from exile the *Lavalas* affiliates who still occupied the assembly, as well as the gangs who controlled the capital's populous slums. Demonstrations, usually followed by violence, broke out regularly; they became a daily occurrence after the September 30 anniversary of his 1991 overthrow. The situation was dispiriting. Under Aristide, Haiti had been undemocratic. Now that he was gone, the country was ungovernable.

The Two-Hundred-Year Flood

Echoes of the capital's late-September political battles were only faintly heard in Gonaïves, the birthplace of both Haiti and the current crisis. On September 19, 2004, following the passage of tropical storm Jeanne, Gonaïves awoke to a flash flood that leveled entire sections of the populous city. Gonaïves was the main reason why Aristide and his party *Lavalas* (Creole for flood) had been expelled from office, and Gonaïves was seemingly punished with a deadly flood that broke out on the ten-year anniversary of the 1994 U.S. invasion and the two-hundred-year anniversary of Haiti's independence. For adepts of Voodoo, the numerological references left no place for doubt: Aristide had evidently secured the help of Agwe, the Voodoo *loa* of the sea.

Jeanne left a devastating trail behind her. When she hit, rain gushed down the denuded Haitian hillsides, taking the precious topsoil with it. Rivers swelled, overflowed their banks, and buried low-lying coastal cities such as Gonaïves under six feet of muck and brackish water. Jeanne was a mere tropical storm when she hit Haiti, but early tallies estimated that fifteen hundred Haitians had died, another thousand were missing, and three hundred thousand were left homeless. Fields and orchards of the Artibonite Valley, traditionally Haiti's breadbasket, were ruined. Decades of deforestation and shoddy building practices had left Haiti singularly vulnerable to high winds and tropical downpours. Jeanne had claimed only nine lives in the Bahamas, seven in the Dominican Republic, and two in Puerto Rico. An earlier tropical downpour that affected the town of Mapou near Haiti's southeastern border with the Dominican Republic in May 2004 had killed two thousand on the Haitian side while a mere seven hundred Dominicans had died. One wonders what would have happened if Haiti, rather than Florida, had been hit by four hurricanes during the summer and fall of 2004.

The political convulsions that followed Aristide's overthrow made the relief efforts particularly problematic. Survivors spent days on rooftops, surrounded by a sea of putrid sludge in which the storms' victims lay rotting. Some ventured barefoot in the wreckage, but pieces of broken zinc roofs hidden underwater made the trip a dangerous one. Gangrene threatened the hundreds of people injured in the storm. Amputations were the only answer in such cases, but they had to be performed with minimal hygiene and no anesthetics. Distress and hunger combined with hopes that the capital would soon send a rescue party. The first truck of food and medicine—sent and financed by the World Food Program, not by the Haitian government—finally made its way up the road from Port-au-Prince. Alas, when it reached the outskirts of Gonaïves, the truck was hijacked by *chimères* warlords who looted its cargo and sold it. Those too weak to fight for their share would have to wait (in later days, aid agencies issued a ruling barring all healthy young males from food distribution centers). Food shipments were halted while the UN peacekeeping force assembled all the troops it could spare to escort the convoys. Meanwhile, foreign doctors who had rushed to Gonaïves to prevent the outbreak of a cholera epidemic complained that they were left vulnerable to attacks by local gangs trying to benefit from their countrymen's misery.

Prime Minister Gérard Latortue boarded a UN helicopter, toured the site of the catastrophe from the air, and returned to Port-au-Prince to hold a press conference. There, he declared a state of national emergency and a three-day period of mourning, and predictably concluded that Haiti was in high need of foreign aid. He then moved on to more pressing matters. On October 2, he sent policemen to arrest two *Lafanmi Lavalas* senators and a former deputy as they were speaking on a radio talk show. The justification for these spectacular arrests remained unclear, but they were probably intended as a revenge for the deaths of nine policemen in the previous week's political clashes. A new pattern was set. The *Lavalas* diehards who controlled the capital's slums, probably inspired by the contemporary wave of kidnappings in Iraq, seized and beheaded policemen. The policemen retaliated by raiding the slums and killing bystanders. The survivors of the Gonaïves disaster could wait. As always, Haiti's political class knew where its priorities lay.

Conclusion: Predatory Elites

Haitian expert Robert E. Maguire has coined the expression "predatory elite" to describe the peculiar blend of gangsterism, populism, and outright theft that has defined the country's political superstructure for most of its two-hundred-year history. As mistletoe feeds off a tree, Haitian leaders have sucked away billions of dollars of their starving countrymen's money while offering nothing of discernable value in return. The chaotic situation of post-flood Gonaïves was a particularly egregious example of parasitism; but political bloodsuckers had bled Haiti white, drop by drop, for decades before. They had merely been more discreet while performing this task.

It is always difficult to understand how one can be so cruel and heartless. How can a well-fed gang leader snatch food relief away from hungry children after they have spent three days on a roof mourning their mother's drowning? How can a *restavek* owner beat up a seven-year-old child for forgetting to scrub the floor after she woke up at dawn? How can a president watch a man burn to death and then call for more grisly scenes of necklacing? How can Haiti's first lady spend millions of dollars on a fancy wardrobe when peasants take their children away from school because their precious pigs were slaughtered under the eradication program her husband approved? Such behavior betrays the most basic principles of human decency.

What is even more puzzling in Haiti's case is that several of the most rapacious leaders started their lives as ordinary, even good-hearted, people. Faustin Soulouque was a debonair army officer before an interrupted nap turned him into a ruthless dictator and imperialist. François Duvalier was a doctor who saved thousands of Haitians from the crippling decay of yaws before he turned into a merciless autocrat with a fondness for torture chambers. Jean-Bertrand Aristide was a kindly priest who defended orphans before he reneged on his vow of celibacy, betrayed his country, denounced his foreign allies, and started ruling Haiti as if he were the godfather of one of New York's five Mafia families.

In Haiti, presidential power has a way of possessing the most disinterested individual and turning him into a zombie-like automaton with a single-minded focus on his own political preservation. Political power has a natural tendency to corrupt individuals entitled with it, but Haitian presidents' odd behavior may be attributed to local political mores as well. The Haitian tradition of expecting everything from a president and the lack of powerful counter powers may inebriate the current occupant of the presidential palace and convince him that normal standards of behavior do not apply to him. Continual rumors of an impending coup d'état may convince even the more democratically minded ruler that force, and force alone, is the key to political survival. The country's colonial past may trigger an adversarial approach to normal diplomatic discourse, even when such belligerence further isolates Haiti. Haiti, in a nutshell, confirms Lord John Acton's adage that power can corrupt any human being, and that absolute power corrupts absolutely. The Haitian experience offers insights whose value is moral as well as historical; Haitian political history is a foray into the fallibility of the human soul.

The predatory elites' impact on their country's development is easier to comprehend. Being a dictator is no guarantee that one will remain in power for any length of time; so Haitian rulers constantly feel the need to seduce their core constituency through chimerical quick fixes (such as Aristide's restitution plan) or clientage (such as Aristide's "small presidential projects" handouts). Alternatively, they exploit xenophobia and racism in a desperate attempt to blame anyone but themselves for their misrule. Such ploys are expensive, diplomatically ruinous, and conducive to further instability and racial strife; but they work extremely well in the short term. The fact that Aristide, fourteen years after he was first elected to the presidency, has a good chance of returning from exile and starting a fourth presidential mandate is a testament to the ingenuity of Haiti's rulers when it comes to preserving their own rule. One can only lament the fact that they have not applied the same political skills to their country's more pressing needs, including hunger, unemployment, child slavery, spouse abuse, disease, illiteracy, and environmental devastation.

CHAPTER 12

Settling Down: The Second Préval Presidency (2006–2010)

Three-Card Monte

Haiti's history is generally characterized by extended periods of time during which a powerful individual dominates the political process (such as Jean-Pierre Boyer, Faustin Soulouque, and the Duvaliers), followed by bursts of instability as various pretenders jockey for power and the political system struggles to find a new equilibrium. The aftermath of Jean-Bertrand Aristide's second overthrow was one such moment. Neo-Duvalierist army veterans such as Guy Philippe, lower-class Aristide diehards, and Prime Minister Gérard Latortue's bourgeois supporters could all legitimately seek to gain or maintain power. But with brute force divided between army holdovers, slum gangs, and a weak national police, no single party was strong enough to decisively rout the other.

As the party that had played the leading role in overthrowing Aristide, the neo-Duvalierist camp seemed best positioned to secure power. But it was merely composed of a few hundred demobilized army veterans who could muster enough firepower to dislodge the unpopular Aristide government or disrupt the judicial process, but not enough to impose their views throughout the country (at their height, Bébé Doc's Tontons Macoutes had numbered three hundred thousand individuals). Its leaders' transparent agenda—naked oppression and theft under a thin layer of nationalism—was also largely discredited, and they were thoroughly unpopular, both nationally and internationally.

Though it failed to seize power, the far-right nebula did manage to avoid prosecution for its long record of human rights violations. Prosper

Avril, the former Haitian dictator (1988–1990) accused of master-minding the murder of Jean-Hubert Feuillé in 1995, was arrested in 2001, freed, rearrested, and held without charges in the Port-au-Prince penitentiary; he escaped from prison during the instability that followed Aristide's overthrow. Colonel Hébert Valmon, Colonel Carl Dorélien, and Major General Jean-Claude Duperval, who were accused of mas-sacring Aristide supporters in Raboteau in 1994, were deported from Florida and jailed in the national penitentiary; in February 2004, they too escaped. Louis-Jodel Chamblain, the former FRAPH leader who helped overthrow Aristide, stood trial on August 17, 2004, for his role in the murder of Aristide's friend Antoine Izméry—only to be acquitted.

This record of impunity is far from unusual. The Haitian judiciary rarely brings legal proceedings to a successful end—particularly when they target powerful individuals—and a sprawling diaspora of Haitian ex-oppressors extended from Europe to Central America. Bébé Doc, who after his 1986 exile enjoyed the high life on the French Riviera, was now living penniless in the Parisian suburbs (minus his avaricious wife, who left him after his money had run out). Philippe Biamby and Raoul Cédras, leaders of the junta that had terrorized Haiti during 1991–1994 and who had been sentenced *in absentia* to life in prison for their role in the 1994 Raboteau massacre, lived in a posh suburb of Panama City. The last member of the junta, Michel François, had also received a life sen-tence *in absentia* (which came on top of a 1997 U.S. indictment for drug trafficking), but he settled in Honduras where he ran a home appliance store 110 miles north of Tegucigalpa. Also sentenced to life in prison, Emmanuel Constant, the FRAPH leader who organized the 1993 Harlan County demonstration, lived freely in New York until he was arrested on unrelated charges of bank fraud in July 2006.

The most famous Haitian exile was Aristide, who, after a stay in Central African Republic and Jamaica, eventually settled in South Africa. His physical return to Haiti was unlikely as long as an interna-tional peacekeeping force, intent on preventing a new flare-up of politi-cal tensions, was present in the country. He was also cited in a large drug-trafficking investigation in Florida, making it legally perilous to return to a location anywhere near U.S. shores.[1] But Aristide had many supporters in the slums of Port-au-Prince, where his departure was fol-lowed by much restlessness (that the violence was directly organized by Aristide from his South African exile is plausible but difficult to prove). As late as 2006, entire sections of the capital were beyond the control of the provisional government; not even UN peacekeepers dared to enter the most notorious slums like Bel Air or Cité Soleil.

Though it presented itself as a form of political protest against Aristide's overthrow and the presence of foreign troops on Haitian soil, slum violence was the workings of organized gangs whose motives were primarily financial. The power vacuum in the capital gave them free rein to continue their illegal activities, and as they turned on one another to expand their turf or their share of the drug trade, a reign of terror began for ordinary Haitians. In the midst of full-blown gang wars, shootings and murders became a common occurrence in a country that, political violence aside, had endured relatively little insecurity in the past. By 2005, no one was safe from a seemingly random death; among many similar incidents, a French honorary consul was shot dead on the country's main thoroughfare between Cap Haïtien and Port-au-Prince. Most prevalent was the threat of kidnapping, a scourge that afflicted not only moneyed foreigners and businesspeople but also low-level professionals and even impoverished market sellers, who would be taken hostage for a fistful of dollars. Given the police's limited means, few cases were investigated or even reported; instead, relatives of the victims did their best to collect ransom payments to save their loved ones' lives.

The possibility that Aristide might return and the gangs' restiveness were a thorn in the side of Prime Minister Latortue, a light-skinned Haitian American with little local support beyond the bourgeoisie. To discredit his rivals, Latortue tried various legal expedients, but these proved ineffective. In November 2005, his government sued Aristide in U.S. court, accusing him of condoning drug trafficking and diverting public funds; the case died down when his lawyers proved unable to physically serve Aristide with the papers. Latortue also demanded that Aristide be extradited from South Africa to answer charges of fraud and incitation to political murder—again to no avail. Meanwhile, Aristide's former prime minister, Yvon Neptune, was jailed for two years on charges that he had been involved in a deadly battle between pro- and anti-Aristide supporters in Saint-Marc (the transparently political case never went to trial).

As has often been the case in Haiti's history, political infighting left the government little time to address issues more central to the population. Long-term problems—environmental devastation, underfunding of education and healthcare, poor infrastructures, and now insecurity—were compounded by a string of hurricanes and tropical storms, including Jeanne (September 2004), Dennis (July 2005), and Alpha (October 2005). These generally did not hit Haiti directly or at their full force, but compared with other Caribbean islands, Haiti suffered outsized physical damage, given its poor building practices and denuded hillsides.

Governmental relief in the aftermath of each catastrophe was not forthcoming; international aid agencies did the lion's share of the rescue-and-recovery effort.

Such natural disasters added yet another layer of misery for Haiti's long-suffering people, but they proved advantageous to the political class since they provided a compelling rationale to request more financial aid. In July 2004, an international donors' conference in Washington, D.C. pledged $1.085 billion over the following two years to assist Haiti's political transition after Aristide's overthrow (not counting money spent by NGOs and worker remittances sent by Haitians living abroad). Actual disbursement of the money was initially slow, but it picked up as the Haitian people endured one natural disaster after another. By the summer of 2005, Haiti had already received half a billion dollars, which put it on track to reach $1 billion by 2006.[2]

Whether those sizable contributions contributed to the long-term development of Haiti was a different matter altogether. Little cash made it past the layers of the bureaucracy to reach hurricane victims in Gonaïves and elsewhere. By 2006, Latortue was under fire at home for spending forty-four million gourdes in per diem rates and other expenses during a string of expensive forays overseas (which, he retorted, were justified by the fact that the trips had secured the country a total of $960 million under his tenure).[3] His underlings were also accused of diverting foreign monies earmarked for humanitarian relief, though such accusations were, by nature, hard to assess. The only hard data was provided by Transparency International's annual reports, which use a variety of surveys to identify countries in which corruption is most prevalent. After ranking first in 2004, Haiti slid to third place in 2005 (a mere 0.1 point below top-ranked Chad and Bangladesh), then regained the top spot as the world's most corrupt country in 2006. As is often the case in Haiti, no legal inquiry was ever launched to assess whether any irregular accounting took place under Latortue's regime. When his tenure in office came to an end in the spring of 2006, he abruptly left the country and retired in Boca Raton, Florida.

The international community, which bankrolled most of the Haitian treasury and maintained a large UN peacekeeping force in Port-au-Prince, could conceivably have acted as a kingmaker in the three-way struggle between army veterans, popular groups, and the bourgeoisie. But after a decade of near-constant involvement, "Haiti fatigue" had set in among foreign diplomats, and foreign powers played a largely passive role. During 2001–2004, U.S. conservatives had maneuvered behind the scenes through the International Republican Institute to foster resistance to Aristide, and possibly assist those who overthrew him.[4] But as the Bush administration entered its second term, and the simultaneous wars in Iraq and Afghanistan took their toll, Washington's enthusiasm for regime change began to wane.

The UN peacekeeping mission in Haiti (MINUSTAH), the single most powerful military force in the country and an entity that could easily have tipped the balance in favor of one of the competing parties, largely contented itself with a narrow agenda: maintaining order in downtown Port-au-Prince, facilitating the distribution of humanitarian aid, and organizing democratic elections. Imperialists they most certainly were not; all that MINUSTAH and its international backers hoped for was someone with decent democratic credentials to take over the thankless task of governing Haiti. In 2006, the commander of MINUSTAH, overwhelmed by much-delayed efforts to stage elections and two years of popular criticism of the peacekeeping effort in Haiti—which had cost the lives of ten of his blue helmets—simply shot himself in his hotel room.[5]

Embrace Thy Enemy

After multiple postponements—no doubt linked to the Latortue government's reluctance to cede power—presidential elections were finally held on February 7, 2006, nearly two years after Aristide's overthrow and on a day meant to commemorate previous presidential inaugurations. The odds-on favorite was René Préval, a former agronomist and president whose term, however unsatisfactory in many ways, seemed like a golden age in contrast with the ongoing chaos. As a former friend and ally of Aristide, Préval was a suitable substitute to Titid in the eyes of many Haitian poor. He was also a low-key political figure who had distanced himself from Aristide over the years, making him far less controversial than the deposed statesman to the bourgeoisie and foreign powers.

As in all recent elections, the electoral process was largely financed and monitored by the international community. The counting process, however, was distinctly Haitian. After hovering above 50 percent for nearly a week, Préval's share of the vote suddenly dropped to 49 percent in preliminary results, which if confirmed, would have forced a second round of balloting at some future, undetermined date. Angry Préval supporters, complaining that thousands of ballots cast in his favor had been found in a dump, began setting up barricades throughout major cities. With a major outbreak of political violence seeming likely, a group of diplomats led by the Organization of American States made a deal with the provisional government to discard eighty-five thousand blank ballots from the total. The procedure, though legally dubious, pushed Préval's share of the remaining ballots over the 50 percent threshold and narrowly avoided a dangerous political crisis.

For the first time in two years, Haiti had a president—though it would have been hard to tell from Préval's behavior. In contrast to Aristide, who, like most politicians, loved to speak and be heard, Préval was soft mannered, even secretive, and remained largely absent from public view. Even as his supporters erupted into celebrations across Haiti, he delivered no rousing victory speech, granted no interviews, and limited himself to a belated press conference on February 22.

Haiti has had its fair share of charismatic leaders whose outspokenness needlessly sparked domestic and international tensions, so Préval's low-key style, however unimpressive, had the advantage of facilitating national reconciliation and cooling the political process. Days after his election, while attending a private party in Port-au-Prince's wealthy Pétionville suburb, he encouraged two black leaders of Aristide's Lafanmi Lavalas party and two light-skinned scions of the elite to embrace so as to symbolize his intention "to reconcile Haiti."[6] Later during his tenure, Préval set free Aristide's former prime minister, Yvon Neptune, who had been held for two years without trial in an attempt to undermine the Aristide camp. In a "Plan d'Apaisement Social" designed to placate potential critics, Préval also decided to keep paying former Aristide bureaucrats and former army members their salary—in other words, he bought out his enemies on the far left and right.

Reaching out to one's foes is highly unusual in Haiti's winner-takes-all political culture, but Préval's conciliatory tactics bore fruit. Within a month, the association of Caribbean states, CARICOM, readmitted Haiti—which it had expelled in 2004 to protest Aristide's overthrow—into its ranks. In April, parliamentary elections quietly took place, and the country's legislative process resumed normally after a three-year hiatus. Then in May, Préval was officially inaugurated as president in one of Haiti's few peaceful transitions of power.

Préval's main priority as he assumed office was to quell the wave of insecurity that was at the forefront of every Haitian's concerns. Aside from its immediate human toll, insecurity had a sizable economic cost, making it impossible to attract foreign investments or to convince expatriates to return to Haiti. For the difficult task of reining in the gangs who had overtaken parts of the capital, Préval characteristically resorted to the carrot as well as the stick. Rather than attacking gang leaders as political extremists and drug warlords, he described criminality as a sad by-product of poverty and created the National Commission of Disarmament, Demobilization, and Reintegration (CNDDR) to foster small-scale social projects in the slums. Faithful to his strategy of defusing opposition, Préval even went as far as appointing gang leaders implicated in the murderous "Operation Baghdad" as members of the commission. Then in the fall of 2006, the national police and UN forces jointly entered Cité Soleil in force to combat the gangs that had controlled the area, unimpeded, for over two years. The kidnapping rate ebbed in the following months and years, and though still high, it no longer had the paralyzing effect on the social and economic life of the capital as it had during 2005–2006.

Happy Times Are Here Again

Préval's conciliatory manners extended to the international community, which he did not attack in the strident tone Aristide had employed before his downfall; in turn, the international community responded generously to his calls for continued assistance. In July 2006, shortly after his inauguration, a donors' conference in Port-au-Prince offered $750 million in aid for the following year. Another conference in Washington, D.C. in April 2009 offered another $324 million; a few days later, a U.S. pledge of $300 million followed. Then came the news in June 2009 that the International Monetary Fund had arranged for Haiti to receive $1.2 billion in debt relief under the Heavily Indebted Poor Countries (HIPC) program.

The sums were notable for a government deriving 65 percent of its operating budget from foreign monies, but given international aid's mixed record in fostering long-term growth in Haiti, the real piece of good news came from the U.S. Congress, where the Haitian Hemispheric Opportunity through Partnership Encouragement (HOPE) Act was passed in 2006. The act offered Haitian-made garments customs-free access to the United States and was further extended in 2008 (HOPE II).

Given the size and proximity of the U.S. market and the vast untapped supply of low-wage labor in Haiti (where the unemployment rate hovers around 70 percent), labor-intensive light manufacturing had always been a potential area of growth in Haiti. The HOPE acts made it economically attractive for entrepreneurs to use Haiti as a manufacturing base in the textile industry, as they had done in the early 1980s before political instability destroyed the nascent assembly sector. Inferior transportation infrastructures, corruption, red tape, and an unreliable energy supply remained major impediments to business, but the assembly sector soon passed the twenty-thousand-employee mark and continued to grow.

With time and a more congenial business environment, topping the high-water mark of eighty thousand employees last reached under Bébé Doc seemed likely. In 2009, the financier George Soros announced his intention to develop a free-trade zone in Haiti, and in October of that year, despite a severe worldwide economic downturn, hundreds of businesspeople gathered in Port-au-Prince for a two-day investment conference. Though organized by former U.S. president Bill Clinton (whose wife served as U.S. secretary of state), the conference was qualitatively very different from the many foreign-backed aid gatherings that had taken place in Haiti in the past. The attendees included representatives of Gap, Levi Strauss, and other U.S. apparel makers who had come not to offer short-term charity but a lasting investment and durable jobs. By the end of the conference, a first batch of ten projects worth $5 million was under way. Haiti was still a long way from turning into Singapore, Taiwan, or China—but then again, these countries had also begun their economic takeoff with a few low-wage factories.

The tourism industry, which had also peaked under Bébé Doc, was another path to economic rebirth. This sector was a leading employer throughout the Caribbean, with Haiti being the one glaring exception (even communist Cuba had become a notable destination for non-U.S. tourists since the 1990s). A major impediment was Haiti's horrendous reputation acquired over decades of political turmoil; a U.S. State Department travel warning advising against all nonessential travel to Haiti remained in effect until 2009. Practical considerations, in a country with fewer than one thousand hotel rooms and poor-quality infrastructures, were another obstacle.

In the short term, acting as a stopover for cruise ships was the most likely starting point, since it required no facilities on the ground aside from a few acres of fenced-in, secured sand. The many cruise ships sailing out of Florida could not visit Cuba due to the U.S. embargo, so Haiti was the nearest logical destination after stopping in the Bahamas. Only Haiti's unstable political life had prevented it from cashing in on the booming cruise industry.

Before 2004, Royal Caribbean began making tentative stops on Haiti's northern coast—though it described the port of call as "Labadee, Hispaniola," in its brochures to avoid scaring off its geography-challenged passengers. After canceling such stops altogether in the chaos that followed Aristide's overthrow—during which one of the security personnel guarding the beach was killed—Royal Caribbean resumed its activities when the political situation quieted down. In the years that followed, the increasingly popular port of call finally appeared under its real name of "Labadie, Haiti," and in 2009, the company prepared to invest $55 million for more extensive facilities on shore.

With Royal Caribbean paying a $6 tax for every tourist getting off of its ships in Haiti—not to mention the jobs created locally in the tourism, food, and handicraft industries as a result—the nascent cruise-ship business was an important source of hope. With time and contin-ued political stability, other cruise companies might follow suit. Throngs of tourists on day trips would begin to venture as far east as Cap Haïtien or into the interior to visit Henri Christophe's Citadel and Sans Souci Palace. Haiti would then turn into a standard stopover for Florida-based cruise ships wanting to offer their customers access to Haiti's cultural and architectural riches—a development that, if it had happened, would have brought a large, steady influx of foreign cash.

During 2006–2009, an increasingly tranquil Haiti largely disap-peared from international news—always a good sign for a country that is rarely mentioned when things go well. With political turmoil receding into the background, the economic potential of Haiti's civil society slowly began to unfold. After four years of recession (2001–2004) linked to the decline and fall of the Aristide regime, the Haitian economy began to grow again—by 2.3 percent in 2006, 3.4 percent in 2007, and 1.2 percent in 2008—and long-term estimates topped 3 percent.[7]

Haiti's growth rate would likely have been much higher had three external shocks not unfortunately hit the country in rapid succession. The first, a spike in world food prices in the spring of 2008, sparked a series of food riots and a political crisis that led to the dismissal of Prime Minister Jacques-Edouard Alexis. The demonstrations quieted down after Préval put rice subsidies in place to lessen the impact of the price increases on the Haitian poor. Solving the political impasse took longer, until after three months of wrangling (largely caused by lawmakers jock-eying for cabinet positions), a new government led by Prime Minister Michèle Pierre-Louis was voted in. The second shock was a string of four hurricanes and tropical storms in 2008—Fay, Gustav, Hanna, and Ike—that buried Haiti, and particularly low-lying Gonaïves, under a sea of mud and caused untold economic damage. The third shock was the most tragic—the January 12, 2010, earthquake, which leveled Port-au-Prince, took over two hundred thousand lives, and temporarily erased much of the progress Haiti had made in previous years.

CONCLUSION

Is There Any Hope for Haiti?

Paradise Lost

The small town of Jacmel, nestled on Haiti's beautiful southern coast, features all the picturesque qualities associated with a Caribbean locale. Located at the end of a small enclosed bay, alongside a mile-long beach of fine sand, Jacmel boasts a covered ironworks marketplace, garden fences graced by flowering bougainvilleas, and some fine, if faded, examples of gingerbread architecture. Aside from local sights, tourists can sample flavorful dishes of the French-inspired Haitian cuisine, purchase some Haitian art (including the local specialty, papier-mâché masks), or arrange a visit to nearby natural wonders. Bassins Bleus, a string of blue-colored pools of water perched above the city, is a popular destination, with the two-hour horse ride in the hills offering beautiful views of the Bay of Jacmel framed by *flamboyants* (tropical trees renowned for their colorful flowers).

When in Jacmel, tourists may also trek through the nearby La Visite National Park, which boasts some of the last forests remaining in Haiti and offers a foray into the inimitable atmosphere of Haiti's countryside: low huts (*kay*), men doing communal work in their fields (*konbit*), women balancing on their heads the goods they bring to market (*marchandes*), and throngs of chattering children (*ti moun*). As the elevation rises and the turquoise waters of the Caribbean Sea recede into the distance, the air becomes dry, pure, and cool—even for a tropical island. A few springs offer welcome refreshment along the way, as do bars stocked with Prestige and La Couronne, the local beer and soft drink. After two days of arduous climbing that give meaning to the Haitian proverb "Beyond the mountains, more mountains," the most adventurous tourists can reach Kenscoff, the breezy town of Swiss-like chalets overlooking the hustle and bustle of

Figure C.1 The bay of Jacmel as seen on the way to *Bassins Bleus*.

the capital. When visiting decrepit Port-au-Prince, it can be hard to understand why colonial Saint-Domingue was known as the Pearl of the Caribbean; but Jacmel and its surroundings (and many other areas along Haiti's coast) amply warrant the label.

Oddly, as I visited Jacmel in 2001, the only thing missing from this paradisiacal setting was tourists. Foreigners were virtually absent, as was the case throughout Haiti. Save for the occasional room reservation by a diplomat or aid worker, hotel rooms stayed empty for months on end, as did beaches and handicraft shops. Just a few hundred miles away in the Dominican Republic, all-inclusive resorts were jam-packed with European and North American visitors, as were many other islands whose natural and historical heritage paled in comparison with Haiti's. How could it be that the Caribbean's most beautiful isle, located a few hours by plane from major population centers in North America, had completely missed the tourist boom that was enriching the rest of the region?

Looking back into colonial times to explain Jacmel's economic limitations sheds no light on the issue. Jacmel suffered much during the Haitian Revolution—particularly in a lengthy 1799–1800 siege during the War of the South—but such events are too distant to explain current tourism trends (the siege of Jacmel, it should also be noted, was conducted by Jean-Jacques Dessalines, not a French imperialist). Natural phenomena do not explain the town's limitations either. Jacmel was hit hard by tropical storm Fay and hurricane Gustav in August 2008, then the January 12, 2010, earthquake, but the town's tourist industry was already ailing before these dates.

Rather, it seemed clear to me that Jacmel's inability to tap into the tourist bonanza was the result of profound political and structural problems—not just bad luck, the colonial legacy, or racist bias on the part of some foreign tourists. Jacmel's gingerbread houses were lovely, but its roads were potholed messes lined with uncollected garbage. The main river bordering the town doubled as a public latrine and a laundry-washing spot. The brackish, waste-filled water reached the beach unfiltered. But this was not all: the lovely fine sand was buried under a thick layer of trash, complete with a rusty cargo ship that had somehow ended its life on the town's waterfront. Broken glass, begging children, and survivors of the great 1982 swine massacre that lived off the beach's refuse added a final touch sure to scare away any tourist who had ventured so far.

Just getting to Jacmel was a struggle. A small pier was still under construction, making it impossible to reach the town by ferry or cruise ship. Though Port-au-Prince was just a few dozen miles away, traveling by land took hours on antiquated American school buses, devoid of regular schedules, which left when filled beyond capacity and stopped every few miles. Port-au-Prince's bus "terminals" were even less welcoming (the main one, for buses due north, was located in the midst of a slum).

Most discouraging to potential tourists was the fact that as of 2001, Haiti's perennially chaotic political life showed no sign of improving. Jean-Bertrand Aristide—in his antiforeign, late-career mode—had just returned to power, and his enemies were openly talking about removing him from office by force. Before the year was out, there would be two attempted coups d'état—one in July and one in December. Misrule—in this case, the lack of investments in infrastructure and sanitation—and political instability were clearly the main culprits of Jacmel's economic shortcomings. Haiti's rulers, not foreign exploiters, were to blame for transforming a lovely bay into a soiled basket case of unemployment, emigration, and hunger.

What Is Wrong with Haiti?

Writing a book on the history of Haiti can be a depressing experience. One must consult the thesaurus regularly to find synonyms for *cruelty*, *poverty*, and *thug*, while looking in vain for an opportunity to mention *hope* and *success* unaccompanied by *lack of*. Just as the Inuit tribes who employ dozens of words to describe varieties of snow and ice, Haitians have developed a rich vocabulary related to the political oppression that characterizes their own environment. The word *paramilitary* alone can be translated into a dozen different words that range from *piquet* to *zinglin, caco, cagoulard, macoute, attaché, FRAPH,* and *chimère.* Because of the ceaseless ballet of revolutions, often comical and bloodless in the late nineteenth century, more tragic and violent in recent times, Haitians like to say that the presidential seat is *rangé,* or cursed.

Probably the single most dispiriting aspect of Haitian history is that one can actually chart the price of a human being over time, starting with the slaves of colonial times, then continuing with the Royal Dahomey soldiers imported under Henri Christophe, the victims of the 1937 massacre, the cane cutters exported under the Duvaliers, the corpses sold by Luckner Cambronne to U.S. medical schools, the prostitutes of the 1970s sex tourism trade, and the *restaveks* of modern times. Drafting such a chart would be tasteless, but the fact remains that the overall trend goes downward. Buying a slave was an expensive proposition in the eighteenth century, much akin to a car purchase today. By the twentieth century, Sténio Vincent was willing to accept an indemnity for the 1937 massacre that valued each dead Haitian at the price of a good pig. In 2004, when former president Bill Clinton

Figure C.2 A close-up view of the bay of Jacmel shows the impact of decades of human neglect.

published his autobiography, *My Life,* he explained that he had invaded Haiti in 1994 in part because his government had spent $200 million to keep Haitians *out* of his country. Over the course of two hundred years, Haitians had gone from a valuable, though abused, resource to an equally exploited people whose overall value was negative in a U.S. president's eyes.

This book started with the question that is central to the Haitian experience: how did Haiti, a country that is small and mountainous but otherwise devoid of any major natural impediment to economic development, go from being the "Pearl of the Caribbean" in the eighteenth century to its current status as a Third World hot spot? To put it more bluntly, what is wrong with Haiti? The previous chapters should have made it clear that the racist argument that dominated Western historiography until recently is not valid: that Haiti is so poor has nothing to do with the fact that its inhabitants are of African ancestry. Haitians have adapted remarkably well to the adversity they have faced, proving time and again that they are a resourceful people whose sole limitation (due to a lack of schools) is widespread illiteracy. Members of the Haitian Diaspora, when transplanted to a more congenial environment, have done just as well as other immigrants—one of them, Michaëlle Jean, currently serves as governor general of Canada. Even Haitian leaders have proved remarkable for their intellectual gifts, though they have too frequently used them for political preservation rather than good governance.

When race has played a role in Haitian history, it has not been a biological factor, but rather a convenient excuse to further the political and economic ambitions of the elite at the expense of the public good. When racial theories first hardened in the late eighteenth century, they were meant as a way to help white planters supplant their mixed-race rivals. In later years, ambitious black and mulatto statesmen employed racial rhetoric to gather supporters in a struggle for political supremacy (the Louverture-Rigaud war that so ravaged Jacmel in 1799 was typical of a personal feud waged under the banner of racial war). Race again featured prominently in Dessalines's calls for revenge against French planters in 1804—though his eagerness to seize the estates of deceased planters suggests that financial gain, not racial purification, was his primary objective. Even the black nationalism of the *noiriste* school—and its legitimate celebration of Haiti's African past—has been perverted by rulers like Papa Doc and Jean-Bertrand Aristide, who borrowed the popular slogans of black nationalism so as to gain and maintain office while ignoring the economic needs of their black supporters.

Hypocritical calls for racial strife have cost Haiti greatly in the international arena as well. Interpreting the world through a racial prism has greatly complicated Haiti's relations with its white and mixed-blood partners in France, the United States, and the Dominican Republic. The *blan* (white person, but also a foreigner in Haitian Creole) was the original source of Haiti's ills and the solution to its problems, claim the most strident nationalists. This is, at least, what they express in public. Blaming white outsiders has always been a popular rallying cry, so rulers can be suspected of resorting to xenophobic rhetoric as needed so as to hide their own shortcomings (the most nationalistic rulers, Papa Doc and Aristide included, are always prompt to call for foreign military assistance behind the scenes when it suits their political ambitions). It should come as no surprise that Dessalines, Faustin Soulouque, and Papa Doc, three of the most brutal dictators in Haiti's history, were also three of the most outspoken advocates of racial pride, cleverly accusing white and mulatto rivals of racism and black critics of disloyalty to their race to silence opposition to their rule. Aristide followed a similar, though less brutal, path, carefully timing his anti-imperialist speeches so that they would coincide with periods when he was under attack for his poor economic record. Haiti cannot escape from its current slump until its leaders look at themselves and at foreigners as human beings, not as members of specific racial groups, and start drafting a development policy instead of constantly finding excuses in some alleged foreign or mulatto racial bias.

Decades of misguided rhetoric have taken their toll. With television and the Internet offering instant access to the outside world—albeit the television world of soccer stars earning multimillion-dollar salaries—many Haitians mistakenly assume that Americans and Europeans have access to untold riches gained by pilfering weaker nations rather than slowly and laboriously accumulating capital. Aristide's fantastic request for $21 billion must be understood in this context; he knew that France would never pay up, but he also knew how easy it would be to convince his supporters that the former colonial power could easily lift Haiti out of poverty by donating a minute portion of its misbegotten wealth, and that the compensation claim would direct popular anger away from his embattled regime. One may call this reliance on sudden, outside wealth the "borlette mentality" after the popular national lottery, the stands for which dot the Haitian landscape and bear revealing names like "Miami Bank" or "Brooklyn Express." "Colombia mentality" would be an adept expression as well, for many desperate peasants now think that their best chance of ever escaping poverty is to wait for a drug plane to mistakenly drop its cargo in their backyard. Little has changed, it seems, since the pirates of Tortuga Island banked on Spanish galleons for a quick windfall in gold.

A series of bad political decisions are to blame—more than racially motivated imperialism on the part of France and the United States—for Haiti's disastrous two centuries of independent rule. Dessalines first killed Haiti's skilled white cadres in 1804. Alexandre Pétion and Jean-Pierre Boyer selected small-scale agriculture as Haiti's main economic sector in the 1810s and 1820s, thus missing the Industrial Revolution that transformed other nations into economic powerhouses. Political instability at the turn of the century turned away potential investors and resulted in a poor allocation of resources as the national treasury financed constant wars and graft instead of education and infrastructures. The two Duvalier presidencies turned oppression and corruption into a science, thus chasing away Haiti's educated citizens, frightening away foreigners, and plundering national coffers to the last gourde. In the 1990s, Aristide was so busy provoking his rivals, then preparing his return from exile after they overthrew him, then grandstanding as a Haitian patriot, to hide the fact that he had returned with U.S. help, that he never took the time to invest the billions of dollars in foreign aid promised to him. Corruption, instability, and xenophobia: these are the main causes of Haiti's decline. Christopher Columbus, Bertrand d'Ogeron, and Admiral William Caperton can rest in peace: their stints as colonial stewards of Haiti brought bad times as well as good ones, but whatever mistakes they made took place too long ago to predetermine Haiti's current political and economic situation.

Sadly, once in place, political violence and poverty tend to become self-perpetuating. Because political murders are rarely investigated or punished, victimized groups often resort to extrajudicial killings to avenge their dead, further convincing the dominant group that repression is the only way to remain in power. Similarly, Haitian politicians would embrace elections if they had a fair chance of winning, but manipulations such as the ones that marked the 2000 elections leave opposition politicians convinced that they cannot prevail at the ballot box, thus setting the tone for more upheavals like the February 29, 2004, coup.

Poverty also begets poverty. Haitian peasants, who traditionally made great sacrifices to pay their children's tuition, started skimping on educational costs in the 1980s when they had to choose between feeding their children and nourishing their minds. As a result, an entire generation grew up without proper schooling. Aristide liked to remind his interlocutors that "illiterate people are not stupid" (*analfabet pa bet*).[1] This makes for a nice populist slogan, but it obscures the fact that uneducated Haitians fare poorly in the economic arena. Peasants have routinely been the victims of crooked lawyers taking advantage of their inability to read land titles, loan sharks demanding monthly 50 percent interest rates, urban bourgeois promising that their children would be well treated as *restaveks,* or, more recently, swindlers peddling the cooperatives' pyramid scheme.

Desperate to raise cash to feed his family, a peasant will cut down all of his trees to make charcoal, even though he is aware that doing so will ruin the topsoil and make valley towns more vulnerable to flash floods similar to the one that ravaged Mapou and Gonaïves in 2004. Such mudslides also bring pollution to Haiti's rivers and coral reefs, crippling fishermen's income after destroying that of farmers. Decades of economic setbacks have also convinced many Haitians that their only chance of ever escaping misery is to leave Haiti altogether, thus depriving the country of valuable human capital. Something—anything—must be done to stop this cycle of poverty.

A Development Plan

Haiti's sobering historical record does not mean that it is a hopeless country that will always remain as desperately impoverished as it is now. Haiti was the richest colony of the Western Hemisphere when its slave revolt began in 1791 and only fell from its pedestal through a worst-case scenario of continuous misrule. Conjointly, Haiti's current status as a concentrate of all the Third World's problems should not be an indication that Haiti is forever doomed. Virtually all of Haiti's current ills are man-made and can be "man-corrected" (AIDS, hurricanes, and earthquakes are more unpredictable, but even these "acts of God" can be combated with proper proactive measures). Recent East Asian history has seen many instances in which a tiny, overpopulated, resource-poor country surmounted a seemingly intractable history of underdevelopment to transform itself into an "Asian tiger" within a generation.

South Korea was one such economic miracle. When it emerged from the bloody Korean War, it was a backwater corner of the world, ruined beyond recognition and lamenting the fact that most of its heavy industry and coal mines were located in Communist North Korea. Both South Korea's and North Korea's 1960 GDP per capita were equivalent to that of Haiti at the onset of the Papa Doc presidency ($880). Today, South Korea is one of the world's richest countries with a GDP per capita of

$19,000. North Korea, with an estimated per capita GDP of $1,000, is on the verge of starvation because its dictators mismanaged the economy while wasting resources on an oversized army and military nuclear programs. Haitians, with an average GDP of $1,400, are hungry too, but they cannot find solace in the fact that their nuclear capabilities are a source of great angst for U.S. military planners (these statistics take into account purchasing power parity; in nominal terms, Haiti has an annual GDP of $550 per person, or $1.50 a day on average).

A span of fifty years was sufficient to transform three countries of comparable size and wealth into three vastly different economies. Political factors—in this case, the disastrous rules of Kim Il Sung, Kim Jong Il, the Duvaliers, and Aristide—bear most of the blame for these differing paths. Conversely, good government could radically alter North Korea's and Haiti's fortunes in the near future. The Asian tigers' examples show that in the current integrated world economy, a dramatic turnaround can take as little as one generation (Europe's industrial revolution took about one hundred years; the United States' and Japan's, fifty; and China's, twenty). Haiti has a large industrious population, no major threat to its territorial integrity, and a strategic location next to the world's largest market.

Terrorism, crime, retirement and health care costs, right versus left, and abortion: these are the issues that monopolize U.S. news. But the central issue of our age, one that is often ignored, is underdevelopment. However horrible terrorism might be, history's worst terrorist attack, on 9/11, killed fewer than three thousand people. Underdevelopment affects billions and kills millions every single year. Two and a half billion people, including most Haitians, live on two dollars a day or less. An estimated twenty-seven million people are victims of modern-day versions of slavery like Haiti's *restavek* system. One million people die every year of malaria, a disease that pharmaceutical companies spend little time trying to cure because 90 percent of its victims are penniless children who hail from impoverished African nations (the Bill and Melinda Gates Foundation is now financing research into a potential vaccine). Why are some countries so poor? Can they ever change for the better? These are the central questions of our age. Haiti's descent into the abyss of underdevelopment—and its possible rebirth—can serve as a model for many other countries facing similar predicaments.

How to effect drastic change is the $21 billion question. Suffice it to say, the vast program of aid advocated by Aristide is no more likely to work than the steady influx of aid over the past forty years, the combined value of which is fast approaching Aristide's requested amount. It might spark a short-term boost in Haitians' income, but it would encourage instability as politicians fought over the massive windfall, destroy the local industry by making the creation of wealth unnecessary, and most likely not result in long-term, self-sustaining growth. Despite its generosity, it might even result in Haitian charges of foreign neocolonialism—a common refrain in Haiti today despite the aid donors' good intentions.

For some enlightened Haitian ruler to emerge is a possibility, but history shows that it is no surefire panacea. Haiti has seen a few benevolent dictators (such as Christophe and Lysius Salomon) who forcibly improved their compatriots' lot, but nothing sustained this growth save the sheer will of its initiators, and economic decline immediately followed their demise. Haiti has also seen many a promising leader whose good intentions were sidetracked by the easy money of state funds and the thrill of power. A broad-based economic development springing from Haiti's grassroots, not strongman rule, is Haiti's best chance for lasting growth.

Historical examples show that economic development generally starts with an initial phase of agricultural modernization during which mechanization and better farming techniques eliminate famine and surplus rural workers are forced to migrate to the cities. The second stage sees the growth of labor-intensive light industries such as textile or (in modern times) electrical assembly. Working conditions tend to be bad in this economic model, but it is uniquely adapted to a large, unskilled urban population that can do few tasks, but can do them cheaply. As education levels, saving rates, and business acumen increase, factories are able to switch (often with government subsidies) to a third stage of heavy industry like shipbuilding and steel mills that require capital investments and engineering know-how that were unavailable prior to the economic take-off. Finally, labor-intensive industries decline due to competition from countries with lower salaries, "rust belts" decline, and economies move into a fourth stage in which service-oriented sectors, such as information technology, make good use of the well-educated workforce.

Whether economic development takes place in a dictatorial or democratic environment remains open to question. The Industrial Revolution unfolded as England and the United States were relatively democratic for their age, but similar growth in East Asia and continental Europe took place under dictatorial regimes. History only offers three insights. First, dictatorial regimes can coincide with economic growth only if they impose internal competition, protect entrepreneurs, invest in education and infrastructure, and generally create an environment that rewards success.

Second, countries usually install high tariff barriers in the early stages of development to protect their nascent industry, then progressively embrace free trade as productivity rises to force domestic manufacturers to remain competitive and allow them to export (Haiti's rush to drop its tariff barriers in 1986 and again in 1991 is an unusual case of a country submitting weak domestic producers to devastating foreign competition before they had a chance to mature). Third, economic progress has always resulted in long-term democratization as newly educated, prosperous middle classes—as in the case of the people of Taiwan and South Korea—demand a say in government (hopes of future political progress have been the rationale for the United States' economic involvement with China since Bill Clinton's presidency).

These historical precedents offer a blueprint that could easily be adapted to Haiti's specific strengths and weaknesses. Eliminating the predatory class that has been the main cause of Haiti's misfortunes is an essential prerequisite in Haiti's case, as are weaning Haiti off its reliance on foreign aid and combating the xenophobic streak that regularly perverts public discourse. During the takeoff stage, key industries have often been nationalized in countries like Russia and France, but due to the dearth of qualified public servants and the high level of corruption, a large government role is unlikely to work in Haiti; a free-market, even libertarian, approach seems better suited. Haitians get virtually nothing from their government as it is—neither education, nor health care, nor infrastructure maintenance, nor disaster relief, nor policing and national defense. Restricting the government's role to a narrowly defined sphere would provide the same level of services, minus the cost.

Haiti also has some unique assets. As soon as the business environment becomes more welcoming, Haiti will be a prime candidate for industrial outsourcing when rising wages in China and elsewhere force U.S. importers to find alternate sources of cheap labor. Haiti's population is large and young; this demographic imbalance makes the first stage of economic development (agricultural self-sufficiency) a challenge, but it will prove essential during the second stage (light industry requiring a lot of unskilled labor). Haitian women in particular have long proved resourceful and hard working and are typically export businesses' employees of choice. Haiti's proximity to the U.S. mainland, which led to two U.S. invasions in the twentieth century and countless cases of political interference, could finally prove to be a boon to Haiti.

Critics might complain that becoming another country's workshop is a form of economic neoimperialism or point out that low wages and difficult working conditions are the norm in assembly factories. The reality is that Haiti has little choice. An overpopulated island with no available land is destined to trade or starve; exporting manufactured goods for food is one of the few realistic economic paths Haiti can take. Low wages and long hours have been the lot of all nascent industrial powers, but even these conditions can be mitigated by good enforcement of labor laws (the U.S. Congress's HOPE II Act contained labor protection clauses). Paradoxically, the best way to improve the lot of Haitian workers is to build more assembly factories. As long as a mere twenty thousand assembly jobs are available in Port-au-Prince and 70 percent of Haitians are unemployed, employers will have no incentive to raise wages and treat workers well. Should the number of employees surpass one million, however, market forces will dictate that employers cater to an increasingly limited labor pool by eliminating sweatshop conditions.

The rise of a service economy—the final and most lucrative stage in the development blueprint detailed in this chapter—could take place earlier than expected in Haiti because of this country's immense tourism potential. Haiti's natural beauty is equal or superior to any of its more popular Caribbean rivals. To this, Haiti can add architectural masterpieces such as the Citadelle Laferrière and Sans Souci Palace, the thrills of fake Voodoo ceremonies, a chance to buy Haitian art or sample Creole cuisine, and the ineffable joys of five-star Barbancourt rum. Columbus's first voyage, pirate lore, and an (idealized) version of the plantation world would give entrepreneurs numerous opportunities to design hotels and theme parks inspired by Haiti's distinctive history. Such a tourist boom would allow Haiti to move quickly from the low-margin, low-pay assembly sector to other activities, such as creating artwork for foreign tourists, that require more skills and provide higher wages (Haitian-produced art is already ubiquitous in the Dominican Republic's souvenir shops). None of this will happen as long as Haiti is known for the brutality and short life expectancy of its leaders, but a turnaround can happen quickly. Greece, Portugal, and Spain—some of Europe's favorite tourist destinations—were all under dictatorships in the 1970s, and it took merely a decade for Ireland to transform itself from a terrorism-plagued nation divided by sectarian strife to roaring Irish Tiger. By 2009, after just a few years of stability, the backwater derelict Jacmel of 2001 was already turning into a budding tourist destination, complete with annual festivals and two hotels in the last stages of obtaining a Comfort Inn franchise. The 2010 earthquake was a major setback, but it is not impossible to imagine that within a decade's time, the city could become a popular stopover for cruise ships or a location for several all-inclusive resorts. All that is needed is lasting political stability and decent infrastructure.

When I mention that I specialize in the history of Haiti, U.S. interlocutors typically begin by telling me how shocked they are by Haiti's gut-wrenching poverty, then proceed to ask what they can do to help lift the country out of its misery (despite the prevalent Haitian narrative of foreign exploitation, I have yet to encounter a person, even in U.S. government ranks, who asked me for the best method to expand U.S. hegemony over Haiti). People usually assume that I will give them a list of my favorite charities, but the answer to this oft-mentioned question—what the United States should do to help Haiti—is simple: as little as possible. U.S. farmers do not need to donate rice to hungry Haitians—this will undercut the local rice industry. U.S. taxpayers do not need to bankroll the Haitian government—this will make the business of running Haiti too lucrative and desirable. U.S. troops do not need to patrol the streets of Port-au-Prince—this will give rise to an understandable nationalist outcry. U.S. ambassadors do not need to select politicians they deem to be best suited for Haiti's future—it is up to Haitians to set up their own government. The history of Haitian-U.S. relations is so politically explosive that anything the United States does, however well intentioned, could be viewed with suspicion in Haiti and may likely backfire.

Aside from short-term disaster relief in the case of a major hurricane or earthquake, the United States should limit itself to creating the conditions for lasting self-driven economic growth in Haiti. The U.S. government should open the U.S. market, tax free, to Haitian-made goods (as the HOPE acts already do for garments), while eliminating the hefty subsidies to the U.S. farming sector that make it so difficult for farmers in Haiti and other poor countries to compete on an equal footing. U.S. businesses should invest in areas where Haiti has a competitive advantage (like labor-intensive industries, handicrafts, and tourism). U.S. customers and tourists should purchase Haitian-made products—artwork, rum, coffee, T-shirts—and visit Haiti. The rest, as in any other sovereign nation, is up to Haitians. Two centuries after 1804, what Haiti truly needs is a second declaration of independence.

Over the long run, favorable developments such as the growth of the assembly and tourism sectors should create a virtuous cycle that would generate further economic growth and end the vicious circle of self-perpetuating poverty. Members of the Haitian Diaspora should return and bring with them much-needed capital and expertise once a stable regime is put in place and business opportunities appear in Haiti. The first tourists to venture back into Haiti—most likely the adventurous, backpacking kind—would convince local hotel owners to modernize their rooms and create vacation packages catering to the affluent throngs who long for reliability and safety more than authenticity. The presence of several assembly factories in a given area would attract more business people desirous of tapping into existing energy and transportation facilities.

Even Haiti's political life should benefit from rising income levels. Judges and civil servants would be less swayed by bribe offers if they actually received their monthly salary. Voters would less likely embrace a radical populist agenda if moderate policies offered them a reasonable hope for a better future. With lucrative careers available in the private sector, the vicious battle to control the spoils of government would take on a less desperate tone. Maybe, fifty years from now, daydreaming will pay off. Maybe, fifty years from now, Haiti will once again be known as the Pearl of the Caribbean.

EPILOGUE

Where Are They Now?

Jean-Bertrand Aristide, the priest-turned-president who has dominated Haitian politics since he was first elected president in 1990, fled to the Central African Republic after he was overthrown in February 2004. He later went to Jamaica, ostensibly to visit his daughters, but probably in the hope of returning to power in Haiti as well. Regional unrest following his return convinced him to move to South Africa. South Africa has so far declined Prime Minister Latortue's demands to extradite Aristide to Haiti where he could be indicted for fraud and incitation to political murder.

Prosper Avril, the former Haitian dictator (1988–1990) who was accused of masterminding the murder of Jean-Hubert Feuillé in 1995 and who fled into exile to escape prosecution, returned to Haiti in 2000. He was arrested in 2001, freed, rearrested, and kept in the Port-au-Prince penitentiary even though he was never formally sentenced for a specific crime. He escaped from prison during the instability that followed Aristide's overthrow in February 2004.

Bébé Doc (Jean-Claude Duvalier) and his wife **Michèle** fled for a luxurious exile on the French Riviera after they were overthrown as dictators of Haiti in February 1986. Michèle divorced her husband in 1990 and Bébé Doc moved to a less exuberant lifestyle near Paris. Both were probably indications that he had run out of money. Some Haitians nostalgic of the 1970s called on Bébé Doc to return to Haiti during the Préval presidency; Bébé Doc even announced in 1997 that he intended to return to Haiti to create a "pluralist democracy."[1] Thankfully, nothing came out of it.

Philippe Biamby followed **Raoul Cédras** to his Panamanian exile. They stayed at a Panama City palace, then moved to Contadora Island, renowned as a former vacationing hot spot for the Shah of Iran, and then returned to a posh suburb of Panama City. In 2000, the two were tried *in abstentia* for their role in the 1994 Raboteau massacre and sentenced to life in prison. Panama turned down Haiti's request that Cédras and Biamby be extradited; so neither of them ever spent time in prison for the thousands of political murders they condoned as members of the military junta that ruled Haiti in 1991–1994.

Jean-Robert Cadet, the author of a moving autobiography on his life as a *restavek* slave, moved to the United States along with his owner. Afraid of being prosecuted for child exploitation, she kicked him out of her home a few months later. He finished his studies, briefly served in the U.S. army, and now teaches French literature in Cincinnati, Ohio. He is married with children.

Louis-Jodel Chamblain, the former FRAPH leader who was implicated in the 1993 murder of Aristide's friend Antoine Izméry and who later helped Guy Philippe overthrow Aristide in 2004, stood trial on August 17, 2004 for his role in the Izméry murder. He was acquitted.

Emmanuel Constant, who organized the 1993 *Harlan County* demonstration and led the FRAPH death squads, entered the United States three months after the 1994 U.S. invasion on an invalid visa. He was later arrested in New York and sent to an immigration jail, but bizarrely was not deported as is routinely the case with illegal Haitian immigrants. Instead, he was released in June 1996. Constant apparently concluded a deal with U.S. immigration authorities under which he would remain silent on his past role as a CIA informer in exchange for the right to remain in the United States. He now lives in New York. He was also sentenced to life in prison *in abstentia* in the 2000 trial on the Raboteau massacre.

Katherine Dunham, the African American artist and Dumarsais Estimé lover who helped popularize Haitian dance in the 1960s and described the *restavek* system in her memoirs, was a prime supporter of Aristide during his years in exile. In August 2004, she sailed on the "Cruising into History" cruise that transported five hundred friends of Haiti intent on celebrating the country's bicentennial. She was ninety-five years old.

Maj. Gen. Jean-Claude Duperval, who served as Cédras's second-in-command during the 1991–1994 dictatorship and was implicated in the 1994 massacre of Aristide supporters in Raboteau, settled in Orlando, Florida, where he worked on tourist ships for the Walt Disney World resort. Also in Florida were his former colleagues Col. **Hébert Valmon**, who worked as a security guard in Tampa, and Col. **Carl Dorélien**, who lived in Port St. Lucie off income from a $3.1 million gain at the state lottery. All three were deported in 2003–2004 for lying on an immigration form about their criminal past. Jailed in Port-au-Prince along with Prosper Avril, they escaped during Aristide's overthrow in February 2004.

Michel François, the third member of the military triumvirate that ruled Haiti in 1991–1994, fled to Honduras after the U.S. invasion. A U.S. court indicted him in 1997 for helping to smuggle thirty-three metric tons of cocaine into the United States before and during his tenure in power, but he was never extradited. He was also sentenced to life in prison *in abstentia* during the 2000 trial on the Raboteau massacre. He now runs a home appliance store 110 miles north of Tegucigalpa.

Emile Jonassaint, the eighty-one-year-old president who signed the Carter–Jonassaint agreement on the eve of the 1994 U.S. invasion, died a year later in October 1995.

Brian S. Latell, the CIA analyst who was accused of passing on Cédras's anti-Aristide propaganda, facts unchecked, to members of Congress during a 1993 briefing, has since retired from the agency. He now is adjunct professor at Georgetown University's School of Foreign Service. His colleagues include **Madeleine Albright** and **Anthony Lake**, who served as secretary of state and national security adviser in the Clinton administration.

Lawrence P. Rockwood, the U.S. captain who was court-martialed for single-handedly investigating human rights abuses in Haitian prisons, received a dishonorable discharge as a result. He earned a Ph.D. at the University of Florida and now teaches history at the University of California in San Marcos and at Grossmont College. He ran for the U.S. Congress in 2004.

Notes

Introduction: Haiti in Ruins

1. Frantz Duval, "Les secondes qui ont tout changé," *Le Nouvelliste* (February 12, 2010), 2.
2. Pat Robertson interviewed by Kristi Watts, Christian Broadcasting Network (January 13, 2010).
3. Interview by Samuel Baucicaut, "Entrevue avec le premier ministre Jean-Max Bellerive," *Le Nouvelliste* (February 13, 2010).
4. "Haïti et l'arme sismique," *Haïti Progrès* vol. 27 no. 35 (February 3–9, 2010), 1.
5. Leslie Péan, "Obama pris entre deux feux et Haïti," *Haïti Observateur* (February 3–10, 2010), 8.
6. Frantz Douyon, "Seul l'État haïtien a la légitimité pour faire la promotion de l'intérêt national," *Le Nouvelliste* (February 13, 2010).
7. Peter Bosch and Yves Colon, "Haiti's Prisons: Inside the Gates of Hell," *Miami Herald* (March 25, 2001), 1L.
8. Clarens Renois (AFP), "Haïti: un mois après le séisme, une crise politique se dessine," *Le Nouvelliste* (February 14, 2010).
9. "Desgraça no Haiti está sendo boa para nós aqui, diz cónsul no Brasil; assista," *Folha Online* (January 15, 2010), http://www1.folha.uol.com.br/folha/mundo/ult94u679672.shtml.
10. David Brooks, "The Underlying Tragedy," *New York Times* (January 14, 2010).
11. Comment by Christopher Dodd, "Haiti: From Rescue to Recovery and Reconstruction" (January 28, 2010), http://www.c-spanvideo.org/program/291699-1.

1 The Pearl of the Caribbean: Haiti in Colonial Times (1492–1791)

1. Christopher Columbus, *The Four Voyages* (New York: Penguin Books, 1969; translated by K. M. Cohen), 116.
2. Quoted in Robert D., Nancy G., and Michael Heinl, *Written in Blood: The Story of the Haitian People, 1492–1995* (New York: U. Press of America, 1996), 4.
3. Quoted in Eric Williams, *From Columbus to Castro: The History of the Caribbean* (1970; reprint, New York: Vintage Books, 1984), 34.
4. Quoted in Heinl et al., *Written in Blood*, 18.
5. Aristide and Christophe Wargny, *Jean-Bertrand Aristide: An Autobiography* (New York: Orbis Books, 1993), 143. From 1500 to 1650, Spanish imports of gold and silver from the entire New World (including Mexico and Peru) were 80 tons and 16,000 tons, respectively. See Henry Kamen, *Empire: How Spain Became a World Power, 1492–1763* (2002; reprint, New York: HarperCollins, 2004), 287.

2 The Slaves Who Defeated Napoléon: The Haitian Revolution (1791–1804)

1. Quoted in Laurent Dubois, *Avengers of the New World: The Story of the Haitian Revolution* (Cambridge, MA: Harvard University Press, 2004), 100.
2. Laurent Dubois and John Garrigus, *Slave Revolution in the Caribbean, 1789–1804: A Brief History with Documents* (New York: Bedford / St. Martin's, 2006), 86–93.
3. Antoine Métral, *Histoire de l'expédition des Français à Saint-Domingue sous le consulat de Napoléon Bonaparte (1802–1803), suivie des mémoires et notes d'Isaac l'Ouverture* (1825; reprint, Paris: Karthala, 1985), 325.
4. Napoléon Bonaparte to Victoire Leclerc, July 1, 1802, *Correspondance de Napoléon Ier*, ed. Jean-Baptiste Vaillant (Paris: Plon, 1858), 7:640.
5. Toussaint Louverture to Jean-Baptiste Dommage, February 9, 1802, CC9B/19, Archives Nationales, Paris.

3 Missed Opportunities: Haiti after Independence (1804–1915)

1. Quoted in Laurent Dubois, *Avengers of the New World: The Story of the Haitian Revolution* (Cambridge, MA: Harvard University Press, 2004), 298.
2. Jean-Jacques Dessalines, "Proclamation" (January 1, 1804), AB/XIX/3302/15, Archives Nationales, Paris.

4 Benevolent Imperialism: Haiti during the First U.S. Occupation (1915–1934)

1. Quoted in Hans Schmidt, *The United States Occupation of Haiti, 1915–1934* (New Brunswick, NJ: Rutgers, 1971), 48.

5 Hearts of Darkness: The Duvaliers' Black Revolution (1957–1986)

1. Quoted in Bernard Diederich and Al Burt, *Papa Doc: Haiti and its Dictator* (1969; reprint, Maplewood, NJ: Waterfront Press, 1991), 80.
2. Quoted in Elizabeth Abbott, *Haiti: The Duvaliers and Their Legacy* (1988; reprint, New York: Simon and Schuster, 1991), 133.
3. Graham Greene, *The Comedians* (1966; reprint, New York: Bantam Books, 1967), ii (emphasis added).

6 A Glimmer of Hope: Aristide's Rise to Power (1988–1991)

1. Robert Pastor in a telephone interview with the author (December 10, 2001).
2. Jean-Bertrand Aristide and Laura Flynn, *Eyes of the Heart: Seeking a Path for the Poor in the Age of Globalization* (Monroe, ME: Common Courage Press, 2000), 16.
3. Speech reproduced in "Aristide Address 27 September after Visit to UN," *Federal Broadcast Information Service Daily Report* (October 7, 1991), 17–19.

7 The Haitian Invasion of the United States: Haitian Boat People (October 1991–October 1993)

1. Quoted in Pamela Constable, "US Relations With Aristide Enter New Phase," *Boston Globe* (April 10, 1994), 15.
2. Quoted in Catherine S. Manegold, "Innocent Abroad," *The New York Times* (May 1, 1994), section 6, 38.
3. Quoted in Elaine Sciolino, "Clinton Says U.S. Will Continue Ban on Haitian Exodus," *The New York Times* (January 15, 1993), A1.

8 Invasion on Demand: The Second U.S. Invasion of Haiti (October 1993–October 1994)

1. "Newsmaker Interview, Jean-Bertrand Aristide," *MacNeill-Lehrer News Hour* (October 22, 1993).
2. Quoted in Steven Greenhouse, "Aristide Condemns Clinton's Haiti Policy as Racist," *The New York Times* (April 22, 1994), A1.

3. Quoted in Howard W. French, "Doubting Sanctions, Aristide Urges US Action on Haiti," *The New York Times* (June 3, 1994), A3. See also "Pdt. Aristide's Address to TransAfrica's 13th Annual Foreign Policy Conference, 3 June 1994," blue folder, box 320.04 SIT, Collège St. Martial library, Port-au-Prince; "Acta de la séptima sesión (5–6 Junio 1994)," OEA/Ser. F/V. 1 MRE/ACTA 7/94, Organization of the American States Library, Washington, DC; Philippe Girard, *Clinton in Haiti: The 1994 U.S. Invasion of Haiti* (New York: Palgrave-MacMillan, 2004), 98.

9   Gratitude Is the Heart's (Short-Term) Memory: The Second Aristide Presidency (October 1994–February 1996)

1. "Meeting of the Multinational Force Coalition in Haiti," *U.S. Department of State Dispatch* vol. 5 no. 38 (September 19, 1994), 609.
2. Katherine Dunham, *Island Possessed: Haiti and the Story of a Woman Whose Life Became One with Her Island* (New York: Doubleday, 1969), 42–44 (Creole spelling updated).
3. Jean-Robert Cadet, *Restavec: From Haitian Slave–Child to Middle-Class American; An Autobiography* (1998; reprint, Austin: University of Texas Press, 2002), 4–5 (Creole spelling updated).
4. Quoted in "Tipper Gore's Staff Scared, but Unhurt in Stone-Throwing Incident," *Associated Press Wire* (October 15, 1995).
5. Signal FM, "Aristide Speaks out on Privatization," *Federal Broadcast Information Service* (October 4, 1995), 8.
6. Radio Galaxie, "Aristide Announces Upcoming Change of Government," *Federal Broadcast Information Service* (October 23, 1995), 39–40.

10   Divide and Founder: The Préval Presidency (1996–2001)

1. Quoted in "Nul ou médiocre?," *L'Express* no. 2321 (December 28, 1995), 7.
2. Quoted in Michael Norton, "Back on Center Stage, Haiti's Aristide is Frustrating Washington—Again," *Associated Press Wire* (June 13, 1997).
3. Quoted in Jean-Michel Caroit, "En toute impunité, les 'chimères' font régner la terreur en Haïti," *Le Monde* (April 11, 2000), 4.

11   Boss Titid: The Third Aristide Presidency (2001–2004)

1. Quoted in "'Tolérance Zéro' pour tous les malfaiteurs?," *Haïti Progrès* vol. 19 no. 15 (June 27, 2001), 1.
2. Quoted in "Célébration de l'indépendance: le chef de l'état aux Gonaïves," *Haïti Progrès* vol. 20 no. 43 (January 8, 2003), 1.
3. Quoted in "1803–2003: restitution et réparation," *Haïti Progrès* vol. 21 no. 4 (April 9, 2003), 1.

4. Quoted in "Vertières au sommet des victoires de la liberté," *Haïti Progrès* vol. 21 no. 36 (November 19, 2003), 1.
5. Quoted in "La déclaration du bicentenaire," *Haïti Progrès* vol. 21 no. 43 (January 7, 2004), 1.

12 Settling Down: The Second Préval Presidency (2006–2010)

1. Jay Weaver and Jacqueline Charles, "Haiti's Ex-president Is Main Focus of Investigation of Bribes from Drug Traffickers, but Paper Trail Is Lacking," *Miami Herald* (July 2, 2006), 1A; Ben Fountain, "Addicted to Haiti," *New York Times* (February 7, 2010), WK12.
2. Maureen Taft-Morales, *Haiti: International Assistance Strategy for the Interim Government and Congressional Concerns* (US Library of Congress: Congressional Research Service, 2005), 16, http://fpc.state.gov/documents/organization/57461.pdf.
3. Gérard Latortue, "En guise de réponse au journal Le Nouvelliste," *Haïti Observateur* (July 26–August 2, 2006), 7.
4. Walt Bogdanich and Jenny Nordberg, "Mixed US Signals Helped Tilt Haiti toward Chaos," *New York Times* (January 29, 2006).
5. Ginger Thompson, "Chief of UN Troops in Haiti Is Found Dead in Hotel Room," *New York Times* (January 8, 2006).
6. Ginger Thompson, "Préval's Silence Obscures Quiet Bid to Reunite Haiti," *New York Times* (February 20, 2006), www.nytimes.com/2006/02/20/international/americas/20haiti.html.
7. International Monetary Fund and International Development Association, *Haiti: Enhanced Initiative for Heavily Indebted Poor Countries: Completion Point Document* (Washington, DC: International Monetary Fund, 2009), 64, http://imf.org/external/pubs/ft/scr/2009/cr09288.pdf.

Conclusion: Is There Any Hope for Haiti?

1. Quoted in Patrick Forestier, "La démocratie chimérique d'Aristide," *Paris Match* no. 2851 (January 8, 2004), 47.

Epilogue: Where Are They Now?

1. Quoted in Lisa Hoffman, "Where Are They Now: Bloody Former Dictators," *Scripps Howard News Service* (January 23, 2003).

Bibliography

Abbott, Elizabeth. *Haiti: The Duvaliers and Their Legacy*. 1988; reprint, New York: Simon and Schuster, 1991.

Aristide, Jean-Bertrand and Christophe Wargny. *Jean-Bertrand Aristide: An Autobiography*. New York: Orbis Books, 1993.

Aristide, Jean-Bertrand and Laura Flynn. *Eyes of the Heart: Seeking a Path for the Poor in the Age of Globalization*. Monroe, ME: Common Courage Press, 2000.

Cadet, Jean-Robert. *Restavec: From Haitian Slave-Child to Middle-Class American; An Autobiography*. 1998; reprint, Austin: University of Texas Press, 2002.

Clinton, Bill. *My Life*. New York: Knopf, 2004.

Columbus, Christopher. *The Four Voyages*. New York: Penguin Books, 1969; translated by K. M. Cohen.

Danticat, Edwidge. *Breath, Eyes, Memory*. New York: Soho, 1994.

———. *Krik! Krak!* New York: Soho, 1995.

———. *The Dew Breaker*. New York: Knopf, 2004.

Diederich, Bernard and Al Burt. *Papa Doc: Haiti and Its Dictator*. 1969; reprint, Maplewood, NJ: Waterfront Press, 1991.

Dubois, Laurent. *Avengers of the New World: The Story of the Haitian Revolution*. Cambridge, MA: Harvard University Press, 2004.

Dunham, Katherine. *Island Possessed: Haiti and the Story of a Woman Whose Life Became One with her Island*. New York: Doubleday, 1969.

Duvalier, François. *Mémoires d'um leader du Tiers Monde: Mes Négociations avec le Saint-Siège; ou: Une tranche d'histoire*. Paris: Hachette, 1969.

Greene, Graham. *The Comedians*. 1966; reprint, New York: Bantam Books, 1967.

Hayek, Friedrich August. *The Road to Serfdom*. Chicago: University of Chicago Press, 1944.

Heinl, Robert D., Nancy G., and Michael. *Written in Blood: The Story of the Haitian People, 1492–1995*. New York: U. Press of America, 1996.

Kamen, Henry. *Empire: How Spain Became a World Power, 1492–1763*. 2002; reprint, New York: HarperCollins, 2004.

Maguire, Robert E. *Demilitarizing Public Order in a Predatory State: The Case of Haiti*. Coral Gables: North-South Center Press, 1995.

Métral, Antoine. *Histoire de l'expédition des Français à Saint-Domingue sous le consulat de Napoléon Bonaparte (1802–1803), suivie des mémoires et notes d'Isaac l'Ouverture*. 1825. Reprint, Paris: Karthala, 1985.

Morquette, Marc-Ferl. *Les nouveaux marrons: Essai sur un aspect de la crise politique, 1989–1998*. Port-au-Prince: L'Imprimeur II, 1999.

Parkinson, Wenda. *"This Gilded African": Toussaint l'Ouverture*. New York: Quartet Books, 1978.

Price-Mars, Jean. *Ainsi parla l'oncle*. 1928; reprint: New York, Parapsychology Foundation, 1954.

Ricardo, David. *Principles of Political Economy and Taxation*. 1817; reprint, Amherst: Prometheus Books, 1996.

Roumain, Jacques. *Les gouverneurs de la rosée*. Port-au-Prince: Imprimerie de l'Etat, 1944.

Schmidt, Hans. *The United States Occupation of Haiti, 1915–1934*. New Brunswick, NJ: Rutgers, 1971.

St. John, Spenser. *Hayti: Or, The Black Republic*. New York: Scribner and Welford, 1889.

St. Méry, Moreau de. *Description topographique, physique, civile, politique et historique de la partie française de l'isle Saint-Domingue*. 1797–1798; reprint, Paris: Société de l'histoire des colonies françaises, 1958.

Weber, Max. "The Protestant Ethic and the Spirit of Capitalism (1905)." In *Working: Its Meaning and Its Limits*, edited by Gilbert Meilaender. Notre Dame, IN: University of Notre-Dame Press, 2000.

Williams, Eric. *From Columbus to Castro: The History of the Caribbean*. 1970; reprint, New York: Vintage Books, 1984.

Wimpffen, Baron Alexandre-Stanislas de. *Haïti au XVIIIème siècle: Richesse et esclavage dans une colonie française*. 1797; reprint: Paris, Karthala, 1993.

Index